Niccolò Machiavelli's *The Prince*
New interdisciplinary essays

No work has attracted more controversy over the centuries than *The Prince*. This stimulating collection of essays offers a challenging sequence of close readings of Machiavelli's text. The essays, by international scholars and critics, form a rich mix of traditional and modern critical approaches, including feminist and deconstructive criticism.

The volume consists of an introduction outlining some of the problems *The Prince* raises as a cultural text. Then follow seven essays, ranging from a discussion of *The Prince*'s first reception and its concern with history and dialogue, through the text's concern with language, power and gender, on to discussions of its contradictions and its place in cultural history. A select bibliography and chronological table are also included.

The result is a volume full of ideas and insights; indeed, an essential companion for anyone studying Machiavelli's text.

Martin Coyle is Senior Lecturer in English at the University of Wales, Cardiff.

TEXTS · IN · CULTURE

Series editors

Stephen Copley and Jeff Wallace

Advisory editors

David Aers, Duke University
Lynda Nead, Birbeck College, London
Gillian Beer, Girton College, Cambridge
Roy Porter, Wellcome Institute for the
History of Medicine
Anne Janowitz, University of Warwick
Bernard Sharratt, University of Kent

This new series offers a set of specially commissioned, cross-disciplinary essays on a text of seminal importance to Western culture. Each text has had an impact on the way we think, write and live beyond the confines of its original discipline, and it is only through an understanding of its multiple meanings that we can fully appreciate its importance.

Adam Smith's *The Wealth of Nations*
Stephen Copley, Kathryn Sutherland (eds)

Charles Darwin's *The Origin of Species*
David Amigoni, Jeff Wallace (eds)

Sigmund Freud's *Interpretation of Dreams*
Laura Marcus (ed.)

Simone de Beauvoir's *The Second Sex*
Ruth Evans (ed.)

Niccolò Machiavelli's *The Prince*
Martin Coyle (ed.)

TEXTS·IN·CULTURE

Niccolò Machiavelli's
THE
PRINCE

New interdisciplinary essays

MARTIN COYLE

editor

Manchester University Press
Manchester and New York

*distributed exclusively in the USA
and Canada by St Martin's Press*

Published by Manchester University Press
Oxford Road, Manchester M13 9NR, UK
and Room 400, 175 Fifth Avenue, New York, NY 10010, USA

Distributed exclusively in the USA and Canada
by St Martin's Press, Inc.,
175 Fifth Avenue, New York, NY 10010, USA

British Library Cataloguing-in-Publication Data
A catalogue record is available from the British Library

Library of Congress Cataloging-in-publication Data applied for

ISBN 0-7190-4195-3 *hardback*
ISBN 0-7190-4196-1 *paperback*

First published in 1995

99 98 97 96 95   10 9 8 7 6 5 4 3 2 1

Typeset in Apollo by Koinonia, Manchester
Printed in Great Britain by Biddles Limited, Guildford and King's Lynn

Contents

Series introduction

Texts are produced in particular cultures and in particular historical circumstances. In turn, they shape and are shaped by those cultures as they are read and re-read in changing circumstances by different groups with different commitments, engagements and interests. Such readings are themselves then re-absorbed into the ideological frameworks within which the cultures develop. The seminal works drawn on by cultures thus have multiple existences within them, exerting their influence in distinct and perhaps contradictory ways. As these texts have been 'claimed' by particular academic disciplines, however, their larger cultural significance has often been obscured.

Recent work in cultural history and textual theory has stimulated critical awareness of the complex relations between texts and cultures, highlighting the limits of current academic formations and opening the possibility of new approaches to interdisciplinarity. At the same time, however, the difficulties of interdisciplinary work have become increasingly apparent at all levels of research and teaching. On the one hand the abandonment of disciplinary specialisms may lead to amorphousness rather than challenging interdisciplinarity: on the other, interdisciplinary approaches may in the end simply create new specialisms or sub-specialisms, with their own well guarded boundaries. In these circumstances, yesterday's ground-breaking interdisciplinary study may become today's autonomous (and so potentially circumscribed) discipline, as has happened, it might be argued, in the case of some forms of History of Ideas.

The volumes in this series highlight the advantages of interdisciplinary work while at the same time encouraging a critical reflexiveness about its limits and possibilities; they seek to stimulate consideration both of the distinctiveness and integrity of individual disciplines, and of the transgressive potential of interdisciplinarity. Each volume offers a collection of new essays on a text of seminal intellectual and cultural importance, displaying the insights to be gained from the juxtaposition of disciplinary perspectives and from the negotiation of disciplinary boundaries. Our editorial stance is avowedly 'cultural', and in this sense the volumes represent a challenge to the conception of authorship which locates the significance of the text in the individual act of creation; but we assume that no issues (including those of disciplinarity and authorship) are foreclosed, and that individual volumes, drawing contributions from a broad range of disciplinary standpoints, will raise questions about the texts they examine more by the perceived disparities of approach that they encompass than by any interpretative consensus that they demonstrate.

All essays are specially commissioned for the series and are designed to be approachable by non-specialist as well as specialist readers: substantial editorial introductions provide a framework for the debates conducted in each volume, and highlight the issues involved.

Stephen Copley, University of York
Jeff Wallace, University of Glamorgan

A note on references

Machiavelli's original manuscript of *The Prince* has not survived. Modern editions often combine readings from a number of manuscripts and editions. References to *The Prince* in the present volume, both in Italian and in translation, are given both by chapter (in Roman numerals) and page number so that readers can make cross-reference to their own texts. In some cases, indicated in the notes, contributors have translated the text themselves.

Chronology

1469 Machiavelli born (3 May) in Florence

Lorenzo de' Medici succeeds his father as unofficial ruler of Florence

1481 Machiavelli attends Paolo da Ronciglione's school

1480s Attends University of Florence

1492 Death of Lorenzo de' Medici (Lorenzo 'the Magnificent'); succeeded by his son, Piero
Cesare Borgia made archbishop of Valencia

1494 Charles VIII of France takes Florence; Piero de' Medici exiled; Girolamo Savonarola, a Domician friar, becomes head of new republican government

1498 Cesare Borgia becomes Duke of Valentinois (Duke Valentino)

1498 Savonarola falls from power

1498 Machiavelli made second chancellor of the Florentine republic by the Great Council
Elected secretary to the Ten of War
Undertakes first mission to Piombino on behalf of the Ten

1500 Mission to court of Louis XII of France

1501 Marries Marietta Corsini

1502 Mission to court of Cesare Borgia at Imola

1503 Mission to papal court at Rome on election of Julius II

1504 Second mission to court of Louis XII

1504 Cesare Borgia flees to Naples, is arrested and sent to imprisonment in Spain

1505 Machiavelli's scheme for Florentine militia accepted

1506 Second mission to papal court

Elected secretary to the Nine of the Militia

1507 Mission to Emperor Maximillian's court (where Francesco Vettori was Florentine envoy)

1510 Third mission to court of Louis XII

1511 Fourth mission to court of Louis XII

1512 August: Spanish troops attack Florentine territory
September: Florence surrenders, return of the Medici
September: Dissolution of the republic
November: Dismissed (7th) from the Chancery

November: Sentenced (10th) to confinement within Florentine territory for a year

1513 Giovanni de' Medici becomes Pope Leo X (the first Medici pope)
Francesco Vettori Florentine envoy to the papal court

1513 February: Machiavelli accused of role in anti-Medici conspiracy; tried, tortured and imprisoned.
March: released from prison
April: retires to his farm at Sant'Andrea, 7 miles from Florence

1513 Writes draft of Il Principe (The Prince)

1515 Begins to attend literary, political discussions at Cosimo Rucellai's gardens (the Orti Oricellari) in Florence

1515 Erasmus: Institution of a Christian Prince

1517 Luther pins 95 'Theses' on church door at Wittenberg

1518 Machiavelli writes Mandragola (a play)

1518 or 1519: Completes Discorsi sopra la prima Deca Tito Livio (Discourses on the First Decade of Titus Livius)

1520 Writes Arte della guerra (The Art of War)
Writes La vita di Castruccio Castracani da Lucca (The Life of Castruccio Castracani)
Is commissioned by Cardinal Giulio de' Medici (later Pope Clement VII) to write history of Florence

1521 Arte della guerra (The Art of War) published

1521 Pope Leo X confers title of Defender of the Faith on Henry VIII

1525 Machiavelli presents finished Istorie fiorentine (The History of Florence) to Pope Clement VII (Cardinal Giulio de' Medici)
Writes Clizia (a play)

1527 Rome sacked by troops of Charles V of Spain

1527 Medicean regime overthrown in Florence and republic (temporarily) restored

1527 Machiavelli dies 21 June, buried in Santa Croce, Florence

1528 Castiglione: Il Cortegiano (translated as The Courtier in 1561 by Sir Thomas Hoby)

1531 Discorsi published

1531 Sir Thomas Elyot: A Book Named the Governor

1532 Il Principe and Istorie fiorentine published

1550 First collected works of Machiavelli published (Testina edition)

1553 First foreign edition of Il Principe: translated into French by Guillaume Capel.

1559 Machiavelli's works placed on the Index of Prohibited Books by the Holy Inquisition

1560 *Il Principe* translated into Latin by Sylvester Telius Fulginatus, and published at Basel

1576 Innocent Gentillet: *Discours sur les moyens de bien gouverner* ... *contre Nicolas Machiavel, Florentin*

1602 Gentillet's *Contre-Machiavel* printed in English, translated (1577) by Simon Patericke

1640 *The Prince* published in English, translated by Edward Dacres.

This chronology is based on that of Quentin Skinner and Russell Price in their edition of *The Prince* (Cambridge: Cambridge University Press, 1988).

1

Introduction

MARTIN COYLE

> The 'voyage' that has us meet strange foreigners remained never-
> theless a privileged means for showing our individual flaws or
> the political weaknesses of our own countries.
>
> Julia Kristeva, Strangers to Ourselves

> Every text *participates* in one or several genres, there is no genre-
> less text, there is always a genre and genres, yet such participa-
> tion never amounts to belonging.
>
> Jacques Derrida, Acts of Literature[1]

The image of Machiavelli has played an important part in
Western cultures since the early sixteenth century. Take, for
example, the demonised figure who opens Marlowe's *Jew of
Malta* (1589-90) and acts as prologue to the play, announcing
its themes of religion, poison and politics:

MACHEVILL: Albeit the world think Machevill is dead,
   Yet was his soul but flown beyond the Alps;
   And, now the Guise is dead, is come from France,
   To view this land, and frolic with his friends.
   To some perhaps my name is odious;
   But such as love me, guard me from their tongues,
   And let them know that I am Machevill,
   And weigh not men, and therefore not men's words.
   Admir'd I am of those that hate me most:
   Though some speak openly against my books,
   Yet will they read me, and thereby attain
   To Peter's chair; and, when they cast me off,
   Are poison'd by my climbing followers.

I count religion but a childish toy,
And hold there is no sin but ignorance.[2]

If Marlowe's figure conjures up the stereotype of the Italian poisoner-politician that was to prove so convenient to Renaissance dramatists, he also glances at recent events through the reference in line 3 to the Duke of Guise, a leader in the massacre of Protestants (Huguenots) by French Catholics on St Bartholomew's night 1572. Though Machiavelli had been put on the Index of Prohibited Books by the Inquisition in Rome in 1559, and therefore was forbidden to Catholics to read, the treachery of the Saint Bartholomew's Massacre was blamed on Machiavelli by Protestants – after all, was not the French King's mother, Catherine de' Medici, a member of that same Italian family to which Machiavelli had dedicated *The Prince*? That blame was compounded in 1576 when the French Huguenot Innocent Gentillet's book *Discours ... contre Nicolas Machiavel* (*The Discourse ... against Niccolò Machiavelli*) was published. Ironically, Gentillet's volume, which was translated into English in 1602, some thirty-eight years before *The Prince*, also proved to be the means by which Machiavelli came largely to be known throughout Europe, and helped to establish his name as a byword for the cunning and unscrupulous politician.

It is in this sense, of course, that modern popular culture uses Machiavelli's name – 'Last gasp of a Machiavelli' reads the byline in *The Observer* 26 June 1994 as it reviews the career of the retiring French President François Mitterand. Underpinning such usage is a whole range of literary and non-literary texts. Bacon, for example, in *De augmentis scientiarum* (1623) writes of how 'we are much beholden to Machiavelli and other writers of that class, who openly and unfeignedly declare or describe what men do, and not what they ought to do'.[3] The English Civil War (1642-49) was fought both on the battlefields between armies and between writers drawing on Machiavelli's writings about princes and republics, while later Cromwell was presented as the very type of the machiavellian ruler rising through his own *virtù*. Harrington's political romance *Oceana* (1656) similarly conducts its analysis of government by way of Machiavelli. In 1740 Frederick the Great of Prussia, aided by Voltaire, published his *Anti Machiavel*, an attack on *The Prince*.

With the French Revolution of 1789 Machiavelli comes to take on yet other significances as first a text supporting republicanism and the people, but then secondly as a text supporting Napoleon's ending of the Revolution. 'Machiavelli', too, appears in George Eliot's novel *Romola* (1862), set in late fifteenth-century Florence, while more recently Alistair McAlpine's *The Servant* (1992) supplies a satiric version of *The Prince* applied to Margaret Thatcher's premiership.

As we might expect, the image of Machiavelli that such appropriations offer is based almost exclusively on *The Prince* rather than works like *The Discourses on Livy* or *The Art of War* or, indeed, the *History of Florence*. Nor does this image take much cognisance of Machiavelli's poetry or his plays or his correspondence. This is not to argue, however, that *The Prince* itself has not been read in a wide variety of ways, and this for obvious reasons which have to do with the complex nature of the text and its problems. One of these is the very ordinary fact alluded to in Brian Richardson's opening chapter in this volume, that we do not have a definitive text of *The Prince*, which was printed only after Machiavelli's death. Coupled with this is the further point that in the manuscripts the work we call *The Prince* is entitled *De principatibus* (*Of Principalities*). This may account for something of the ambiguous focus of the work, which seems initially concerned less with advice to the Prince than with an analysis of kingdoms and states.

At the same time, it is worth noting for the reader who has no Italian and who relies purely on translated editions that the titles to Machiavelli's chapters are in Latin, and that throughout the text Machiavelli inserts occasional words of Latin. The significance of this seems to lie in the way the text positions itself in relation to other works offering advice to princes and in relation to its educated readers. However new Machiavelli's approach in its time, the form of *The Prince* remains overtly traditional.[4] It may be, however, that what is also being signalled is how that form is under pressure. Indeed, we might push this point a little further and see *The Prince* not just as the product of a specific individual but also as the product of a shift in cultural values, a shift which begets a new kind of political thinking but one still represented in a traditional (educated, Latin) format.

The question of translations of *The Prince* is obviously too large to deal with here, but many modern readers know Machiavelli's work only through translation, and this itself poses several problems. For example, here are five versions of the opening sentences of the dedicatory letter of *The Prince*:

> *Men who are anxious to win the favour of a Prince nearly always follow the custom of presenting themselves to him with the posses- sions they value most, or with things they know especially please him: so we often see princes given horses, weapons, cloth of gold, precious stones, and similar ornaments worth of their high position.*
>   tr. George Bull

> Those that court the favours of a prince generally come before him bearing presents from their own most treasured possessions, or such as they see him to delight in: hence we often see princes receive horses, arms, cloth of gold, precious stones and other such ornaments, worthy of their greatness.   tr. Bruce Penman

> It is customary most of the time for those who desire to acquire favor with a Prince to come to meet him with things that they care most for among their own or with things that they see please him most. Thus, one sees them many times being presented with horses, arms, cloth of gold, precious stones and similar ornaments worthy of their greatness.   tr. Harvey C. Mansfield

> Those who wish to be viewed with favour by a ruler usually approach him with things from among their possessions that are very dear to them, or with things that they expect will please him. Hence, it often happens that they are presented with horses, weapons, a cloth of gold, precious stones and similar ornaments, which are worthy of their exalted position.
>   tr. Quentin Skinner and Russell Price

> It is a frequent custom for those who seek the favor of a prince to make him presents of those things they value most highly or which they know are most pleasing to him. Hence one often sees gifts consisting of horses, weapons, cloth of gold, precious stones, and similar ornaments suitable for men of noble rank.
>   tr. Robert M. Adams[5]

It is clear that these translations differ in tone, vocabulary, syntax, indeed almost every detail, and that all translation involves not a little critical interpretation. The problem for the reader of a translation is somehow to remain conscious of the fact that what we are reading is not 'Machiavelli' but an edition which belongs as much to our own modern culture as to the fifteenth- and sixteen-century Florence we construct. This, of course, also holds good for readers working on Italian texts: there is no access to a pure, real Machiavelli; there are only editions of his works, and in that sense all readings of *The Prince* remain provisional.

There is one further point I wish to make which has to do with reading *The Prince* as a cultural text. It is a point raised in Maureen Ramsay's chapter, that many of the key terms in *The Prince* have a plurality of meaning which undermines any monolithic definition we may seek to give them. This is particularly the case with the word *virtù*, but it also applies to words like *fortuna*, *libertà*, even *principe*.[6] To this extent *The Prince* seems an inherently unstable text subject to the ambiguity of its own language and open to many different readings and interpretations, as a glance at Silvia Fiore's six-hundred-page bibliography of studies of Machiavelli reveals.[7]

Such is the scale of writing about Machiavelli that it might seem all but impossible to think of a topic that has not been exhausted. And yet this is not really the case. Much of the writing about *The Prince* is often at a certain distance from the text, not engaging with it in a critical or textual way. One of the features of the chapters in this book is the extent to which they focus on the complex texture of Machiavelli's writing and on the complex reading processes this in turn calls forth. Indeed, we might argue that it is not simply, as modern theorists have it, that the reader creates the meaning of the text but that certain texts in our culture – texts like *The Prince* – create and demand a more complicated response from readers as well as different kinds of reading. In other words, they demand a plural approach.

This last point ties in with the aim of this book and the interdisciplinary nature of the series in which it appears. Underlying the series is the recognition that many texts cut across disciplinary boundaries as well as across cultures and historical periods. Included in this book, for example, are chapters by scholars and critics from departments of French, Italian, English, History, Politics, Philosophy and Government. But it would have also been possible to seek out essays from a whole range of other disciplines, and this because of the way in which *The Prince* belongs to a broad set of interests. In turn this helps us understand why we read such texts and what their importance is as cultural documents: they are places where we find ourselves thinking about the way we organise society and what sort of implications that has for us both as individuals and as members of society. Such thinking goes beyond the confines of particular disciplines, though necessarily it is through those particular disciplines that we gain the most acute insight into the issues and problems that we are interested in.

In assembling this book, then, I was conscious of the need to bring together both a variety of critical viewpoints and a variety of disciplines but also a series of arguments which would allow the reader to engage in a debate that was at once broadly based and intensely focused. That debate has to include proper recognition of the particular circumstances of Machiavelli's writing, an awareness of the modern critical approaches now being explored in relation to *The Prince*, and a sense of the connection between Machiavelli and the twentieth century. More simply, what I have sought to achieve is a sequence of chapters by critics and scholars which locates the text both in its own history and in ours, a set of chapters that create a sense of both past readers and present but also a set of chapters which, through their similarities and differences, offer a sense of the dynamic effect interdisciplinary approaches can have.

The book itself continues with Brian Richardson's chapter on '*The Prince* and its early Italian readers'. Noting that *The Prince*, though drafted in 1513, 'was not printed until 1532, nearly five years after Machiavelli's death', Richardson begins by sketching in what he calls the later 'deforming readings' of Machiavelli's texts before examining how the work was perceived by its first audience and then appropriated by other writers. Usefully, Richardson summarises what we know about the various early manuscripts of *The Prince* and the marginal notes made by early readers, at the same time pointing out that in contemporary Florence most texts would have circulated in manuscript rather than in printed form. No less revealing of the actual production of the work are Richardson's remarks about its style, which resembles Machiavelli's 'routine chancery writings', in which 'a sprinkling of Latin jargon ... is mixed with colloquial Florentine forms'. Yet despite this apparently casual style the work, Richardson argues, was undoubtedly intended to impress, as suggested by its dedicatory letter and its links with the genre of books advising princes on how to rule. Both the questions of *The Prince*'s genre and of its opening letter (Machiavelli changed the dedication in favour of Lorenzo de' Medici after the original dedicatee, Giuliano de' Medici, died) are themes taken up in later chapters, as is the question of Machiavelli's style and its implications. Richardson's particular point, though, is that Machiavelli, through his 'blunt, business-like style', wished to shock his 'well-educated readers' into an awareness 'that fine words were not enough, that they had to stop dreaming about imaginary states and start listening to the voice of practical experience', and that this emphasis in the text should be put in the context of Florence's turbulent history which had seen it only recently lose its republican freedom and find itself again under the Medici family and the threat of absolute rule.

The government of Florence is something that is self-evidently important in Machiavelli's writing both in *The Prince* and in his other works. As Richardson goes to demonstrate, Machiavelli shared this concern with other writers of the period, who seem to have drawn upon *The Prince* both for their material and for their method of argument in the debate about the Florentine constitution. Not necessarily, however, to agree with it. As in the cases of Francesco Guicciardini (the most significant of Machaivelli's contemporary historians and writers on politics) or Agostino Nifo and Antonio Brucioli, writing slightly later, what we see are writers borrowing from, adapting and rewriting Machiavelli but at the same time seeking to counter the arguments of *The Prince* about the nature of princely rule and 'reassert conventional political ethics'. Such borrowing, as Richardson shows, is evidence of the powerful effect of Machiavelli's writings as well as the 'ambiguous attitude' that marked its reception, for while in private letters 'Florentines could reveal their fascination with Machiavelli's

analysis of effective statecraft ... in public it was not possible
to approve what he had dared to say'.

Such, in brief, is Richardson's argument which provides
both a lucid overview of *The Prince* and an important perspective on the immediate reception of the text and its place in the
political debate of Florence. What Richardson also alerts us to
is the intricate interplay between Machiavelli's text and other
texts of the time. Such interplay or intertextuality goes beyond
mere verbal borrowing and relates to the generic expectations
that *The Prince* is built on and alludes to. As Janet Coleman
shows in the third chapter in this volume, these expectations
involve not just a type of writing or a type of content but an
attitude towards history and language that binds Machiavelli
much more closely to the Middle Ages than to the modern
world we often assume he heralds in.

Coleman begins her chapter by suggesting that the problem
Machiavelli is dealing with in both *The Prince* and his *Discourses*
centres on the subtle question of 'what Machiavelli means by
"history"'. More specifically, she suggests that while contemporary practioners of law and medicine 'knew how to read history
correctly and benefit from that reading', those engaged in politics
– princes, governors as well as 'new men' not from the traditional ruling elite – were lacking this skill. What Machiavelli
seeks to show is how this 'already established way of reading
history' could be be applied to contemporary problems. For
Machiavelli, Coleman argues, this method of reading was
entirely different from modern historical readings of the past:
where these see events as over and finished, for Machiavelli the
past is 'alive and capable of imitation. It is a past for the
present.' Implicit in this conception is the idea that history is
not so much a record of facts and events as a matter of language
which can convey the nature of experiences which others could
then read as a literal account. Through reading, a later audience 'could ... be as though "present" and witnessing the past'.

Under this medieval and, indeed, Renaissance approach to
history, Coleman continues, lie several important assumptions:
first, that 'the world to be experienced is and always has been
stable'; second, 'that the human mind' and human nature remain
constant and the same; third, that language alone changes;

fourth, that there are some universally shared characteristics such as the incredulity and ingratitude of men. In turn this means that it is possible to construct probable laws of human behaviour but also to imitate past actions provided they are chosen carefully. 'In short', writes Coleman, 'Machiavelli is giving us an epistemology, a psychological theory of how humans learn and understand', but it is not a theory Machiavelli invented – its roots lay in the sort of observation and experience that Aristotle promulgated as the basis of judgement and faith (the *via moderna*) as opposed to Platonism with its notions of what the ideal might be (the *via antiqua*). What is new in Machiavelli is the application of the theory and method of reading to contemporary politics.

Coleman's argument is enormously illuminating of the logic behind Machiavelli's mode of writing and why it draws both upon personal experience and upon reading of ancient texts as two complementary ways of knowing about the past. At the same time the chapter highlights the fallacy of thinking of Machiavelli as a 'new man' of modern attitudes. Or rather, the fallacy of thinking in terms of a crude division between medieval and Renaissance as if some bifurcation occurred at a particular moment. A minute's reflection will show up the weaknesses of separating historical periods totally from each other, but it may also lead us to consider the way in which, far from trying to divide off the old from the new, Machiavelli's method sees the two in close relationship. At the same time, we might want to argue that, paradoxically, and ironically, the effect of seeing the way in which contemporary Italy and ancient texts were related seems to have brought about the writing of a work which, precisely because it applies traditional thinking to the practical world of government, itself signalled the end of that way of seeing. Even as Machiavelli constructs his correspondences between ancient texts and contemporary figures we may be more struck by the differences than by the similarities, but equally we may be aware of the way in which Machiavelli's historical method is being used to construct a politics that works by using past examples to justify itself rather than to maintain any sort of continuity.

Coleman's analysis provides a bridge between Richardson's

chapter and John Parkin's discussion of the topic of dialogue in *The Prince*. Starting with an outline of the different types of dialogue that we might consider in thinking about *The Prince* – the clash, for example, between the discourse of humanism and the realities of practical politics, or the various addressees conjured up by the text, including Lorenzo de' Medici and the 'political student' who reads the work as a text book – Parkin goes on to explore some of the nuances in Machiavelli's letter to his friend and correspondent Francesco Vettori which describes the composition of *The Prince* as 'a kind of dialogue with the dead' of classical Rome.[8] As Parkin notes, one of the extraordinary features of *The Prince* is the way in which it seems simultaneously to address both the student of political science and the humanist reader alert to its rhetorical strategies, so that what we have is a sort of 'dialogic web', a rich inter-weaving of discussion, debate and different voices and strands. More particularly, what Parkin is interested in analysing is the way *The Prince* works in its 'double structure' of humanist culture and contemporary Medici readership and how this relates to the processes and procedures of the text.

Those procedures, Parkin suggests, involve Machiavelli set-ting up general rules or guidelines which are then modified or countered by examples and further distinctions. This 'dialogic structure' is seen, for example, in chapter XII, dealing with mercenaries (Machiavelli, it will be recalled, advocated that Florence should abandon relying on mercenaries and organise its own citizen army), where Parkin argues that Machiavelli's intention is 'less to present reality scientifically' than to equip his princely reader with ideas on how to analyse problems. At the same time Parkin suggests that the text is working on a number of levels at once – philosophical, technical, personal – so that its various dichotomies such as that of *virtù/fortuna* are inherently unstable. They are so partly at least because *The Prince* is a piece of persuasion rather than a logical argument, with its shifting dialogue itself reflecting the kind of flexibility needed to cope with changing circumstances – needed both by the Prince and by his adviser. In this sense, Parkin suggests, *The Prince* takes on an almost dramatic quality, with Machi-avelli acting as skilled political servant to his reader/listener, demonstrating his competent grasp of relevant examples and his power of analysis. Through such dramatic features the text, Parkin concludes, acts to prompt further dialogue outside and beyond itself.

Informing Parkin's analysis are the theories of Mikhail Bakhtin, and in particular the notion of the dialogic text, which Parkin shows must be central to any reading of *The Prince* if we are to make sense of the variousness of its language. No less concerned with the question of language, though in a significantly different yet complementary way, is John Najemy's chapter, which takes up a number of the issues referred to in the first three chapters and places them in the light of Renaissance attitudes to rhetoric as the foundation of politics. Evident in the dedication to *The Prince*, however, and in the letters to Vettori, Najemy suggests, is a 'fundamental worry about language', a worry about 'a certain indeterminacy or inexactness of language', about the lack of correspondence between *cose* and *discorsi*, between events, actions, purposes and the language used to understand, represent, describe them. While this worry, Najemy suggests, is not theorised, it troubles the text, as does the idea (advanced by Lorenzo Valla in the fifteenth century) that language depends upon common usage and is open to change over time. Najemy argues that one of the objects of *The Prince* is to seek to stabilise and control the meaning of words, and that this underlies one of the text's 'best known features: its almost obsessive reliance on differential pairs or binary oppositions', including, of course, its most famous pairing of *virtù* and *fortuna*.

Najemy suggests, however, that behind this concern with language lies, in part, Machiavelli's correspondence with Vettori and in particular the latter's argument that we cannot know what princes think. Set against this, Najemy contends, is Machiavelli's claim in chapter XV to be able to get to the 'effectual truth' of things rather than having to rely on imagination or the interpretation of appearances, a claim that leads him to redefine the terms used to blame or praise princes and, indeed, the meaning of 'vices' and 'virtues'. Common understanding, Machiavelli argues, falls short of a proper understanding of these words, but as Najemy demonstrates, Machiavelli's own argument at this point is caught in a labyrinth of contradictions, which make themselves felt again in chapter XXIII, where Machiavelli takes up the question of who should advise the Prince. Such advice, Machiavelli proposes, must exclude contact with ordinary speech and language, but also depends upon the Prince being able to know the truth through his own discourse. In *The Prince*, then, Najemy suggests, Machiavelli constructs a sort of 'linguistic fantasy', that there is 'another kind of language practice possible and necessary for survival in power', a fantasy Najemy argues that Machiavelli rejected in his later work, especially in *The Discourses* and their analysis of republican rule.

What is striking about Najemy's chapter (and obviously the summary above omits much of its important detail) is its combination of Renaissance scholarship with a deconstructive analysis that foregrounds the way in which *The Prince* is deeply conscious of the problem of language and politics. As I noted above, the chapter itself implicitly looks back to the first three essays and their concern with contemporary readings of the text, but Najemy's argument also acts as a sort of preface to the three essay that follow it, and in particular to Maggie Günsberg's challenging discussion of 'the discourses of power' in *The Prince*, a discussion that draws both upon modern feminist theory and upon post-structuralist theory more generally. Like Andrew Mousley's and Maureen Ramsay's chapters that follow it in the second part of the volume, Günsberg's argument focuses much more on the ideology of *The Prince* and on modern readings of the text than the earlier chapters, yet it nevertheless echoes some of their concerns.

Günsberg begins her chapter by providing an overview of the economic and social processes specific to *The Prince* – the early capitalism and emerging state identity of Florence – as well as its genre. This then leads into the first part of the chapter which examines *The Prince* not as a political treatise but as narrative, a narrative composed of a main story centring on the would-be Prince whose goal is to gain power, and a series of closed sub-stories illustrating failure or success. Both main and sub-stories are, Günsberg suggests, end-orientated, that is they emphasise achievement, the gaining and maintaining of power, and she goes on to show how this sort of linear quest narrative is associated with epic and the reinforcement of certain gender and class values. More particularly, Günsberg argues that *The Prince*, with its stress on combative action and male valour, situates the text in a tradition of stereotypical masculine values, values shared by the author in his own quest to conquer knowledge. Such values depend on the positing of a set of binary oppositions which build in gender stereotyping, so that, for example, *fortuna* is associated with the feminine and weak, *virtù* with prowess and the masculine. Importantly, Günsberg suggests that these features of the text are connected with its realism, with its purport to offer a sense of things as they are, to be a work of *realpolitik*.

Informing the narrative structure and process of *The Prince*, Günsberg suggests in the second part of her chapter, are a set of discourses and power relations. The latter includes the sense of the text itself as a piece of persuasion intended to bring about certain outcomes through its rhetorical strategies. Central to those strategies is the way power is presented in terms of domination and subordination, reinforcing a hierarchical ordering of both class and gender. Machiavelli seeks to naturalise this ordering, Günsberg suggests, through various tactics, such as presenting it as universal or true, most often through the use of generalisation. The final part of the chapter is itself taken up with an analysis of these rhetorical strategies, including generalisations about human nature, the use of binary oppositions and analogies to structure reality and engineer the 'truth', as well as cause and effect arguments and the discourse of history.

Günsberg's aim, as she says at the end of her chapter, is to offer a radical critique not just of *The Prince* but also of the Western epistemological traditions in which Machiavelli was writing. The critique is followed by Andrew Mousley's complementary chapter on '*The Prince* and textual politics'. Machiavelli, Mousley suggests, faces readers with a dilemma, for though he seems to have a 'definite position in cultural history' as the founder of modern politics, his writing remains elusive, resistant to 'any single identifiable "Machiavellism"'. It is this contradiction between 'doctrinal clarity' and 'diversity of perspective' in the text that Mousley explores, beginning with

Machiavelli's status as the founder of modern political science. That status, Mousley contends, is bound up with the way *The Prince* is offered as a 'readable manual', something to be used which makes the art of government unproblematic, something outside language in the realm of things that can be done. Power in *The Prince*, Mousley suggests, is made tangible, a matter of cause and effect that can be controlled, with mastery being shown as achievable through, for example, the skilled use of war or, in the opening chapter, though the text's system of classifications of principalities.

However, threatening such systematising of power, Mousley continues, is the almost endless list of variations Machiavelli gives so that we begin to see all such states as provisional, as sites of struggle and therefore of ambiguous significance. There is, we start to realise, no universal system, no certainty, despite the demystification of politics in the text. Undermining the realist project of *The Prince*, Mousley proposes, is thus another perspective, a view based on common opinion, itself dismissed yet also sometimes appealed to, with the result that the text is seen to point in 'conflicting directions', simultaneously supporting and undermining its own propositions. This is evident again, Mousley suggests, in the theatrical metaphors which destabilise the text by their multiple effects. One of these is to present the Prince as alienated 'from any single stable identity', with the result that, despite Machiavelli's apparent intention, we may begin to speculate about the price of power. Similarly the very contradictoriness of the text may cause us to read Borgia's story in more than one way or to see that the examples given are in themselves arbitrary and open to different interpretation. In the end, suggests Mousley, the text cannot close itself off or isolate meaning; it cannot simply be a piece of 'apparatus writing': 'In this sense *The Prince* is a failure. There is too much going on in the text for it to be straightforwardly effective.'

Like other contributors in the volume Mousley builds his analysis on close reading of the text, teasing out the implications of Machiavelli's deceptively plain language. Similarly in the final chapter in the book Maureen Ramsay explores Machiavelli's political philosophy in *The Prince*. The chapter

offers a further perspective on several of the issues raised elsewhere in the book, in particular the questions of means and
ends, of Machiavelli's understanding of human nature, of the
relationship of *The Prince* to other writings offering advice to
the Prince and of Machiavelli's praise of *virtù*. Ramsay's chapter,
however, places these issues in the context both of the history
of political thought and of the present day.

Ramsay begins by noting that although Machiavelli is sometimes regarded as the founder of political science his work is
not systematic enough to warrant such a title. Rather what we
have in *The Prince* is an embryonic form of modern analysis
which is, as Machiavelli says in chapter XV, a new approach in
that it is applied to the real world. Central to this approach –
although, as Ramsay points out, Machiavelli never actually puts
it this way – are the questions of 'the doctrine that "the end
justifies the means"' and of the 'relationship between politics
and morality'. Ramsay suggests that in examining these issues
Machiavelli was not seeking to define moral rules but 'those
qualities … rulers must have to establish, restore or maintain
order and stability'. Again, Machiavelli does not reject conventional morality, Ramsay contends; rather, he recognises that
sometimes it is necessary for the Prince to act contrary to
conventional morality in order to bring about a public good.
This consequentialist ethic, Ramsay goes on to suggest, means
that 'to bring about beneficial results the Prince must cultivate
not conventional virtue but Machiavellian *virtù*', itself a flexible, plural concept with several meanings.

Behind Machiavelli's argument, Ramsay reminds us, lies a
pessimistic view of the unchanging nature of human behaviour
and desires and the need to construct a political morality for
the way human beings are. Machiavelli, however, was not
unique in airing these problems, and Ramsay shows how the
questions raised by political realism were recognised if not
explicitly stated by other writers. The difference between these
writers and Machiavelli lies partly in the dramatic force with
which he presents them but mainly in the fact that for
Machiavelli expediency becomes 'the norm of political activity',
a norm which implies the obsolescence of conventional morality in politics. But if Machiavelli has affinities with some of the

writers of his own age, some of his assumptions, Ramsay argues, are shared by the liberal tradition of our own modern period, including, for example, the separation of the individual and society or the idea that human beings are endlessly ambitious. And, second, Ramsay suggests that the clash that Machiavelli highlights between consequentialist ethics – the justification of means by ends – and other ethical forms such as Christianity is a clash that we live with and debate in our daily lives at almost every level of activity. That debate, Ramsay ends her chapter by noting, has recently been infused by feminism and its alternative values, yet even these values or indeed others no less desirable, she suggests, may sometimes have to be sacrificed to Machiavelli's expediency for the sake of the common good.

Ramsay's chapter, like those that precede it, raises a number of large issues which bear upon the place of *The Prince* both in the history of political ideas and in culture more widely. In the terms of the Julia Kristeva quotation at the start of this introduction, Machiavelli was a stranger to his own time after the return of the Medicis, cast outside the sphere of power. From that stranger position he seems to have been able to create a work that overturned conventional political morality and placed him (fictionally, at least) back at the centre of power. This moving between centre and margins is repeated through the text's subsequent cultural history, with Machiavelli by turns being demonised by moralists and canonised by political thinkers.

Where Machiavelli belongs – at the centre or the margins – depends on the position from which we read him, on what kind of work we think *The Prince* is. A political treatise? A diabolic handbook for tyrants? A work of literature? A philosophical work? The quotation from Derrida at the start of this introduction puts this same question, though more elegantly: that texts are not confined to or bound by the rules of a single genre. As we read *The Prince* from different angles and different disciplines, so its genre seemingly changes; and so perhaps it becomes a different text, or a different kind of work not quite belonging to any one genre. What is clear, however, is that *The Prince* remains an important text in the attempt to understand cultural history and one that reminds us how difficult but rewarding that task is.

Notes

1 Julia Kristeva, *Strangers to Ourselves*, tr. Leon S. Roudiez (London: Harvester Wheatsheaf, 1991), p. 114; Jacques Derrida, *Acts of Literature*, ed. Derek Attridge (New York, London: Routledge, 1992), p. 230.

2 *Christopher Marlowe: The Complete Plays*, ed. J. B. Steane (Harmondsworth: Penguin, 1969), p. 347.

3 Sir Francis Bacon, *De augmentis*, quoted in Felix Raab, *The English Face of Machiavelli: A Changing Intepretation* (London: Routledge & Kegan Paul, 1964), p. 74.

4 Earlier works on political rule include: Plato, *The Republic*; Aristotle, *Politics*; Cicero, *De officiis* (*On Moral Obligation*); Seneca, *De clementia* (*On Mercy*); Sir Thomas Aquinas, *De Regime Principium* (*The Government of Princes*). For a full discussion of the topic, see Allan H. Gilbert, *Machiavelli's 'Prince' and its Forerunners: The Prince as a Typical Book de Regimine Principum* (Durham, NC: Duke University Press, 1938).

5 The translations are from: *Niccolò Machiavelli: 'The Prince'*, tr. George Bull (Harmondsworth: Penguin, 1961), p. 29; *Niccolò Machiavelli: 'The Prince'*, tr. Bruce Penman (London: Dent, 1981), p. 17; *'The Prince': Niccolò Machiavelli*, tr. Harvey C. Mansfield (Chicago: University of Chicago Press, 1985), p. 3; *Machiavelli: 'The Prince'*, ed. Quentin Skinner and Russell Price (Cambridge: Cambridge University Press, 1988), p. 3; *Niccolò Machiavelli: 'The Prince'*, tr. Robert M. Adams (New York: Norton, 1992, Norton Critical Edition), p. 3.

6 For a helpful discussion of the vocabulary of *The Prince*, see *Machiavelli: 'The Prince'*, ed. Quentin Skinner and Russell Price (Cambridge: Cambridge University Press, 1988), pp. 100-13.

7 Silvia Ruffo Fiore, *Niccolò Machiavelli: An Annotated Bibliography of Modern Criticism and Scholarship* (New York: Greenwood, 1990).

8 A translation of the letter appears in the Appendix – see p. 196.

2

The Prince and its early
Italian readers

BRIAN RICHARDSON

The Prince, conceived in 1513, was not printed until 1532, nearly five years after Machiavelli's death. Writing of the early criticism of the work, L. Arthur Burd noted that while *The Prince* was circulating in manuscript it aroused some opposition but no surprise; when, however, it became generally known through the medium of print, reaction grew stronger and interpretations more divergent, so that 'it was either attacked in unmeasured invective, or it was defended on the supposition that it contained a hidden meaning'.[1] The first defence of *The Prince* on the grounds that it dealt with 'poisons' as well as 'herbs and medicines', in other words that it warned of what to avoid as well as teaching remedies to be followed, appeared in the dedication of the second printed edition (Florence, 1532). As the Reformation and Counter-Reformation grew in strength, so attacks on *The Prince* became bound up with the defence of religious values and with Catholic and Protestant propaganda. Disagreement about Machiavelli's political intentions continued. Innocent Gentillet insisted that the Florentine's aim was to teach the Prince to be a true tyrant.[2] But the theory of what Rousseau called the 'secret intention' (*Du contrat social*, III, 6), that Machiavelli was really giving a warning against tyranny, lived on tenaciously.

The purpose of this chapter is to go back beyond these deforming readings of *The Prince* and to look at the reactions of its early Italian readers, chiefly in the two decades before it appeared in print, in order to see how it was perceived in the intellectual world in which and for which it was created. We can ask, first of all, who were *The Prince*'s first readers and at what readership (apart of course from the dedicatee, Lorenzo de' Medici) Machiavelli was probably aiming. We will look at two sorts of evidence: the surviving manuscripts and the literary form and style of the work. Then, by examining the influence of *The Prince* on contemporary written works, we can consider which aspects of it attracted most attention and how it was appropriated in Florence and elsewhere.

It is clear that *The Prince* was quite widely known and appreciated even before printing. Many manuscripts must have been lost, but at least seven of the survivors are datable to before 1532.[3] Naturally, the work was copied in Florence: three of these manuscripts were written by Machiavelli's former chancery colleague Biagio Buonaccorsi.[4] The other four were transcribed elsewhere. The Vatican copy is particularly interesting because it was made in Rome and evidently for a wealthy owner who valued the work highly. Unlike the others, it is on parchment. It was commissioned from the outstanding scribe working in Rome in the 1520s, Ludovico degli Arrighi, and entrusted by him to his Spanish colleague Genesius de la Barrera, probably between 1521 and 1523.[5] The elegant italic hand of the Charlecote manuscript is also related to that of Arrighi.[6] The Corsiniano manuscript was copied and edited in Siena by a notary, Teofilo Mochi, with a letter addressed to his readers which shows that he planned to have the work printed. He was careful to correct some of Machiavelli's idiomatic Florentine forms and took the trouble to collate the text with another manuscript and to emend it. That *The Prince* also circulated in northern Italy is shown by the northern forms found in the Gotha copy and in another manuscript which may have been transcribed to be printed in Venice.[7]

Marginal notes in these manuscripts reveal something of what early readers found especially interesting in *The Prince*. A few of those in Buonaccorsi's copies and the Vatican manuscript draw attention to passages considered noteworthy. These include the enthusiastic summary of Cesare Borgia's achievements in chapter VII, the conclusion of chapter VIII on doing injuries together and not varying one's conduct, the distinction in chapter IX between reaching power with the support of patricians or the *popolo* (roughly, the middle classes), and some generalisations, for instance that causing someone else to become powerful leads to one's downfall (chapter III) or that new kindnesses do not make great men forget old injuries (chapter VII). In chapter VIII, on those who came to power by crime, Machiavelli's account of Agathocles and Oliverotto was too neutral for some: the words 'nefandum scelus' ('abominable crime') were added by Buonaccorsi to describe Agathocles's slaughter of his fellow-Syracusans and by Genesius to describe Oliverotto's murder of the citizens of Fermo.

As well as providing evidence of the popularity of *The Prince*, the number and spread of the manuscripts also gives us a first indication that, just because his treatise was not printed, Machiavelli did not necessarily intend it for a limited readership. Only one of his non-literary prose works, the *Arte della guerra* (*Art of War*), was printed during his lifetime; and such an edition was exceptional in contemporary Florence, whose prose writers were simply not yet in the habit of writing for the printing industry, still less than half a century old in Italy.

What, though, can the form and stylistic register of *The Prince* tell us about Machiavelli's intentions for its readership? One of the striking features of his language in most of the work is its lack of the polish which one would expect in artistic prose. His style resembles that of his routine chancery writings. A sprinkling of Latin jargon ('in exemplis', 'praesertim', 'tamen' and so on) is mixed with colloquial Florentine forms – for example 'stiavo' for 'schiavo' ('enslaved') or 'mia' for 'miei' ('my', masculine plural) – and with informal syntax, such as the omission of 'che' as a relative pronoun or conjunction and the use of the 'left dislocation', characteristic of the spoken language, in which the object of a verb is moved to the start of a sentence and then referred to again with a personal pronoun, as in '*li stati* ordinati come quello di Francia è impossibile posseder*li* con tanta quiete' (chapter IV, p. 263; 'states organised like that of France, it's impossible to hold them so peacefully').[8] This could be taken as a sign that Machiavelli intended *The Prince* merely as a practical advice document whose circulation was to be limited to a small circle of politicians.

But it is important to consider these stylistic features in a broader context. Machiavelli undoubtedly intended the work to make a dignified initial and concluding impression which would appeal to anyone with a humanistic background. The title (originally *De principatibus*) links the work with the long-established genre of advice books on princely rule. The dedicatory letter is impressively eloquent, beginning with the same phrase, 'Sogliono, el più delle volte' ('They are usually wont'), as a contemporary literary classic, Sannazaro's *Arcadia*. The extraordinary concluding chapter has passages of high rhetorical skill. However, the dedication also contains signals to educated readers that they should expect a change of stylistic level in the rest of *The Prince*. Machiavelli tells them that he has chosen to leave the work unadorned 'with verbose phrases or with pompous and magnificent words, or with any other embellishment or extraneous ornament' ('di clausule ample, o di parole ampullose e magnifiche, o di qualunque altro lenocinio o ornamento estrinseco', p. 257). He is rejecting, then, what Horace called *ampullae* or bombast (*Ars poetica*, 97). Instead, he says in the letter that he wants his work to be appreciated for 'the diversity ["varietà"] of its matter and the dignity ["gravità"] of its subject'. Here he is deliberately using two terms from the technical vocabulary of rhetoric. *Gravitas* was a quality associated by Cicero and by the author of the *Rhetorica ad Herennium* with the highest of the three levels of style. In the *De oratore* Cicero recommended both *gravitas* and *varietas* for the orator's language and advised that the two qualities should be found together in a public speech. But at the same time he suggested that they would be superfluous in a speech made to an intelligent audience and when time pressed.[9] Machiavelli would have felt that his was a parallel situation. But he goes further and transfers the terms away from style to content. He wants *varietà* and *gravità* to be found in what he has to say, not in the way in which he says it. This rejection of a superficially attractive style in favour of allowing the subject to speak for itself, unadorned, complements the crucial distinction in chapter XV between the states imagined by others and Machiavelli's focus on the actual truth of the matter. The humble style which, by implication, he is adopting is entirely appropriate, since it is the style which Quintilian associated with teaching (*Institutio orato-ria*, XII, 10, 59). What one should note, then, is that Machi-avelli's adoption of rhetorical terminology in order to justify his blunt, businesslike style did not mean that he was addressing only those used to reading Florentine chancery documents. On the contrary, he was addressing all well-educated readers in terms which they would recognise and respect, but he wanted to shock them into awareness that fine words were not enough, that they had to stop dreaming about imaginary states and start listening to the voice of practical experience.

This experimental use of a plain style was, however, aban-doned in Machiavelli's later prose works as he became conscious of his responsibility for upholding the traditional prestige of Florentine prose in competition with writers from Naples, Venice and elsewhere. The publication of his *Arte della guerra* in 1521 by the leading Florentine press, that of the Giunta family, had great significance. This was only the third vernacular prose work which the Giunta had printed and the first by a Florentine; and the two previous ones were the two major examples of contemporary prose literature, Bembo's *Asolani* and Sannazaro's *Arcadia*. In the *Arte*, Machiavelli used a conventional dialogue form and a prose style which was still without superfluous ornamentation but nonetheless more complex and leisurely than that of *The Prince*. One can measure the change of approach by looking at a case in which Machiavelli rewrites a sentence from *The Prince*:

> Sforza, suo padre, sendo soldato della regina Giovanna di Napoli, la lasciò in un tratto disarmata; onde lei, per non perdere el regno, fu costretta gittarsi in grembo al re di Aragona (chapter XII, p. 276; 'Sforza, his father, being hired as a soldier by Queen Giovanna of Naples, left her suddenly unarmed; so that she, in order not to lose her kingdom, was obliged to throw herself into the lap of the King of Aragon').

In the *Arte della guerra* this becomes:

> Sforza, padre di Francesco, costrinse la reina Giovanna a gittarsi nelle braccia del re di Ragona, avendola in un subito abbando-nata e in mezzo a' suoi nimici lasciatala disarmata (book I, p. 306; 'Sforza, father of Francesco, forced Queen Giovanna to throw herself into the arms of the King of Aragon, having suddenly

abandoned her and in the midst of her enemies having left her unarmed').

Here, in place of the original sentence with its two main verbs ('lasciò', 'he left' and 'fu costretta', 'she was obliged') and its change of subject (from Sforza to Giovanna), Machiavelli uses a subordinate construction with a gerund which reverses the logical order of the two actions ('costrinse la reina ... avendola ... disarmata'). In another case the sacrifice of directness is even greater:

> Il re Luigi ... spense quella [ordinanza] de' fanti e cominciò a soldare Svizzeri: il quale errore, seguitato dagli altri, è, come si vede ora in fatto, cagione de' pericoli di quello regno (*The Prince*, chapter XIII, p. 278; 'King Louis abolished that [ordinance] concerning infantry and began to hire Swiss soldiers: an error which, continued by the other [kings], is, as one sees now in practice, the cause of the perils of that kingdom').

> Quanto allo errore che fa il re di Francia a non tenere disciplinati i suoi popoli alla guerra ... non è alcuno, deposta qualche sua particolare passione, che non giudichi questo difetto essere in quel regno e questa negligenza sola farlo debile (*Arte della guerra*, book I, p. 312: 'As for the error which the King of France makes in not keeping his peoples trained for warfare, there is nobody, having set aside any personal partiality, who will not judge that there is this defect in that kingdom and that this negligence alone makes it weak').

The straightforward statement of *The Prince* is replaced by a Latinising sentence which is, for Machiavelli, unusually long-winded and ungainly.[10]

The *Arte della guerra* was certainly successful: it was soon reprinted in Florence (1529) and helped establish Machiavelli's reputation as a military expert.[11] However, the immediacy and crispness of Machiavelli's prose style in *The Prince* evidently did not deter readers. In fact, it seems to have attracted in the 1520s the most elegant Tuscan prose writer of the day, Claudio Tolomei, a Sienese then in exile in Rome. In late 1524 or early 1525 he composed the dialogue *Il Polito* on a subject about as remote as possible from Machiavelli's, the reform of the Italian alphabet. At one point Tolomei observes that different peoples have had an independent alphabet, an 'alfabeto proprio', to suit the needs of their own language ('lingua propria'); they did not want to wear a jacket or shoes belonging to others, which, not being made to one's measure ('fatte a suo dosso'), are either too tight ('stringono') or crippling or too wide, and in short never fit. He must have had in mind what Machiavelli had written in chapter XIII of *The Prince* on one's own forces, *armi proprie*, using the image of borrowed armour which either falls off your back ('ti caggiono di dosso') or weighs you down or is too tight ('stringono', p. 278) Then, towards the end of *Il Polito*, Tolomei warns of the difficulties of introducing spelling reforms: 'I can see nothing which requires such courage to attempt, which is so dangerous to carry out, or more doubtful to achieve ["di pericolo eguale nel maneggiarla, o di dubbio maggiore nel finirla"], than wanting to make any innovation in the institutions ["ordini"] of one's ancestors'.[12] In Tolomei's mind, and probably before his eyes, was what Machiavelli had written in chapter VI on the problems of establishing a new regime if one has become prince through *virtù:* 'one must realise that there is nothing more difficult to arrange, more doubtful to succeed in, nor more dangerous to carry through, than making oneself a leader to introduce new institutions' ('debbasi considerare come non è cosa più difficile a trattare, né più dubia a riuscire, né più periculosa a maneggiare, che farsi capo a introdurre nuovi ordini', p. 265).

We can look next at the influence of *The Prince* on works linked with the question of the government of Florence. Machiavelli's treatise was written and began to circulate during a period of intense debate on the way in which Florence should be controlled by the Medici. Their restoration in September 1512 had soon been followed by a return to their traditional method of exercising authority by filling the key institutions of the republic with their supporters. The abolition of the Great Council also represented a return to a more narrowly based form of government. In spite of this, the new Medicean regime was regarded with misgiving by some patricians. On the one hand, there were those who feared that the Medici would mistrust and ignore the leading citizens, so that they would lose all influence. On the other hand, some were impatient with the ambiguity of the system and wanted the Medici to establish a true principality in Florence under the young Lorenzo, grandson of Lorenzo il Magnifico. The election of Lorenzo's uncle Giovanni as Pope Leo X in March 1513 had brought exciting new possibilities for the Medici and for Florentines, but also created a new anxiety for the patricians: would the new power base of the Medici in Rome lead them to neglect the government of Florence and to concentrate too much of their attention on establishing their authority in the Papal States?

Early in 1516 a member of a distinguished Florentine family, Francesco Guicciardini, voiced his fears in a *Discorso del modo di assicurare lo stato ai Medici* (*Discourse on Securing the Medicean Regime*), written to clarify his own thoughts.[13] He argues that the position of the Medici is unstable: the *popolo* is hostile, the Medici have no powerful supporters and it is dangerous to rely on the support of the papacy. He therefore proposes that the Medici should base their regime on three 'foundations': they should concentrate on their position in Florence rather than on new states elsewhere; they should favour and consult with experienced and well-established citizens; and they should keep the population as a whole content, as far as possible, by paying due attention to communal finances and civil justice and by ensuring that the weaker were not oppressed by the stronger. Some details in the *Discorso* suggest that Guicciardini was using ideas from *The Prince* but adapting them freely to his own purposes. His comments on the difficulty of keeping new states, caused by the opposition of neighbouring powers ('vicini potenti') and the hostility of the inhabitants ('pessime disposizione di populi', p. 269), have some resemblance to Machiavelli's reflections on the same topic in chapter III of *The Prince*. Guicciardini uses the advice in chapter XXIII of *The Prince* on giving ministers free power to tell a prince the truth ('libero arbitrio a parlargli la verità', p. 293) in order to support the cause of his own class, and says that the Medici would receive good guidance if there were some trusted citizens whom they encouraged to speak the truth freely ('a' quali dessino animo di parlare liberamente el vero', p. 271). When Guicciardini warned the Medici that excessive taxation would have two effects, arousing universal hatred and making the city weak and poor through the running down of 'its life

which consists in commerce and occupations' ('la vita sua, che
sono la industria e li esercizi', p. 277), he was perhaps drawing
together the connection made in *The Prince* between high taxes
and hatred (chapter XVI), Machiavelli's praise of German cities
for protecting those occupations which are their strength and
life ('quegli esercizii che sieno il nervo e la vita di quella città',
chapter X, p. 273), and his advice that the Prince should encourage his subjects in their occupations ('esercizi', chapter XXI).

But Guicciardini also takes issue with Machiavelli by insert-
ing what he admits is a digression on Francesco Sforza and
Cesare Borgia (pp. 270–1). In *The Prince*, chapter VII, Machiavelli had contrasted the two, intending to support his thesis
that it is hard to gain a principality through *virtù* but easy to
keep it, while it is easy to gain one through fortune but hard
to keep it. For Guicciardini, Machiavelli's account was simplistic, a generalisation which did not stand up to a historian's
scrutiny. He points out how difficult it is for private citizens
like Cesare to acquire great states. Then he says that, if Sforza
succeeded in the even more difficult task of keeping his state,
it was because of a rare combination of circumstances: Sforza's
exceptional prowess, the ending of the Visconti line, the
Milanese being accustomed to servitude, and their hostility to
the alternative of being ruled by Venice.

Guicciardini ended his *Discorso* with a warning against
those who believed that it would be safer for the Medici to take
absolute power officially rather than ruling under a pretence of
liberty, through magistrates ('per mezzo de' magistrati', p. 269)
whose appointments they had manipulated. One cannot be
certain that Lorenzo seriously intended to become lord of the
city, but his style of control was undoubtedly becoming more
despotic. It is quite possible that Guicciardini thought that *The
Prince* was being used to encourage Lorenzo in this tendency,
for the last section of chapter IX discusses the problems of
making the leap from ruling 'per mezzo de' magistrati' to
absolute power (p. 272).[14] Whether or not Machiavelli believed
that Lorenzo should become prince in Florence – and again
there is no firm evidence – the combination of his dedication
and Lorenzo's autocratic style probably made it inevitable that
Florentines should jump to the conclusion that, as Benedetto

Varchi put it in mid-century in his *Storia fiorentina* (IV, 15), Machiavelli addressed *The Prince* to Lorenzo 'so that he should make himself absolute lord of Florence'.[15]

Among those who urged that the Medici should move towards a principality was Guicciardini's brother-in-law Lodovico Alamanni. Late in 1516, in Rome, he wrote two letters to the imperial ambassador, Alberto Pio of Carpi, on the need for Lorenzo, increasingly absent from Florence and withdrawn from involvement in government, to take the Florentine state seriously and on how Lorenzo should go about ruling it and increasing its power.[16] The influence of *The Prince* can be seen in Alamanni's method of argument (the formulation of clear-cut alternatives, the concise weighing up of their advantages and drawbacks), in his choice of examples, and in some of his advice. In the first letter, for instance, he warns of the danger of putting off securing one's position (*assicurarsi*) until necessity makes certain actions excusable. There are two ways of securing the regime: by winning over enough supporters or by getting rid of opponents. One can get rid of men either with or without a pretext, and in one of two ways, by exile or death. Alamanni draws on the eighth chapter of *The Prince* for the advice not to put off winning over people by benefiting them (a concept for which both writers use the phrase 'guadagnarseli con beneficarli') until one's favour is judged to be done under duress. There is another similarity of terminology between Alamanni's use of a graphic but generic verb, *spacciare*, in the same sense of 'to eliminate politically' as Machiavelli's characteristic *spegnere*. The eighth chapter of *The Prince* also provides Alamanni with the examples of Agathocles and Oliverotto, and, like Buonaccorsi, he explicitly condemns such actions, saying that Lorenzo must not imitate them. In the second letter, Alamanni borrows from *The Prince*, chapters XII and XIII, when he contrasts the use of one's own army and of mercenaries, attributes the rise of the latter to the clergy and the middle classes, and rejects the conventional attribution of military failure to divine punishment for Italy's sins. He cites the thriftiness of Louis XII, as did Machiavelli in chapter XVI; and he repeats Machiavelli's advice (in chapter XXI) on the dangers of neutrality, using the same example of Antiochus and the Romans.

Alamanni's letters are important because they show not just the early impact of *The Prince* on contemporary political writing but also the way in which its ideas were soon diffused outside Florence and appropriated for purposes which had nothing to do with those of Machiavelli. Unlike Guicciardini, Alamanni was writing in another city, addressing himself to a non-Tuscan who represented a major European power, the Emperor Maximilian, and seeking to promote at the same time his own career and his views on the Medicean state and its foreign policy. Machiavelli would have been horrified at the suggestion of this Florentine, nearly twenty years younger than him, that, since the older citizens would never give up their tradition of liberty (or rather, as he calls it, 'asininity', 'asineria'), Lorenzo should use favours in order to entice the leading young citizens to become his courtiers.

Later examples of the use of *The Prince* in Florence, but by a critic of Lorenzo de' Medici's autocratic tendencies, are found in two writings by Francesco Guicciardini's nephew Niccolò. One is a letter dated 29 July 1517 to his father Luigi, dedicatee of Machiavelli's *Capitolo dell'ambizione*. Niccolò was born only in 1501 and, as the letter shows, was still receiving lessons in 1517. But he was already familiar with *The Prince*. Luigi was Florentine commissioner in Arezzo, and Niccolò was concerned at the news of the movement of Spanish troops towards the city because this might provide the Aretines with an opportunity to rebel. 'It would be necessary, in order to make sure of them', the young man wrote, 'to do as Machiavelli says in his work *De principatibus* that Ivriotto da Fermo did when he wanted to become lord of [Fermo], and even then one could not be completely sure of the others' ('bisognerebbe, a volere assicurarsene, fare come dice el Machiavello in quella sua opera *De principatibus* che fece Ivriotto da Fermo, quando se ne volle insignorire, et anche poi non sarebbe da fidarsi al tutto degli altri').[17] Niccolò was taking totally out of context Machiavelli's account in chapter VIII of the slaughter of the leading citizens of Fermo when Oliverotto (as he was usually known) seized control of the town. One would like to know how Luigi reacted to receiving such advice from his son.

Niccolò used *The Prince* again in an essay written a year or so later, between 1518 and 1519. Given his youth, his views at this stage probably reflected those of his father and of his uncle Francesco.[18] After recounting in detail how Lorenzo had (regrettably, he implied) become lord of Florence in all but name, Niccolò explained that the most common causes of a prince losing his state are a popular uprising, a conspiracy, or an external threat, and that there were three measures which Lorenzo ought to take in order to make his regime secure: to dispose all his subjects favourably towards his rule, to establish a good militia recruited above all from Florentine territory, and to acquire good and powerful allies. This advice appears to be a reworking of Machiavelli's analysis in chapter XIX of the internal and external threats to a prince. The young Guicciardini subdivided the internal threat into uprisings and conspiracies, whereas Machiavelli considered only the latter. But Machiavelli had given all three countermeasures: a prince can guard against conspiracies by avoiding hatred or contempt and keeping the people satisfied with him; and he can defend himself against external powers in two ways, with a good army and with good allies. According to Niccolò Guicciardini, Lorenzo's only protection against the three threats was his powerful ally Pope Leo; Lorenzo was not suited to organising a militia and he had antagonised the people, partly because he did not abstain from women as he should, thus going against Machiavelli's advice at the start of chapter XIX.

So far, looking at works written for private circulation between 1516 and 1519 in the context of the Florentine constitutional debate, we have seen some selective use being made of ideas and examples from *The Prince*, some evidence of a feeling that an account of Agathocles or Oliverotto should carry a warning against imitation of their actions, and some criticism of Machiavelli's interpretation of historical evidence, but no apparent hostility to the argument that what are traditionally considered virtues can be politically harmful and that vices can be politically beneficial. If, however, we go outside this context, a few years forward in time and into the world of print, we find a work which uses *The Prince* extensively but which at the same time reasserts conventional political ethics: the *De regnandi peritia* (*On the skill of ruling*) by Agostino Nifo of Sessa

Aurunca.[19] Nifo had a close relationship with Leo X. He was invited by the Pope to teach philosophy in Rome in 1514. After dedicating to Leo in 1518 his polemic with Pomponazzi on the immortality of the soul, he was sent by Leo to teach philosophy at the university of Pisa (controlled by Florence), where he remained from 1519 to 1522. He was also granted the right to use the name of Medici. In this period Nifo began astutely to cultivate and exploit the interests of Medicean Florence, writing in particular on the question of princely rule, still topical though less charged with controversy since the death of Lorenzo in 1519. The Giunta press brought out in 1521 Nifo's *Libellus de his quae ab optimis principibus agenda sunt* (*Pamphlet on what the Best Princes must Do*). This described one by one the virtues – clemency, piety and so on – of the ideal prince, reinforcing the message of the *Institutio principis christiani* (*Education of a Christian Prince*) of Erasmus which had been printed by the Giunta in 1520. Since the Florentine branch of the Giunta press normally published only literary works, Nifo may, it has been plausibly suggested, have been encouraged to write and publish the *Libellus* in reaction to Machiavelli's *Prince*.[20] But in 1522, after Pope Leo's death, Nifo returned to Sessa, taking with him a manuscript of *The Prince*. In the Kingdom of Naples he was free to treat the Florentine work as a quarry of new ideas and examples which would attract the interest of the court and of other intellectuals; and he immediately used it in order to create the *De regnandi peritia*, completed in October 1522 and printed in Naples by Caterina Mayr in the following March. It was dedicated to the same person as was Erasmus's *Institutio*, the Emperor Charles V, though in 1516 Erasmus had been addressing a sixteen-year-old prince. The first four books transformed and reorganised the material of *The Prince*. Books I (on acquiring states) and III (on protecting them against threats from their subjects) were based on chapters I–XI of *The Prince*, book II (on military defence against external threats) adapted chapters XII–XIV and XX, while book IV (on further questions arising from the previous two books) used chapters XVI–XXIII. Sections of *The Prince* were rewritten, whole chapters (XV, XXIV–XXVI) and parts of others were omitted, and much new material was added. There

was also a fifth book which brought readers back to reassur-
ingly familiar territory by dealing 'with the honourable type of
ruling' ('de honesto regnandi genere').[21]

Nifo was able to take over some of Machiavelli's ideas
unchanged. He evaluates in book II (2–8) the different types of
soldiers just as Machiavelli did in chapters XII and XIII. He
agrees with what Machiavelli says in chapter IX on the civil
Prince's need for popular support (III, 10–12). At the same time,
Nifo was careful to adapt his material to the political context of
the south. He added a number of contemporary Neapolitan
examples. However, most of his alterations and additions were
intended to ensure that the *De regnandi peritia* would win praise
for originality of approach (perhaps particularly in comparison
with Erasmus's work) but without incurring condemnation for
breaking abruptly with traditional ethics.

In this respect, his most important addition was the distinction on which Erasmus had insisted in the first section of his
Institutio but which Machiavelli had deliberately omitted in *The
Prince*, that between tyrants and kings. For Nifo, the deeds of
tyrants were to be treated as poisons, those of kings as anti-
dotes. Nifo's definition of a tyrant is at times a legal one. In the
first chapter of book V, a tyrant is a ruler who has reached the
throne neither through succession nor through election; the
opposite, then, of Charles V, who had inherited the throne of
Naples in 1516 and had been elected emperor in 1519, though
admittedly with the help of bribes. Even a civil prince tended
to become a tyrant, since he lacked a legitimate title to rule (III,
10). A regime which was technically a tyranny could be benign
('iucunda tyrannis', I, 10), like that of Lorenzo il Magnifico.
However, tyranny also had strongly pejorative overtones for
Nifo. He followed Aristotle (*Politics*, 1279a–b, 1295a, 1311a) in
defining a tyrant as someone who rules for his own rather than
the common good (I, 1). The tyrant is associated with the
neglect of peaceful occupations (II, 11), with injustice (II, 13),
with merely pretending to keep one's word and with what is
done out of political expediency ('regnandi causa', IV, 11). His
fate is to suffer in this world and the next, while the king will
be rewarded with lasting fame and eternal glory (V, 5–6). The
importance of a ruler's moral attributes means that it is possible

for a king to become a tyrant and vice versa, which is why the Prince must have virtues like liberality and piety (V, proem).

This framework allowed Nifo to take over from *The Prince* various passages on harsh rule which could not have figured in conventional works on princes, since he could present them as tyrannical 'poisons'. He could cite the effectiveness of the Romans' destruction of previously independent cities, commenting that such things are tyrannical and wicked ('tyrannica et impia', III, 5). He could use the close of Machiavelli's chapter IX, on the transition from a civil to an absolute principality, without having to add any adverse comment, because by his criterion this was a transition between types of tyranny ('ex civile ad absolutam tyrannidem', III, 13). In IV, 4, similarly, he could accept Machiavelli's view that it is safer to be feared than loved, given that bad men outnumber good ones, as long as this applied to the voluntary love which is given to a tyrant; for a king, it was of course preferable to be loved with the natural love which his subjects have for him.

Nifo could also simultaneously follow his Florentine source and distance himself from it by adding moralising comments. When in I, 5 he used the same two examples from *The Prince*, chapter VIII, of those who came to power through crime, he stressed the debauchery of Agathocles as a young man, first catamite then womaniser, and he said that Oliverotto met his end, after he had been created tyrant, through divine vengeance ('ulciscente Deo'), because of his treachery and disloyalty to Cesare Borgia. Nifo noted the effectiveness of Cesare's murder of Ramiro de Lorqua (*Prince*, chapter VII) but condemned Cesare for using cruelty and crimes and added that Cesare too lost his principality through God's revenge (III, 7 and 9).

Another technique used by Nifo was to cite Machiavelli's views but to disown them by attributing them to others. Sometimes he was not specific about his source, as when he borrowed Machiavelli's comments in chapters XVI and XVII on the dangers of liberality (IV, I) or the 'good' use of cruelty by Cesare Borgia (IV, 3). Sometimes he gave 'historians' ('historici') as his source. This was the case when he repeated, from chapter III of *The Prince*, the ways of ruling annexed principalities (III, 2), adding that the use of colonies was tyrannical; or when he gave the explanation, from chapter VIII, that cruelty used once and for all can keep someone like Agathocles in power (III, 8); or when he gave Machiavelli's advice in chapter XVIII on being prepared to fight by force as well as by laws, even though the former is proper to beasts (IV, 11). For Nifo, clearly, historical knowledge was not enough for a proper analysis of the correct course of action. His ideal counsellor should certainly be skilled in history but should also be able to distinguish right from wrong, and he criticised the error of princes in not using philosophers or lawyers known for their prudence, virtue and goodwill (IV, 15). The views which he endorsed himself were those of philosophers (IV, 17; V, 6), or more precisely moral philosophers (IV, 3 and 11), and of 'holy men' ('sacri viri', IV, 3). *The Prince*, then, was for Nifo a work which lacked a philosophical, legal and religious dimension. But his reservations did not prevent him from using it opportunistically in order to create a stir in Naples. He must have met with some success, for he reused both his *Libellus* of 1521 and the *De regnandi peritia* to create a third work, the *Libellus de rege et tyranno* (*Pamphlet on the King and the Tyrant*), printed in Naples in January 1526.

Another work of the 1520s whose teaching countered *The Prince* was written by a Florentine, Antonio Brucioli. In 1522, when a plot to assassinate Cardinal Giulio de' Medici was discovered, Brucioli had to flee his city. He was not one of the leading conspirators but was closely associated with one of them, Luigi Alamanni, younger half-brother of Lodovico. Brucioli settled in Venice. Here he was quick to realise that a well-educated person, even with a lower-class background like his own, could earn a living with the help of the city's thriving printing industry. His first publication was a collection of dialogues (*Dialogi*) on moral philosophy, printed in 1526 and revised in two later editions of 1538 and 1544.[22] Machiavelli's *Arte della guerra* must have been Brucioli's main inspiration to write dialogues in the vernacular, and indeed it is one of the unacknowledged sources on which Brucioli tended to depend heavily: there are several close correspondences between it and his eighth dialogue, on the military captain. Given Brucioli's close links with the circle of intellectuals, including Machiavelli, which met informally in the Orti Oricellari (the gardens of the

Rucellai family in Florence), it is very probable that he had read *The Prince* by 1522, though he may not have had access to a copy when writing the first version of the *Dialogi*. The hypothesis that he already knew the work is supported by a passage in the fifth dialogue, *Della republica* (*On the Republic*). The main speaker is asked to describe republics according to reality, not according to those impossible ones imagined by some; and this request, which is out of key with Brucioli's idealistic approach, recalls Machiavelli's rejection in chapter XV of those who have imagined republics never seen in fact.

However, Brucioli's *Dialogi* champion traditional standards of political ethics, making use especially of Aristotle's *Politics*, the oration of Isocrates to Nicocles, Xenophon's *Hieron*, and Erasmus's *Institutio*. One of his aims may well have been to combat what he would have seen as Machiavelli's dangerously subversive new thought. Brucioli would have had two main reasons for taking issue with Machiavelli. First, Brucioli was deeply religious and an advocate of strict moral conduct. Second, although in the 1530s he became a secret informer to Duke Cosimo I, in the 1520s he was bitterly opposed to the Medici and in particular to Clement VII, alluded to in 1526 as a tyrannical monster. Brucioli and his fellow exiles would have associated Machiavelli with this tyranny, as author of *The Prince* and then of a Florentine history commissioned by Clement when still a cardinal.

Brucioli used two dialogues to defend the tradition of the virtuous ruler as distinct from the vicious tyrant: *Del governo del principe* (*On Princely Rule*, renamed in the later editions *Del giusto principe*, *On the Just Prince*) and *Della tirannide* (*On Tyranny*). Brucioli argued in the former that the chief foundation for the ruler's authority is religion. This is not just the appearance of religion which Machiavelli advised the prince to seem to have but to be prepared to cast aside if necessary. Brucioli's king had to be truly religious, to hate vices, follow virtues, and to love the truth so much that he is trusted by all. What Machiavelli wrote on going against one's word was also singled out for condemnation in the same period by Luigi Alamanni: his second *Satira* (written between 1524 and 1527 and first printed in his *Opere toscane* in 1532) contained a sarcastic attack on an unnamed but easily identifiable 'golden book of morality' ('l'aureo libro moral'), now in the hands of Italy's oppressors, which advised wise men to keep their promises only when it suited them.[23]

Brucioli's advice on hatred and contempt in *Del governo del principe* is also deliberately different from that of *The Prince*. He imitated a passage of Erasmus's *Institutio* in which the Prince is told to avoid arousing these two emotions, which are caused by traditional vices, and to cultivate their opposites, goodwill and authority, which result from traditional virtues. Machiavelli concentrated on how to avoid hatred and contempt and mentioned the goodwill of the people only some way into chapter XIX. He believed that good deeds, just as much as vices, could lead to hatred, that virtues such as justice and benignity (which for Brucioli were among the causes of goodwill) did not necessarily prevent a ruler's downfall, and that integrity (a source of authority, for Brucioli) was one of the qualities which one should seem to have but be prepared to put aside. At other points Brucioli is a little closer to Machiavelli's position. He agreed that excessive taxation caused hatred, and his addition of effeminacy to Erasmus's list of the causes of contempt could have been suggested by his reading of *The Prince*, chapter XIX. However, these two dialogues remained substantially unchanged in the 1538 edition of the moral *Dialogi*, even though Brucioli, now a collaborator of the Medicean regime, here relaxed his opposition to *The Prince* so far as to add to the *Dialogo della republica* a long passage on mercenaries based on chapter XII, as well as using Machiavelli's *Discorsi*.[24]

Reaction against *The Prince* can also be found in the *Novelle* (first three parts printed in Lucca, 1554) of the Dominican friar Matteo Bandello, who had met Machiavelli in 1526.[25] One character is described as an excellent 'simulatore e dissimulatore', as Machiavelli said the Prince had to be (chapter XVIII, p. 283), but is compared in the same breath with the cruel tyrant whom he served (II, 13). In the dedication of III, 5, Bandello recalls a discussion about the qualities which a good prince should possess if he is to avoid a reputation for tyranny and make himself loved rather than feared, for love is the Prince's greatest fortress. Here he is correcting *The Prince* (chapters XVII and

XX) as Brucioli had done when he quoted Erasmus's distinction in the *Institutio* between the tyrant's wish to be feared and the king's wish to be loved, and when he preferred to identify the safest bodyguard for a prince with the people's goodwill rather than following Machiavelli's more realistic dictum that the best fortress is not to be hated.[26]

Yet Bandello is also attracted to *The Prince*. In another story (II, 16) the narrator begins with a very pragmatic analysis of the problems facing a new prince of a previously free state. It can be no coincidence that the ruler in question is Alessandro de' Medici, first duke of Florence, since *The Prince* had been exploited by Clement VII and the Medicean faction in order to support the establishment of the duchy: hence the printing of the work first in Rome in January 1532, during the period of discussions about the new constitution (with a dedication to Filippo Strozzi, one of Lorenzo's chief advisers, and a reminder that Lorenzo had effectively ruled as a prince), then in Florence on 8 May, less than a fortnight after the establishment of the principality. Bandello's narrator tells us that, in order to establish his dominion, Alessandro is forced to remove all his opponents by death, by exile, or by forced residence. Machiavelli had warned in chapter V of *The Prince* of the extreme measures needed in order to rule cities accustomed to liberty and had recommended that such cities should be 'ruined' and their inhabitants separated and dispersed. If the alternatives of death and exile recall Lodovico Alamanni's letters of 1516, that too may not be coincidental. Bandello had linked Machiavelli and Alamanni in the first story of the *Novelle*, narrated by Alamanni in the friar's presence during the Florentine's embassy to the French commander Lautrec in Milan from 1518 to 1519 and based on an episode in Machiavelli's *Istorie fiorentine*.[27]

Bandello's ambiguous attitude to *The Prince* is typical of the time. In letters or papers written for private circulation, Florentines could reveal their fascination with Machiavelli's analysis of effective statecraft. But in public it was not possible to approve what he had dared to say. The same chapters that had aroused most interest in private – those on reaching power through crime (VIII) and on vices and virtues (XV–XIX) – seem to have been the main cause first of a backlash against *The Prince* in works printed from the 1520s onwards, which reasserted the distinction between the tyrant and the good prince, and then of the deforming readings which I mentioned at the start of this chapter. If *The Prince* failed to bring Machiavelli the personal benefits for which he hoped, being used by the Medici only after his death, this was partly because he had boldly sent his message in a literary form which would circulate widely and in which it would be least expected, that of a treatise. What Bandello made one of his narrators say, referring to the *Discorsi*, about Machiavelli's lack of discretion, his excessive openness about what should remain hidden, must equally have been the reaction of many early readers of *The Prince*:

> I can truly only admire, praise and commend the acuteness of Machiavelli's intelligence; but I feel the lack in him of a very good judgement, and I wish he had been somewhat more moderate and restrained and not so quick to teach many bad and wicked things, which he could and should easily have avoided, keeping silent about them and not revealing them to others.　　　(III, 55)

Notes

1　*Il Principe*, ed. L. A. Burd (Oxford: Clarendon Press, 1891), p. 35. Machiavelli's works are quoted in this essay from Mario Martelli's edition of *Tutte le opere* (Florence: Sansoni, 1971). Translations are my own.

2　In his *Discours sur les moyens de bien gouverner et maintenir en bonne paix un Royaume ou autre Principauté ... contre Nicolas Machiavel Florentin*, [Geneva], 1576; see especially the preface to part III. There is a modern edition entitled *Anti-Machiavel*, ed. C. Edward Rathé (Geneva: Droz, 1968).

3　Those in Florence, Biblioteca Medicea Laurenziana (XLIV 32) and Biblioteca Riccardiana (2603); Rome, Biblioteca dell'Accademia dei Lincei (Corsiniano 43 B 35); Vatican City, Biblioteca Apostolica Vaticana (Barb. lat. 5093); Paris, Bibliothèque Nationale (It. 709); Gotha, Landesbiblio-thek (B 70); and the manuscript at Charlecote Park. See A. Gerber, *Niccolò Machiavelli: Die Handschriften, Ausgaben und Übersetzungen seiner Werke im 16. und 17. Jahrhundert*, 3 vols and facsimiles (Gotha: Perthes, 1912-13), vol. I, pp. 82-100; O. Tommasini, *La vita e gli scritti di Niccolò Machiavelli*, 2 vols (Rome: Loescher, 1883-1911), vol. II, pp. 1013-20; A. E. Quaglio, 'Per il testo del "De principatibus" di Niccolò Machiavelli', *Lettere italiane*, 19 (1967), pp. 141-86; J. H. Whitfield, 'The Charlecote manuscript of Machiavelli's *Prince*', in *Discourses on Machiavelli* (Cambridge: Heffer, 1969), pp. 207-29; and G. Inglese, 'Il Principe (De principatibus) di Niccolò Machiavelli', in *Letteratura italiana:*

le opere, vol. I (Turin: Einaudi, 1992), pp. 889–941 (p. 894), including reference to Munich, Universitätsbibliothek, MS in-4° 787.

4   Those in the Laurenziana, the Riccardiana and in Paris. See D. Fachard, *Biagio Buonaccorsi: sa vie, son temps, son œuvre* (Bologna: Boni, 1976), pp. 158-60, and p. 215 for Buonaccorsi's record of copying the text in 1519.

5   J. Ruysschaert, 'Le copiste Genesius de la Barrera et le manuscrit Barberini d' "Il principe" de Machiavelli', in M. P. Gilmore (ed.), *Studies on Machiavelli* (Florence: Sansoni, 1972), pp. 349-59.

6   Whitfield, 'The Charlecote manuscript', pp. 212, 229.

7   Formerly Phillipps 7375: Whitfield, 'The Charlecote manuscript', pp. 209-10.

8   On Machiavelli's style in *The Prince*, see F. Chiappelli, *Studi sul linguaggio del Machiavelli* (Florence: Le Monnier, 1952).

9   A speech in the senate can be relatively simple, since it is an inherently wise gathering and others have to speak, but 'an oration before a public assembly ['contio'] takes in the whole power and gravity of oratory, and demands variety': *De oratore*, II LXXXII, 334.

10 On the transition from Machiavelli's prose in *The Prince* to that of the 1520s, see also Paolo Trovato's introduction to *La vita di Castruccio Castracani da Lucca*, ed. R. Brakkee and P. Trovato (Naples: Liguori, 1986), pp. 32-40.

11 ·S. Anglo, 'Machiavelli as a military authority: some early sources', in *Florence and Italy: Renaissance Studies in Honour of Nicolai Rubinstein*, ed. P. Denley and C. Elam (London: Westfield College, 1988), pp. 321-34.

12 *Il Polito*, 90-1, 304, in *Trattati sull'ortografia del volgare 1524-1526*, ed. B. Richardson (Exeter: University of Exeter, 1984).

13 In *Dialogo e discorsi del reggimento di Firenze*, ed. R. Palmarocchi (Bari: Laterza, 1932), pp. 267-81; see also R. von Albertini, *Firenze dalla repubblica al principato* (Turin: Einaudi, 1970), pp. 94-5.

14 On Lorenzo's ambitions, see R. Devonshire Jones, 'Lorenzo de' Medici, Duca d'Urbino, "Signore" of Florence?', in Gilmore (ed.), *Studies on Machiavelli*, pp. 297-315, and *Francesco Vettori: Florentine Citizen and Medici Servant* (London: Athlone Press, 1972), pp. 109-42; H. C. Butters, *Governors and Government in Early Sixteenth-Century Florence 1502–1519* (Oxford: Clarendon Press, 1985), pp. 224-5, 301-3. J. N. Stephens suggests that *The Prince* may be echoed in the advice of Lorenzo's secretary, Goro Gheri, that all that matters for a prince is success in maintaining his state: 'Machiavelli's *Prince* and the Florentine Revolution of 1512', *Italian Studies*, 41 (1986), pp. 45-61 (p. 49).

15 Varchi, *Storia fiorentina*, ed. Gaetano Milanesi, 3 vols (Florence: Le Monnier, 1857-8), vol. I, p. 200. On Varchi's evidence, see Burd's introduction to *Il Principe*, pp. 39-41.

16 On these letters, see Albertini, *Firenze dalla repubblica al principato*, pp. 33-6, 376-90 (where the text is given); C. Dionisotti, *Machiavellerie*

(Turin: Einaudi, 1980), pp. 124-7; Butters, *Governors and Government*, pp. 301-2. Lorenzo's lack of involvement with Florence is mentioned by Butters, pp. 278-9.

17 For this letter, see J. Stephens and H. Butters, 'New light on Machiavelli', *English Historical Review*, 97 (1982), pp. 54-69 (pp. 60-2, 68-9).

18 On this essay, see Albertini, *Firenze dalla repubblica al principato*, pp. 32-3, 365-75 (where the text is given).

19 For a biographical sketch and bibliography, see E. P. Mahoney, 'Agostino Nifo', *Dictionary of Scientific Biography*, vol. X (New York: Scribner's, 1974), pp. 122-4.

20 For this suggestion and on Nifo's links with Florentine culture, see Dionisotti, *Machiavellerie*, pp. 127-33.

21 On this work, see Gerber, *Niccolò Machiavelli*, vol. III, pp. 7-12; G. Procacci, *Studi sulla fortuna del Machiavelli* (Rome: Istituto storico italiano per l'età moderna e contemporanea, 1965), pp. 3-26; Dionisotti, *Machiavellerie*, pp. 133-4. The Neapolitan edition of 1523 is reproduced, with facing translation, in *Une réécriture du 'Prince' de Machiavel: le 'De regnandi peritia' de Agostino Nifo*, ed. S. Pernet-Beau and P. Larivaille (Université Paris X-Nanterre: Centre de recherches de langue et littérature italienne, 1987). Larivaille discusses the possible circulation of different redactions of *The Prince* (pp. viii–x); some other contributions on this question, which lies outside the scope of the present essay, are mentioned in Inglese, 'Il Principe', pp. 936-7.

22 There is a modern edition: *Dialogi*, ed. A. Landi (Naples: Prismi, 1982). On Brucioli, see especially G. Spini, *Tra Rinascimento e Riforma: Antonio Brucioli* (Florence: La Nuova Italia, 1940). On Brucioli and Machiavelli, see Procacci, *Studi sulla fortuna*, pp. 26-43, and, arguing persuasively for a different interpretation of the evidence, Dionisotti, *Machiavellerie*, pp. 193-226.

23 This allusion is noted by Dionisotti, *Machiavellerie*, pp. 152-3.

24 On Brucioli's borrowings from Machiavelli in the *Dialogo della republica* of 1538, see Procacci, *Studi sulla fortuna*, pp. 33-42.

25 On Machiavelli and Bandello, see A. Fiorato, 'Bandello et le règne du père', in A. Rochon and others, *Les Ecrivains et le pouvoir en Italie à l'époque de la Renaissance* (Paris: Université de la Sorbonne Nouvelle, 1973), pp. 77-154 (pp. 124-9).

26 See Landi's edition of the *Dialogi*, pp. 267 (*Del governo del principe*) and 219 (*Della tirannide*). In talking of the goodwill of the people, Brucioli was singling out an idea from Isocrates, *Ad Nicoclem*, 21. Machiavelli had adapted Seneca's comment that 'there is only one impregnable defence: the love of one's citizens' (*De clementia*, I, 19.6).

27 On the embassy, see H. Hauvette, *Un Exilé florentin à la cour de France au XVIe siècle: Luigi Alamanni* (Paris: Hachette, 1903), pp. 6-7; Butters, *Governors and Government*, p. 302. It is also mentioned in the *Novelle*, III, 41, dedication.

3

Machiavelli's *via moderna*: medieval and Renaissance attitudes to history

JANET COLEMAN

In the *proemio* (introduction) to the *Discorsi*, Machiavelli speaks of having decided to enter upon a road which, he says, has not yet been followed by anyone.[1] By following this *via*, examples from antiquity could be shown to be useful to those who, in his own day, wished to found a republic, maintain states, govern kingdoms, organise an army, conduct a war, dispense justice and extend empires. He does not mean that this road has *never* been travelled before. Indeed, he tells us that contemporary jurists were prepared to use civil law remedies prescribed by the ancients to direct their decisions and that the current practice of medicine also drew on the experiences of ancient physicians to guide their present judgements (p. 124). Only contemporary princes or republics were unprepared to have recourse to ancient examples (p. 124).

As this is a rhetorical introduction, we may suspect that Machiavelli overstates his case for literary effect. But could it be that Italians, and notably Florentines with political ambition in the latter fifteenth and early sixteenth century, and especially 'new men' who were not from the traditional, hereditary social elites, were not receiving an appropriate grammar and rhetorical education to enable them to read Latin and thereby benefit from what ancient texts could tell them?[2] The lessons of antiquity could be of use especially to republican citizens and, hence, these lessons were to be revealed in a commentary on republics, *The Discourses on Livy*. Machiavelli insists that

everyone knows that history shows us the most virtuous works
('le virtuosissime operazioni che le istorie ci mostrono') of
ancient kingdoms and republics, but when it comes to organising republics ('ordinare le republiche') or ruling kingdoms
('governare e' regni') his contemporaries are more prepared to
admire than to imitate ('essere piu presto ammirate che imitate')
these past exemplary deeds. Here, then, is the problem as he
sees it. It appears that the practitioners of juristic and medical
sciences of his day knew how to read history correctly and to
benefit from that reading[3] but that men engaged in what today
we would call 'political activities' had not developed this skill.
The road Machiavelli intends to follow is clearly one that every
specialist in his society already follows *except* princes and
governors of republics. Hence, the route is not a new one *tout
court*. His aim is to show princes and republicans what other
specialists already know how to do. Machiavelli does not seek
to teach a new way of reading ancient texts; rather, he shows
how an already established way of reading history may be
applied to contemporary problems concerning the governance
of men and the maintenance of states, be they princedoms or,
more to the point in this work, republics. He pursues a similar
purpose in *Il Principe*.

This chapter examines what Machiavelli means by 'history'
and his understanding of the past as exemplary and imitable. It
shows how his examination of historical texts was part of a
distinctive medieval tradition of textual study, still very much
alive in his own day, which rendered the past 'usable' in the
present. He believed that it was from a 'correct' reading of history
that the laws of politics may be induced, just as the 'correct'
reading of 'historical' texts had already provided judicial and
medical practitioners with principles and ' laws' that were appli-
cable to sixteenth-century Italian Renaissance society. Machiavelli's historical analysis of ancient texts and the laws of human
behaviour which he believes can be elicited from past writings
about human action was part of a long tradition of reading texts
that was elaborately developed during the Middle Ages. It was
a method of reading that was not new to the Renaissance. Nor
is it a method that resembles what modern historians are
supposed to be doing when they read and interpret ancient

historical texts to try to understand, in a disinterested way, what ancient authors meant within social contexts that were vastly different from those of the modern world and its values.[4] Modern historians deal with an over-and-done-with past in and for itself, where past-people's actions in the past may be understood but cannot be imitated; Machiavelli's past is, for him, alive and capable of imitation. It is a past *for* the present.[5]

This is made clear in the dedicatory letter to Lorenzo which introduces *The Prince* to its intended reader. Machiavelli writes that among his possessions there is nothing he holds so dear or esteems so highly as the knowledge of the actions of great men which he has learned by long experience of modern things and from a continuous reading of antiquity ('quanto la cognizione della azioni delli uomini grandi, imparta con una lunga *esperienza* delle cose moderne et una continua *lezione* delle antique', p. 13). He presents to his reader the results of his lengthy and diligent examinations and thoughts on these matters now reduced to written form in a little volume ('le quali avendo io con gran diligenzia lungamente escogitate et esaminate et ora in uno piccolo volume ridotte', p.13). The book is meant to substitute in some way for all those things Machiavelli has learnt through long, dangerous *experiences* over many years and, therefore, to provide its reader with an understanding, from a text, what Machiavelli has come to understand through years of *experience and reading*. The small volume is a short cut to the same knowledge which Machiavelli has acquired by other, more lengthy means. The knowledge provided is of things experienced in the modern world as well as information imparted – not through actual experience but by reading the experience of others recorded in ancient texts ('[un] dono che darle faculta di potere in brevissimo tempo intendere tutto quello che io in tanti anni e con tanti mia disagi e periculi ho conosciuto', p.13).

From the very beginning, then, Machiavelli states that he presents, in writing, his understanding or knowledge of great men's actions drawn from two different sources: one from experience of modern things, that is, his personal, eyewitness experience of men's behaviour, and the other from reading ancient texts. His own textual presentation is unadorned with rhetorical ornament, unlike the writings of others who, he says, seek to embellish their material. He has no need for such embellishment. Instead, he sees his efforts as analogous to the representational method of landscape painters who station themselves in the plains in order to consider the nature of mountains and high places or position themselves on high ground and ascend an eminence in order to get a good view of the plains. He explicitly states that painters represent the *nature* of what is there to be seen. They use the learned conventions of artistic representation (not least the 'science' of perspective) to represent through paint on two-dimensional surfaces the *nature* of the world that is seen with the eyes and which, through another learned set of conventions, discourse, can be represented in language. From experience and the representation of the *nature* of that experience in images or words, men draw conclusions and come to understand the *nature* of what they have witnessed and the *nature* of what has been represented in words or painted images of what has been witnessed. Similarly, he says, it is necessary to be a prince to know the nature of the people and it is necessary to be one of the populace to know the nature of princes. Machiavelli has stationed himself in the plains with the populace to observe the nature of princes above him, and then has represented, in words, the nature of what has been and is there to be seen ('perche cosi comme coloro che disegnono e' paesi si pongano bassi nel piano *a considerare la natura* de' monti e de' luoghi alti ... similmente a conoscere bene *la natura* de' populi bisogna esser principe et a conoscere bene quella de' principi bisogna esser populare', p. 14). Men sensually experience the world and come to understand its nature.

If we wish to try to understand what sixteenth-century contemporaries would have understood by Machiavelli's statement of purpose and the method by which he will achieve it, we shall have to suspend some of our own, modern presuppositions about how we think texts, be they ancient or contemporary, relate to 'reality' . Indeed, we must suspend the very notions that texts express relative or, perhaps, intensely subjective and personal truths, or that the meaning they convey is intrinsically bound up with the historical circumstances in which they were produced. Before the nineteenth century and the emergence of historicism, there was another attitude to texts and their truth and another understanding of history. This other, older attitude still survives today: it is sometimes called 'the practical past',[7] and is deployed in sermons and in ideologies. But it is not what is today meant by history which concerns a past experienced by others (who were necessarily *different* from us) and which is now over and done with and can never be repeated or imitated, although it can, to some degree, be understood.[8]

The general theory behind medieval and Renaissance understandings of 'history'

In general terms (I shall be more specific below) what Machiavelli tells us in the introductory letter to Lorenzo comprises one standard medieval and Renaissance way of describing the following relations: between eyewitness experience of the world, thinking about the nature of what one has experienced, and then representing thoughts about the nature of one's experience in writing. The writing down of one's experiences, the construction of a narrative about what one had experienced, was called *historia*. It is not unlike our eyewitness journalism. *Historia* was not necessarily about the long-distance past; indeed, it could be the representation of experiences had yesterday or five minutes ago, but the experiences had to be yours and when you came to convert your memories of the experiences into narrative, freezing the sensual experiences, as it were, by representing them in language on a page, you were thought to be providing for others a literal, unembellished, uninterpreted account of what you had witnessed. This is what historians from antiquity until the sixteenth century were said to be doing when they wrote their histories. This is what it meant to be an historian for anyone who studied grammar and rhetoric in the traditional university arts course or in humanists' schools during the Middle Ages and Renaissance, having learnt this meaning of *historia* from Aristotle's set books on rhetoric and poetry and from various commentaries on Aristotle's works, not least by Cicero (who, however, misconstrued Aristotle's historian and substituted the rhetorician/poet) and Boethius. Increasingly, during the Renaissance, there was much irritation expressed towards certain medieval chroniclers who, it was believed, had not witnessed what they wrote about and hence ought not to be considered true historians. But this had also been debated in Bede's day and during the twelfth century, so the problem as Renaissance historians saw it was not a new one.[9]

These texts from the university arts course on grammar and rhetoric discussed the relationship between the world and the ways in which human languages referred to experiences of it. It was in the study of grammar and rhetoric that one learnt that writing represents *thoughts* about the world; language itself, either written or spoken, refers to the world by means of signs that signify thoughts had about the nature or the kind of thing experienced. To conceptualise experience is not to have mental representations of particular physical experiences that were had at some particular time – these would be images in one's imagination and memory – but rather to be able to think in more general terms about the nature of that kind of experience had before in the past. Thinking about the more general kinds of experiences had is a more abstract or generalising psychological activity. This is how thinking was described: as an activity of human minds engaged in responding to experiences. Writing does not directly signify things in the world; rather, writing, like speaking, constitutes a conventionally established code which refers to or signifies naturally generated human thoughts about the nature of sensual experiences had.

This way of relating experience, thought and texts has its origins in ancient Greek discussions, notably by Plato and Aristotle. These were followed and elaborated upon in the Roman world, especially by Latin grammarians and rhetoricians. The process by which humans were said to come to know what they know through learning and understanding and remembering what they had learnt and understood was, however, explained somewhat differently by Plato and Aristotle. Roman authors, like all authors after them, found themselves either choosing one account as opposed to the other or else synthesising the opposing views into a kind of unity. Especially during the later Middle Ages and again in Machiavelli's Renaissance

Florence there was considerable conflict between 'Platonists' and ' Aristotelians'.

But where Plato and Aristotle were understood by their medieval and Renaissance readers as differing in their explanations of how individuals learn, know and understand their own experiences and thoughts, they were held to agree more or less on how that very individual might learn, know and understand from *someone else's account* of learning, knowing and understanding of 'his' discrete experiences and thoughts. It is this latter issue of learning about someone else's past through some mode of his communication of it to you without your having experienced precisely the same experience, which enables us to achieve some understanding of what they thought of a past which others long ago had experienced but which a present individual could come to some understanding of only through recorded eyewitness accounts of a past that could no longer be experienced. This is what Machiavelli refers to when he speaks in the dedicatory letter to *The Prince* of one of the two sources of his knowledge of the actions of great men: *'una continua lezione delle antique'* ('a continuous reading of antiquity'). Such a recorded eyewitness account was held to be a memorial of someone's experiences, transformed through the words which represented the experiences into a 'frozen memory' on the page. It was believed that language enabled consciously witnessed occurrences to be preserved in a different form, through a conventional code, language itself, which was more enduring than the sense experience, so that, through language, the consciously witnessed occurrence could be considered by future readers who had not been present at the original, now past, event. It had come to be asserted in late antiquity, and accepted thereafter, that the only way the past could be 'touched' was through the medium of language which represented experiences and thoughts of others by means of a code that had been established by convention. In this way a later audience could, through reading an account literally, be as though 'present' and witnessing the past, consciously witnessed occurrence, that is, the experience. What was meant by a *literal* reading was that the words were not to be interpreted as having any higher, symbolic meaning but only pointed to past thoughts about sensual, witnessed experiences which readers could now imagine in their own minds.[10] What language did was represent the thoughts of eyewitnesses who recorded whatever they *experienced* (not simply whatever was there in the world), and when the record was read in some future time in a literal manner, it could enable the later reader to be as though present in imagination at the events described as experienced. It was also argued that you would not understand the conventional code of language, that is, you would not understand what the words represented or pointed to if you had not already had a *similar type of experience* yourself.

From Aristotle until well beyond the sixteenth century, *historia* was understood to be the recording in language of one's own experiences (not pure events), so that fleeting experiences could be preserved, but in words.[11] Herodotus and Thucydides were said to be this kind of historian.[12] So too were all those Roman historians (Sallust, Livy, Tacitus, etc) whose texts were increasingly influential during the fourteenth to sixteenth centuries, especially for Italians. Their texts were read literally by medieval and Renaissance readers who accepted them as eyewitness narrators of their experiences either under the Roman republic or under the imperial principate. The experiences of these witnesses were revived, reread and listened to, notably by early and later humanists. Through the written histories of earlier men future readers could re-experience in their own minds what had been experienced in ancient Rome.

In our modern world the discrete professions of psychologist and historian treat different subject matters: the first deals with individuals' own personal pasts, and the second treats 'the past'. They deploy different methods of investigation of their subject matter. But during the medieval and Renaissance periods both the problems of recalling my personal past and the meaning of another person's past which, not having experienced it myself could not be recalled by me, were problems for a wide range of *overlapping* specialists. Some were theologians, others university logicians, still others were humanist grammarians and rhetoricians. We have become used to speaking of how Renaissance humanists differed from medieval scholastics. But their similarities were much more significant.

What they *shared* was an interest in the relation between human psychology and language, the relation between the intellectual and the sensual aspects of the human soul (*anima*/*animus*) and, in turn, the soul's relation to the body, the relation between the ethical and politically active life and the contemplative life of philosophy. In general, then, a very wide range of professions not only discussed how human minds know, learn, understand and remember but they also treated the representative modes– the thoughts and images– *by which* humans perform these mental acts. And whatever their profession, be it grammarian, rhetorician, philosopher, logician, physician, or lawyer, they spoke about these subjects *in the same ways*, often using the same language and drawing upon Aristotelian and/or Platonist insights. For this reason the historical and every other mode of understanding were treated as having to do with psychology, that is, with the parts of the soul that were actively engaged in intellectual and practical reasoning about sense experiences of the soul that were represented 'in' the soul as images and memories, themselves the consequences of the body's sensual response to the world. From here they discussed the means by which psychological activities (conceptualising, judging, imagining, remembering, etc.) are capable of 'representing' sense experiences of the world. The human mind was discussed as having a capacity to represent that aspect of the world that is experienced by a witness *in the mind's own mode*, that is, as thoughts and images. They then drew analogies with the representative capacities of language which re-presents in spoken and written form the representations in mind of experiences of the world. By focusing on language as a system of signs for thoughts about experiences of the world, they linked the two issues of individuals recalling their personal past and the recalling of the past of others. Language became the key not only to thinking but to all past history which was no longer there to be experienced. Most notably, they discussed thinking as a species-specific activity of humans that is *prior to language*, the latter alone being actually developed as the consequence of culture. Different languages emerged from culture as conventions which were as varied as the different grammars of Greek and Latin and the vernaculars. On this view, all men think alike but, depending on the culture in which a person grows up, each speaks through the different, conventionally established and learned language codes about what they think.

It is important to realise that this medieval and Renaissance approach assumed and was aware of assuming two things. First, the world to be experienced is perceived to be as it is and is presumed to be as it was, that is, the world to be experienced is and always has been stable. This is what enables men to perceive certain conditions in the present and judge them to be similar to those in the past and hence, conditions are thought to repeat themselves. This is what Machiavelli means when he says there is an effectual truth of the way things are ('[una] verita effettuale della cosa', chapter XV, p. 65). Second, the human mind has fixed ways of operating when it experiences and considers experience. What varies over time is not the world that is experienced or mind in its understanding of experiences but *language*. Language conventionally encodes what is there to be understood by us and what is thought by us to be there. This means that for medieval and Renaissance thinkers, language alone has what *we* today mean by a history. The *modi signifi-candi* (the modes of signifying experiences) change over time and from culture to culture but what there is to be known by us and what is known by us to be there do not change. This is why we can imitate past heroic actions but only when the conditions are perceived and then judged to be similar: Machiavelli insisted that we must choose our historical examples carefully (chapters IV and XIX). On this view, there must be presumed to be universal regularities of mind and of 'experienceable things' or conditions, perhaps empirically or logically indemonstrable as such, but at least to be accepted in principle as probably necessary, preliminary hypotheses. For medieval and Renaissance thinkers the world that is experienced (*not* the world 'out there', much of which was not presumed to be experienced or even capable of being experienced by humans in the natural course of life and without divine help), along with abstract categories of thinking about experiences, remains constant.

In practice this meant that Machiavelli's own experiences of the actions of contemporary great men, once represented in words and recorded in unembellished form (as his *historia*, as when he tells of his observations of Louis Xll of France, the Duke of Ferrara opposing the Venetians and Pope Julius, Cæsare Borgia or Pope Alexander VI, etc.) were to be read and understood *in the same way* as one read and understood the actions of heroic actors that were encoded by historian-witnesses in their ancient texts (their *historia*). These acts were the same *kinds* of things, and the conditions which caused men to act in the ways they do and did were perceived and judged to be similar because the world to be experienced by human beings was presumed stable. Hence, Machiavelli's *Prince* literally presents his *historia* and it literally re-presents the *historia* of past experiencers to be read and understood in the present.

We must now distinguish between what they meant on the one hand by man's *nature*, fixed for the species and universally shared, and, on the other, by men's *characters*, which are the consequence of habits built up by experience. For Machiavelli and for all medieval and Renaissance thinkers, man's *nature* does not change over time: ancient, medieval and Renaissance men share the same natures. In all societies throughout history men can be observed to have demonstrated through their actions the same kind of nature, a nature that is specific to humans. Hence, there is one truth for mankind no matter in what period of history or in what culture they have lived.

We can list some of the universally shared characteristics which Machiavelli attributes to human nature as such: men change masters voluntarily believing they can better themselves (chapter III); men walk almost always in the paths trodden by others, proceeding in their actions by imitation (chapter VI); mankind is incredulous, not truly believing in anything new until they have had an actual experience of it (chapter VI); men commit injuries either through fear or through hate (chapter VII); it is the nature of men to be as much bound by the benefits that they confer as by those they receive (chapter X); for it may be said of men in general that they are ungrateful, voluble, dissemblers, anxious to avoid danger and covetous of gain (chapter XVII); love is held by a chain of obligations which, men being selfish, is broken whenever it serves their purposes. Fear is maintained by a dread of punishment which never fails (chapter XVII); men forget more easily the death of their father than the loss of their patrimony (chapter XVII); men love at their own free will but fear at the will of the Prince (or anyone else who has sufficient force at his disposal (chapter XVII); men are bad and would not observe their faith with you (chapter XVIII); men are so simple and so ready to obey necessities that one who deceives will always find those who allow themselves to be deceived (chapter XVIII); men in general judge more by the eyes than by the hands, that is, men see appearances but do not feel what things are (chapter XVIII); the common people are always taken by appearances and the occurence of events and the world consists only of the common people (chapter XVIII); there are three breeds of human brains ('generazioni cervelli'): one which understands things by itself ('l'uno intende da se'), another which learns what others understand ('l'altro discerne quello che altri intende'), and a third which understands neither by itself nor by others ('el terzo non intende ne se ne altri'). The first is most excellent, the second excellent but the third is useless (chapter XXII); men are much more taken by present than by past things and, when they find themselves well off in the present, enjoy it and seek nothing more (chapter XXIV); a common fault of men is not to reckon on storms in fair weather (chapter XXIV); all men aim at glory and riches but proceed in different ways to achieve their aims (chapter XXV).

Let us note, in passing, that there is no historicism here. We can reduce these species-specific characteristics which demonstrate human nature to the following: men are by nature primarily self-interested, and what they take to be their interest is material wealth and glory (reputation, the esteem of others). All their actions are aimed at self-betterment *as they perceive it*. They are inclined by their nature to live in societies but the conditions of society are such that they are fearful of threats to perceived self-interest. Therefore, 'all the qualities that are reputed good cannot all be possessed or observed, human conditions not permitting it' ('ma, perche non si possono avere, ne interamente osservare, per le condizioni umane che non lo consentono', chapter XV, p.65). As a consequence, they are not grateful or faithful to others unless necessity forces them to be; self-interest leads them to look for ways to avoid danger and covet gain. They commit injuries in these conditions through either fear or hatred. They deceive and are deceived.

The heart of the matter is that human nature demonstrates that it has a particular way of coming to know what it takes to be in its self-interest: men judge only by appearances, that is, they know about the world by first having sensed it, and the primary sense used is that of sight. First they see and then they judge what they see and think about what they have judged. They do not believe anything unless they have first experienced it and their experience is founded on perception. Knowledge can be only of what has first been perceived. What men perceive is that on which the eyes focus. Men's senses do not grasp what things really are but only what they appear to be. And they then proceed in their lives by imitating what they see.[13] What they see and then imitate is the actions of others. They cannot know another man's intentions; they can only judge a man by his actions, which may or may not reflect what he is thinking. The knowledge men acquire is the consequence of what appears to their senses to be the case: events and actions. This is why men are more taken by the present than by the past. They see the present. But if one writes down what one has seen and if one reads the writings of others who have recorded what they have seen in their present, then human nature will be shown to be constant over time. The constancy consists in the apparent 'fact' that men have always judged what they take to be their self-interest and how to act to achieve it on the basis of the perception of appearances.

In short, Machiavelli is giving us an epistemology, a psychological theory of how humans learn and understand what they have learnt from sensual experience. And he links a psychological theory of human nature with a theory about how language in its written form can re-present, through words, past perceptions of appearances which are events and actions.

This is not a theory that Machiavelli invented. This theory was one of the two possible alternatives that were current during the medieval and Renaissance periods. In short, it is a kind of Aristotelianism that was developed most influentially by theologians, philosophers and rhetoricians who were grouped together especially from the fourteenth century onwards and known as the *via moderna*. Their main opposition came from another group of theologians, philosophers and rhetoricians known as the *via antiqua* and whose guiding principles were Platonist.[14]

Having spoken of what was meant by the stability of human nature we must now proceed to distinguish human nature from character. Individually and collectively as cultures, men develop their universally shared human natures so that they come to have the discrete characters they have, such characters being the consequence of their individual and collective experiences. These experiences are not random and unconscious events which happen *to* men. Men cannot control contingencies, that is, the times and circumstances they are born in, no matter how prudent they may be. Machiavelli says that 'time brings with it all things and may produce indifferently either good or evil' (chapter III, p. 22). But experiences are the psyche's responses *to* the world of times and circumstances and experiences have effects on men's characters. Men are agents and their experiences are their willed responses to contingent events so that from these willed responses characteristic habits of behaviour become fixed. Hence, Machiavelli notes that the character of peoples varies (chapter VI). Indeed, the characters of individual men also vary: some men proceed cautiously and others impetuously on their way to what they perceive to be their self-interest (chapter XXV). Character is the result of habits built up on a foundational shared human nature. It is these willed responses that constitute their experiences and, taken together over many years, are built up as inclinations to respond to certain conditions in characteristic ways. Men become fixed in their ways. Hence it is *their* acts which, when considered by others, demonstrate to observers - be they contemporaries or future readers - the *kinds* of characters they possess, and from an observation of character (and note this is an observation of appearances) one can predict with a certain degree of probability how such an habituated person will respond in future circumstances, when, of course, the circumstances appear to be similar to those to which he responded in the past.

Here we have two constraints on the randomness or 'freedom' of human behaviour. One is human nature itself, which

is fixed for the species and shows that men always make judgements on the basis of appearances. The other is the fixity of
habituated character: a man has learnt how to proceed in life
through imitation and by developing habits based on the experiences he has had. And the more experiences (willed responses
to contingencies) past or present, the more 'experienced' or
prudent he becomes in recognising similarities in conditions
and acting accordingly to produce like results. This does not
mean an experienced man is infallible. There are no absolutely
safe policies. Machiavelli says it is better to consider the *probable* results of certain policies because the *nature of things* is
such that one never tries to avoid one difficulty without
running into another (chapter XXI). Prudence consists in being
able to know the *nature* of the difficulties and taking the least
harmful as good. Human life proceeds on the basis of the probable, spurred on as it is by judgements founded on appearance.
No matter how many experiences a man may have, no matter
how experienced or prudent he is, he will never be able to
respond freely to the near infinite contingencies of time and
circumstances, for 'time brings with it all things and may
produce indifferently either good or evil'(chapter III, p. 22).
Man remains fixed both in nature and in character 'either
because he cannot deviate from that to which nature inclines
him or else because having always prospered by walking in one
path, he cannot persuade himself to leave it' (chapter XXV, p.
98). No man can change his human nature. And persuasion is
not usually sufficient to change his character. Only necessity
can force a change in character and this necessity is a coercive
imposition from outside his self. If man *could* change his nature
and character to suit *all* times and *all* circumstances, he would
not only *not* be man as he has appeared to be throughout
history, but his *fortuna* would never change, contrary to what
his *historia* appears to show. Man's life is not *determined* (by
God or providence or biological necessity) but his life is
constrained because of the kind of being he is. Some men's *characters*, however, show them to be more ready than others to
meet the needs of the times, largely through preparing themselves by foreseeing a *range of possibilities* and changes in
conditions with which they are likely to be faced. But human

nature being what it is, no man can do this for all times and all circumstances and, as a consequence, great men have been those who have had the kinds of characters that suit most of the contingencies of the time in which they happened to have lived. Moses was one such man whose character suited the times. *When this is the case*, Machiavelli reminds his reader that 'God will not do everything in order not to deprive us of free will and the portion of the glory that falls to our lot' ('Dio non vuole fare ogni cosa, per non ci torre el libero arbitrio e parte di quella gloria che tocca a noi', chapter XXVI, p. 103).

Were a medieval or Renaissance philosopher or theologian to look at what Machiavelli says here, he would recognise that Machiavelli was treating a long-running standard issue of debate: the nature of future contingencies and the degree to which a man can determine not only what will happen in his future but the extent to which he can be held responsible for his own character and fate. During the fourteenth to sixteenth centuries this issue was not only of interest to philosophers and theologians. It was treated by poets and rhetoricians and not least by those who continued to read and comment upon Boethius' *Consolation of Philosophy*, where the whole question of the degree to which man has free will and is responsible for his fate was discussed.[15] Chaucer was much exercised by this issue in fourteenth-century England when he not only translated Boethius but wrote his *Troilus*. In the fifteenth century, Lorenzo Valla (d. 1457) was much exercised by the same Boethian dilemmas in his *Dialogue on Free Will*.[16] Undoubtedly, questions concerning the limits of human action and responsibility were even higher on the agenda of men who lived in Italy, a country that was subject to upheavals from foreign invasions and from alternations of princedoms and republics in cities, and most notably in Florence with its revolutionary changes in government. Life in Italy during the fifteenth and early sixteenth centuries was tumultuous. Those texts from antiquity which were already part of the grammatical and rhetorical education that was followed by literate men on their way to professions and civic or courtly power were made to speak to contemporary issues. But a contemporary learned reader would also recognise that Machiavelli had constructed his argument in a distinctive and recognisable way which would place him as an opponent to all kinds of Platonist idealism. And it was just such Platonism that was being revived by Marsilio Ficino, in Florence, during Machiavelli's own lifetime. Machiavelli insisted that men have always come to whatever knowledge they have as a consequence of appearances, that is, by means of the particular sense experiences they have had, and *not* through receiving authoritative ideas that encompass universal truths that are *divorced* from sense experience and available only to a mind that is 'troubled by' and separated from the body.[17] In adopting this epistemology Machiavelli had indeed chosen one *via* as opposed to another: he had chosen the *via moderna*.[18] I have described elsewhere how the linguistically centred philosophy of William of Ockham and his nominalist adherents during the fourteenth and fifteenth centuries came to influence the works of later writers outside the medieval university milieu. There is no space in this chapter to trace the route of the *via moderna* into the grammar and rhetoric schools of humanists who ideologically wished to distance themselves from scholastic philosophy but, in so doing, grasped hold of the philological underpinning of the Ockhamist enterprise.[19] Valla was a key figure here.[20]

According to Machiavelli, then, past and present experiences are similar in *nature* because men perceive things at one time and judge them to be similar to those at another time, and these conditions, once judged similar, cause them to have what they take to be experiences of like kinds. Thus, when we understand the nature of past experiences narrated or recorded in past texts, we recognise them as kinds of experiences that may be had in the present. The world to be experienced is, as we have seen, stable. (This is a statement not about the world but about men's experience of it.) When we read texts, we observe past and present actors responding successfully or not to contingencies which they have construed as recognisably similar conditions to which they respond by means of having certain kinds of experience, themselves constrained both by human nature and by habituated character. Thereafter, we are able to construct probable laws of behaviour across time which enable anyone in the present to imitate the *nature* of past actions. In imitating past actions one does not do the same thing but things that would appear to be *similar* in apparently similar situations. In imitating eminent past actors you would be seeking to acquire a reputation that was similar to that of a great man in the past. Reputations are based on what appears to be the case to an eyewitness narrator of his experiences. Hence no historian, present or past, tells you ' how it really was' but, rather, how it appeared to be. Consequently, the laws of human behaviour cannot be infallible and necessary; they are hypothetical constructions which tell us of likely, probable outcomes, once the similarities of conditions have been so judged.

It is for these reasons that Machiavelli advises that the Prince should exercise his mind ('quanto allo esercizio della mente', chapter XIV, p. 64) by reading history ('leggere le istorie', chapter XIV, p. 64) and studying the actions of excellent men to see how they acted in warfare and to examine the causes of their victories and defeats in order to imitate the former and avoid the latter. Above all, the Prince should do as some men have done in the past who have imitated someone who has been much praised and glorified and have always kept his deeds and actions before them, as they say Alexander the Great imitated Achilles; Caesar, Alexander; and Scipio, Cyrus. Whoever reads the life of Cyrus written by Xenophon[21] will recognise in the life of Scipio how gloriously he imitated the former (chapter XIV). Machiavelli read the lives of these great men in Latin versions even when some of them had originally been written in Greek and it is clear that some of these 'historians', notably Plutarch, wrote about what they had never themselves witnessed! But Machiavelli is true to his own theory which tells us what *historia* is: it is the narrative representation of appearances. History preserves reputations of men, what they appeared to be and do and not what they were. History is filled with plausible *exempla*. It is not filled with facts. History does not teach how to acquire virtues but, rather, how men acquired the reputation for possessing them.

It remains only to suggest an answer to the question: Where would someone of Machiavelli's generation in Florence learn this background theory to how one reads past and present texts in order to use what they say in pursuing one's own course of action in the present? The short answer is either in the long-established university arts course with its focus on grammar, rhetoric and logic or in the newer humanist schools which like-wise focused on grammar and rhetoric but pruned scholastic logic from their curriculum. In both curricula, Aristotle's works in Latin translation were foundational along with standard commentaries and revisions by Roman grammarians and rhetoricians (Cicero, Quintilian, Boethius, etc.), and these texts constituted a general education, preparing students for higher professional studies in medicine, law and theology. What became the humanist stress on the philological exegesis of past texts had emerged from this university arts course where the grammar of texts was analysed and the 'historical method' of analysing texts was identified with the literal mode. Here one studied the letter, the terms and propositions which rendered a text grammatically coherent or incoherent. The *sensus grammaticus* (the grammatical sense) was identified as the *sensus historicus* (the historical sense). When humanists then called for a *fides historiae* (faithfulness to the historical text) they were calling for a literal reading of coherently constructed grammatical texts in order to get at plausible meaning. Once one analysed a text literally (historically), a student of rhetoric could go on to compose epideictic speeches to praise or blame the literal acts of past or present actors in order to give advice to an audience. As Aristotle taught, 'the "time" of epideictic is the present', for all speakers praise or blame past acts with the intention of celebrating timeless virtues as models of behaviour, reminding the audience of the past and projecting the course of the future.[22] This is what Machiavelli does in *The Prince*.

Once one learned the theory and practice of both grammar and rhetoric, Aristotle's *Nicomachean Ethics* and *Politics*, available in Latin - the former at the end of the twelfth century and the latter from the mid thirteenth century – showed a student how far rhetorical persuasion could extend in matters moral and political. Bruni (1369-1444), who had studied rhetoric, law and Greek in Florence in the 1390s and became Chancellor of the republic in 1427, had provided new translations of the *Politics* and *Ethics* to replace those of the thirteenth-century Dominican,

William of Moerbeke.[23] In book V, 5 of the *Politics*, (1305a 7 f.)
Aristotle was emphatic that oratorical persuasion was *not* enough
if one wished to seize power and maintain it. Indeed, book V
of the *Politics* may be considered a template for Machiavelli's
advice to 'new princes' seeking stability and preservation of *lo
stato*, especially for chapters I–XI of *The Prince*. Aristotle's
Nicomachean Ethics, notably Book 6, is instructive for reading
chapters XII–XXVI.

Fifteenth-century humanist grammarians and rhetoricians,
who wanted to revise if not eliminate university philosophy
and logic and replace these with what Cicero had called the
studia humanitatis, stressed moral inquiry as of great vocational
and civic importance to their students. They developed new
genres, for instance the dialogue and the public speech, to
appeal to a professional but non-clerical, civic audience of
increasingly literate men. They focused on poetry, rhetoric,
ethics and politics to the exclusion of university logic and
natural philosophy. Theirs was a truncated arts course. But the
texts which taught what grammar and rhetoric were, as
subjects, and which explained how oratory worked by the use
of certain kinds of probabilistic arguments that persuaded an
audience by affecting men's emotions and guiding their practical reason were still those of Aristotle and Cicero on oratory,
poetry, ethics and politics, now supplemented by rediscovered
ancient discussions on similar themes and methods. Ancient
Romans and Cicero in particular had referred to the necessity
of an educated man studying those authoritative texts of the
Greeks and their Latin continuators that gave instruction in
grammar, rhetoric, poetry, history and moral philosophy.
Medieval arts students had followed precisely this course of
study in preparation for later ecclesiastical and legal careers.
From the thirteenth century and the foundation of the *univer-
sitas* in various urban centres across Europe, the medieval
university's arts course was vocational in nature, meant to
prepare students for professional public careers in administration of either church or nation state. But especially, although
not uniquely, in later thirteenth-century Italy, ancient Roman
culture and learning were revived by literate and professional
men with even greater enthusiasm than previously as a model

for contemporary life, values and language. During the four-teenth century and even more so in the fifteenth, access to previously unknown literature from ancient Greece and Rome was overwhelmingly improved owing to the efforts (primarily although not exclusively) of Italian scholars who returned to Italy from journeys in Greece prior to the Turkish invasion of Constantinople in 1453.[24] To the standard Aristotelian corpus were now added the works of Plato[25] and a variety of Neoplatonists.[26] Marsilio Ficino's great accomplishment was to have translated or retranslated all of Plato's works by 1469.[27] An increasing familiarity with the Greek language also enabled more accurate Latin translations of Aristotle's works to be made available. From 1470 the new invention of printing made books cheaper, more convenient and in wider circulation so that the growing number of the literate had access to the old *and* new texts, although the Latin language still remained the chief medium by which ancient texts came to be known. Ficino's translations of Plato were printed for the first time in 1484. George of Trebizond prepared a new Latin translation of Aristotle's *Rhetoric* which was then printed *c.* 1477.[28]

Machiavelli, we recall, was in grammar school in 1481. We cannot say whether or not he actually used any of these new translations of either Plato or Aristotle. But it is suggested here that a revived Platonism not only came too late for him but that it could not serve his purpose: which was to follow the *via moderna* and show that *historia*, present and past, teaches that men and their experiences, rather than an inscrutable provi-dence or God, determine the course of politics.

Notes

To avoid anachronism, the reader is asked to remember the following. Machiavelli speaks of human nature and human conditions using *men* as his model of humanity. No woman is taken as a model of action, no women were part of his 'political' world, either as citizens and rulers, or as subjects of past historical narratives. Like his contemporaries and predecessors he does not self-consciously or explicitly exclude women, but his focus is on great *men* of the past and on those male historians who wrote about them, in order that contemporary men might imitate the successful behaviour of great men of the past. Although I refer, at times, to 'people' or 'human beings' in order to indicate the supposed universality of his theory, Machiavelli's general conclusions on human psychology and action come from a study of *men* and are meant to aid *them* in the very male world of Florentine politics. From the text of *The Prince* we have no way of knowing whether Machiavelli thought women behaved in like manner, but given that the politics of ruler–ruled was a male domain, it is unlikely that he ever worried about them, except, of course, to refer rather unflatteringly to Fortuna as a woman, who was not impressed by laws and reason but by young males' impetuousness and violence! No man can ever imitate this female Fortuna, but if he is a great man he can combat her and be prepared for her apparently irrational interventions in men's lives. Machiavelli's *Prince* is about men and for men.

1 Niccolò Machiavelli, *Il Principe e Discorsi sopra la prima deca di Tito Livio*, ed. S. Bertelli (Milan: Feltrinelli, 1960): 'ho deliberato entrare per una via, la quale, nonessendo suta ancora da alcuno trita', p. 123. All further references are to this edition and are given in the text. The translations are my own and are meant to take into account the precise words used because the original Italian words often have a technical meaning that a more impressionistic translation does not render accurately.

2 Robert Black, 'Florence' in Roy Porter and Mikulas Teich (eds), *The Renaissance in National Context* (Cambridge: Cambridge University Press, 1992, p. 34), notes that a private classical education became a status symbol in Florence with patrician families alone engaging teachers to educate their children as a sign of the family's wealth, exclusive social position, ancient lineage, public office and marriage alliances. Without such a private tutor a satisfactory Latin, or what was called 'grammar' education was difficult to come by in Florence. Indeed, grammar suffered such a decline in the fifteenth century for most of the population that only 2 per cent of boys were in grammar school in 1480, precisely the time at which Machiavelli was himself being educated in the school of Paolo da Roncaglia. Classical learning in Florence was a preserve of the aristocracy and it is clear that Machiavelli's own education was that of Florence's social elite (pp. 35-6).

3 See Ian Maclean, *Interpretation and Meaning in the Renaissance: The Case of Law* (Cambridge: Cambridge University Press, 1991) for an excellent study of language theory and textual interpretation amongst medieval and Renaissance lawyers. Also, Anthony Parel, *The Machiavellian Cosmos* (New Haven: Yale University Press, 1992) on contemporary medical practice and an interesting interpretation of the effect of 'humours' on Machiavelli's understanding of *fortuna* and men's characters.

4 See Janet Coleman, *Ancient and Medieval Memories: Studies in the Reconstruction of the Past* (Cambridge: Cambridge University Press, 1992) and Coleman, 'The Uses of the Past (14th-16th Centuries): The Invention of a Collective History and its Implications for Cultural Participation', in Ann Rigney and Douwe Fokkema (eds), *Cultural Participation, Trends since the Middle Ages* (Amsterdam: John Benjamins, 1993) pp.21-37.

5   I disagree with Quentin Skinner, *Foundations of Modern Political Thought* (Cambridge: Cambridge University Press, 1978), vol. 1, p. 86, where he cites the views of Panofsky with apparent approval, that 'the classical past was looked upon for the first time, as a totality cut off from the present'. Skinner then says 'a new sense of historical distance was achieved as a result of which the civilization of ancient Rome began to appear as a wholly separate culture, one which deserved – and indeed required – to be reconstructed and appreciated as far as possible on its own distinctive terms' (p. 86). See instead Lauro Martines, *Power and Imagination: City-states in Renaissance Italy* (Harmondsworth: Penguin, 1983 [1979]), pp. 268-300.

6   This is dated 1515/16 but the first dedicatee, in 1513, was Giuliano, uncle of Lorenzo.

7   See Michael Oakeshott, *On History and Other Essays* (Oxford: Blackwell, 1983).

8   Coleman, *Ancient and Medieval Memories*, pp. 593-9.

9   *Ancient and Modern Memories*, pp. 137-54, 274-324.

10 See the legal texts cited in Maclean, *Interpretation and Meaning in the Renaissance*, pp. 68f., Bartolus on signification and literal meaning, pp. 89-94; Goeddaeus on signification, p. 97; pp. 126, 161, 207.

11 Hegel repeated this in the nineteenth century. G. W. F. Hegel, *Lectures on the Philosophy of World History*, trans. H. B. Nisbet (Cambridge: Cambridge University Press, 1975), First Draft, pp. 12-15.

12 Aristotle, *Poetics*, II, 6, 1451b f. 'It is not by writing verse or prose that the historian and poet are distinguished; the work of Herodotus might be versified but it would still be a species of history. They are distinguished by this: that history relates what has been and poetry what might be. Poetry is the more philosophical since it is chiefly about general truth, while history is about the particular. In what manner any person of a certain character might speak or act, probably or necessarily - this is general, and the object of poetry. But what Alcibiades did or what happened to him, this is particular truth.'

13 Cf. Aristotle, *Poetics*, 1, 5: 'to imitate is instinctive in man from his infancy; by this man is distinguished from other animals and from this imitative instinct he receives his earliest education. To learn [by imitation] is a natural pleasure that is not confined to philosophers but common to all men.'

14 I have discussed this in *Ancient and Medieval Memories*, pp. 463-599.

15 *Ancient and Medieval Memories*, pp. 539-99. William of Aragon's late thirteenth-century 'Aristotelianised' Commentary on Boethius' *Consolation* noted: 'Let us not impute to Boethius the crimes of the Platonists, for he knew Aristotle very well.' Cited in A. J. Minnis, A. B. Scott and D. Wallace (eds), *Medieval Literary Theory and Criticism c. 1100–c.1375, the Commentary Tradition* (Oxford: Clarendon Press, 1988), p. 318, n. 27.

16 L.Valla, *Dialogue on Free Will*, trans. C. E Trinkaus Jr, in E. Cassirer, P. O. Kristeller and J. H. Randall Jr (eds), *The Renaissance Philosophy of Man* (Chicago: University of Chicago Press, 1948), pp. 147-82. Also see Skinner, *Foundations*, vol. 1 on other fifteenth century tracts on Fortune, pp. 120f.

17 This was the underlying thesis of the *via antiqua*. Indeed, the Florentine scholar and leading citizen Gianozzo Manetti, in his *De dignitate et excellentia hominis* (1452/3), 111, p. 97, ed. E. R. Leonard (Padua, 1975), emphasised not only man's sublime dignity but also his envy, pride, ambition and lust for domination which were 'disturbances of the soul' and therefore redefined man, with regrets, as an animal filled with indignation. Machiavelli's version of this rejects a divorce between higher soul and the senses: man is not higher intellect *divorced* from a troublesome body. His access to knowledge comes *through* the senses.

18 I agree with Skinner that Machiavelli was a critic of humanism but only a humanism of the Platonising kind. This would include Cicero, whose Platonist psychology and belief that rhetorical persuasion was capable of winning over men under *all* conditions, if used by a man of genius, Machiavelli could not accept. Nor could Aristotle.

19 For a fuller account, see Coleman, *Ancient and Medieval Memories*, pp. 500–47.

20 On Valla and Machiavelli see Nancy Struever, *Theory as Practice: Ethical Enquiry in the Renaissance* (Chicago: University of Chicago Press, 1992) and John Monfasani, 'Is Valla an Ordinary Language Philosopher?', *Journal of the History of Ideas* 50 (1989), pp. 309-23.

21 Machiavelli knew about the deeds of these famous men from the following ancient texts: Plutarch, *Vita Alexandri* and Q. Curzio Rufo, *Historiarum Alexandri* (on Alexander and Achilles), Suetonius, *Divus Iulius* (on Julius Caesar) Cicero, *Ad Quintum fratrem* (on Scipio) and Xenophon, *Cyropaedia*.

22 Aristotle, *On Rhetoric: A Theory of Civic Discourse*, trans. and introd., George A. Kennedy (Oxford: Clarendon Press, 1991), 1.3, 1 358b f., pp. 47f., 1.3, 1359a f., pp. 50-1: 'And since impossibilities cannot be done nor have been done, but possibilities [alone can be done or have been done] it is necessary for the ... epideictic speaker to have propositions about the possible and the impossible and [about] whether something has happened or not and [about] whether it will or will not come to be.'

23 On Bruni's Aristotelianism in his political works, see Nicolai Rubinstein, 'Florentine Constitutionalism and Medici Ascendancy in the 15th century', in N. Rubinstein (ed.), *Florentine Studies: Politics and Society in Renaissance Florence* (London: Faber & Faber, 1968), pp. 442-62.

24 In general, see Brian P. Copenhaver and Charles B. Schmitt, *A History of Western Philosophy, 3: Renaissance Philosophy* (Oxford: Oxford University Press, 1992). The early excellent chapters are by Schmitt but by the middle of the volume Copenhaver takes over and modifies

Schmitt's insistence on the continuity between medieval and Renaissance philosophy.

25 Most of Plato's major works were hardly known during the Middle Ages even in Latin translation, except for *Meno* and *Phaedo*.

26 Middle and Neoplatonists had been the main and immensely influential source of medieval Christian Platonism which relied on various reinterpretations of Plato provided by Plotinus, Proclus, Porphyry and the early Christian Church Fathers such as Lactantius and Augustine; from the twelfth century, these were supplemented by Latin translations of Arabic commentaries on a variety of Plato's works. See the various studies in Anna Baldwin and Sarah Hutton (eds), *Platonism and the English Imagination* (Cambridge: Cambridge University Press, 1994).

27 P. O. Kristeller in G. C. Garfagnini (ed.), *Marsilio Ficino e il ritorno di Platone* (Florence, 1986), pp. 50-80.

28 Aristotle's *Rhetoric* was previously known to Arabic scholars of Greek philosophy and in the thirteenth century Hermannus Alemmanus in Spain made a Latin translation of an Arabic commentary, attributed to Al-farabi. He also translated Averroes' Commentary on Aristotle's *Poetics*. Two Latin translations of the *Rhetoric* from Greek were also made by Bartholomew of Massina (?) and by William of Moerbeke. For medieval examples, see Minnis, Scott and Wallace (eds), *Medieval Literary Theory and Criticism*, especially Anonymous (late 13th century?): A question on the nature of poetry, pp. 307-13.

4

Dialogue in *The Prince*

JOHN PARKIN

When Machiavelli began writing *The Prince* he was subject to numerous pressures including boredom, poverty, a sense of failure and a loss of self-respect. Such pressures will of themselves generate self-questioning in a writer's personality, and a biographical critic can make it his or her task to examine the ways in which, albeit obliquely, these patterns of doubt and self-enquiry emerge in the book, compensating for their negative effects via the intoxicating sense of constructive activity confidently and lucidly expounded which is the hallmark of Machiavellian prose. The cultural historian would look for a more explicit and broader-based set of dialogues whereby Machiavelli, even knowingly, expresses a sense of the conflict of two political eras: the discourse of humanism, having failed to secure Italian political life against invasion by less advanced societies, had to be replaced by new models, in the process making possible a contact with reality such as he had lived it in his political career and which he now sought to re-evaluate in his imposed idleness. Moreover, a further dialogue operates within these two phases of Machiavelli's life between which the distinction is relative, not absolute: Machiavelli's scholarship infected the professional despatches he composed whilst a career diplomat just as the jargon of his profession invades *The Prince*.

A fourth set of dialogues, intersecting with these others rather than supplanting them, has Machiavelli using different aspects of his personality (for example the trained orator, the experienced diplomat, the flattering courtier, the bar-room wit, the political analyst) to cajole and convince the different addressees they conjure up. Among these latter one recognises Giuliano and Lorenzo de' Medici (in effect the book's dedicatees), the colleagues and opponents with whom Machiavelli had conducted political business, the public authorities who had employed and then discarded him, the princes and peoples of Italy at large whom he chooses to imagine responding to his eloquence and passion, and finally his friends, including in particular Francesco Vettori, a man still in government service and to whom Machiavelli sent a famous letter in December 1513 describing *The Prince* as his recently completed *opuscolo De principatibus* ('little work *On Principalities*').

Two further hypothetical addressees of *The Prince* are, first, Machiavelli's own political student, the person who reads the work as an objectively devised textbook and is thereby persuaded to help found the discipline of political science (although of course the term is never used), and, second, the contemporary scholar, expert less in the science of politics than in the art of rhetoric and who, responsive to the sense of leisured contemplation conjured up for Vettori, would situate the work in the literary contexts established by Renaissance humanism.[1] It is with such scholars in mind that Machiavelli, when outlining to Vettori his preparatory work for *The Prince*, falls back on stock humanist notions like the peaceful cultivation of the study of literature in the contemplative life as mapped out by such as Petrarch, Salutati and Bruni:[2] 'When evening has come I return home and enter my study. And at the doorway I take off my muddy and miry everyday clothes and put on regal and courtly raiment, and, attired appropriately, I enter the ancient courts of ancient men.'[3]

The letter to Vettori has often served as a preamble to *The Prince* itself and it is justifiably famous, expressing poignantly Machiavelli's current distressed state but relieving the pathos with delicious shafts of irony which show a detached self-mocker behind the self-pitying victim of circumstance: as Gundersheimer puts it, 'a threadbare, overqualified outsider' lurks behind 'the robed Petrarchan sage'[4] who enters every evening into a kind of dialogue with the dead (the genre was richly established in the Renaissance), a dialogue which paradoxically animates, indeed justifies his own existence: 'I enter the ancient courts ... where, received lovingly by them, I feed on that nourishment which alone is mine and for which I was born; wherewith I am not ashamed to talk with them and ask them about the reasons for their actions, and they in their kindness answer me.'[5] What is particularly remarkable is the unreserved commitment with which Machiavelli portrays himself engaging in this dialogue, thus making the past live for him in a way which would enrapture his own humanist tutors. And while the exchange between interlocutors has been seen as sterile and one-way,[6] to me its portrayal conveys great power and delight, specifically in the metaphor of political discussion as food and the sense of transferred identity ('tutto mi trasferisco in loro') whereby the past redeems him and cures his depression. It is prose-poetry of a high order expressing Machiavelli's attempts to console himself while amusing and interesting his correspondent.

But in fact the dialogic pattern of the letter is richer still, for alongside the reverential humanist the letter portrays an idle vulgarian who wastes his time by day on petty village squabbles. And this dichotomy is itself an ironic rejoinder to Vettori's own self-portrait as conveyed in his recent missive to Machiavelli depicting what his life is like in Rome ('qual sia la vita mia in Roma') and where he chose to move the dialogue with Niccolò, his 'dear comrade' ('*compar charo*') away from the chronotopes of political action (negotiating chamber, political assembly, battlefield, etc.) into those of the private life.[7] Unlike Machiavelli Vettori is close to the centres of Roman power, both ancient and modern: he lives within sight of Nero's gardens and spends his mornings chatting to those politicians whom Machiavelli desperately wants to impress (cruelly Vettori actually names the Pope and Cardinal Giulio de' Medici). In the evening, however (cf. Machiavelli: 'venuta la sera'), Vettori too studies classical history, meditating on the problems Rome has suffered under imperial and now papal ambitions: like Machiavelli he has a classical library (the names of Sallust, Plutarch and Suetonius are dropped among several others); they also share immediate memories of Julius II and Alexander Borgia.

So far so good, but the whole exchange with Vettori, and specifically Machiavelli's prose-poem on his dialogues with the ancients, ill prepares us for *The Prince* as we have it. For instance, the first classical example in *The Prince* does not come until chapter III, where it punctuates a discussion about Louis XII, a man about whom Machiavelli would clearly have had to inform the ancients rather than vice versa. To this extent the meditative humanist has been replaced by the experienced political agent, the civil servant who has bandied words with Georges d'Amboise (in effect Louis XII's prime minister). Accordingly, Machiavelli's ongoing dialogue with Vettori has not the same contours as his plan for the princes of Italy, specifically the Medici, from whom a resulting offer of employment would certainly dissolve his mood of dissatisfaction and somewhat more permanently than do his nightly excursions to the Elysian fields.

Moreover it is clear that it is not from his dialogue with the illustrious dead that Machiavelli has culled the series of dichotomies that structure the first chapter of *The Prince*. All states that have been or are, Machiavelli writes there, are either republics or kingdoms, the latter being either hereditary or acquired, these latter in turn being either annexations or entirely new – as Milan had been by Francesco Sforza (another unlikely intruder into the classical Elysium). The dialogue here is with the reader of the textbook who looks not for inspiring examples (such as Machiavelli in chapter VI admits to using) or for the kind of pompous and magnificent words (*'parole ampullose e magnifiche'*)[8] of display rhetoric (which he claims in his dedicatory letter not to be using) but for clarity and a transparent correspondence with known reality. Why begin by distinguishing republic from kingdom (rather than say kingdom from tyranny)? Because Naples is a kingdom and Venice a republic. Why then distinguish hereditary possession from possession by conquest? Because France is a hereditary kingdom and Italy full of conquered provinces. Why speak of Sforza (rather than say Romulus)? Because of his immediacy and relevance. As Machiavelli puts it in chapter XIII, 'I did not wish to move beyond recent Italian examples' (p. 278), and were the fact-based discourse of chapter I to continue then the text would be a very remarkable one indeed, though certainly a less complex one, with a far narrower range of addressees.

As I noted above, however, alongside this passive student of modern reality conjured up in chapter I and told, for example, in chapter XII that 'you have therefore to understand' ('*avete dunque a intendere*', p. 276), how Italy has changed,[9] stand the active exponents of humanist learning who would recognise a rhetorical device in the prologue at the very point when Machiavelli is disowning rhetoric, even seeing '*parole ampullose*' in the very terms he uses at that juncture, and approving of posture of humility theme adopted to gain his reader's favour (the technical term for this is '*captatio benevolentiae*') and of the high/low (*alto/basso*) antithesis used to distance him from the Medici, as well as recognising the source (Isocrates) from which he is drawing his introduction. It is to such readers, situated in the private studies of educated contemporaries, the schoolrooms where they gained that education and the erudite discussion groups where they exercised it (like the Orti Oricellari, the Rucellai gardens in Florence, where Machiavelli would one day locate his own extended dialogue on the art of war),[10] that Machiavelli addressed the illustrative topoi culled from his classical reading.

Not only does Machiavelli apply such examples of classical rhetoric, capitalising on their prestige to make his argument more appealing to his humanist readers, but he also theorises the approach itself, creating a metatext in dialogue with his own text. Hence the opening paragraph of chapter VI justifies his application of most eminent examples ('*grandissimi esempli*') – Theseus, Moses and Romulus are among those intended – by creating the extended metaphor of the archer aiming high:

> A wise man must always follow in ways laid down by the great and imitate those who were most outstanding, and act like the wise archers who, on seeing that the place they wish to strike is too far and knowing the strength of their bow, shoot at a point much higher than the intended target so that with the help of such a high aim they can achieve their goal.   p. 264.

Moreover, in chapter XIV he re-engages with the same dialogue when outlining his plan for princely education, promptly retreating to the standard position whereby the pupil is inspired by evaluating and copying the great figures of the past (much as his persona is seen doing in the Vettori letter): 'the Prince must read histories and in them consider the deeds of outstanding men, seeing how they have behaved in war, exam-

ining the causes of their victories and defeats so as to avoid the
latter and emulate the former' (p. 279). The argument could
scarcely be more predictable, and leads into a passage where
Scipio is praised for having used Xenophon to strengthen the
virtues of chastity, courtesy, humanity and generosity (*castità,
affabilità, umanità* and *liberalità*), virtues which in fact
Machiavelli will proceed immediately to reconsider and in the
most deliberately challenging terms. At this point, however, he
is, albeit tritely, readapting the postures of the devoted classical humanist to his own book on princely education and illustrating it with an example of an educated prince (Scipio) himself
studying a classical text of humanist education (the *Cyropaedia*).
So, he tells us, should a wise prince (*'principe savio'*) behave.

Given the rich interweaving of dialogues which *The Prince*
thus displays, it is not surprising that it 'has been read in so many
ways that one must wonder how such diverse interpretations
can be about the same text'.[11] This confusion is predominantly
due to different readers taking up different strands within the
dialogic web and identifying with one of Machiavelli's interlocutors while the remainder are developed elsewhere in separate passages elaborating different dialogues and in alternative
readings by other students. So, for instance, were one to go so
far as to argue that *The Prince* is merely another example of
humanist prince literature, equating classical knowledge with
virtue and seeing both as essential equipment for the aspiring
monarch, then several patterns in the text could be used in
support: does not Machiavelli say 'a prince must also present
himself as a lover of virtues' (chapter XXI, p. 292)? However,
this reading would cut across not only Machiavelli's obvious
violation of the humanist tradition (see the ways in which *liberalità* and *umanità* are questioned in chapter XV following the
famous distinction of effectual truth (*'verità effettuale'*) –
Machiavelli's territory – from imagination (*imaginazione*) –
humanist territory) but also his cultivation of the Medici who,
although receptive to the rhetoric of the dedicatory letter and
the eulogies their house enjoys in chapters XI and XXVI, have
to be lured into making Machiavellian *'verità effettuale'* their
common ground.

If we are to do justice to Machiavelli's method, or rather

methods, in *The Prince*, we have to recognise how this rich structure of dialogue works. The metatextual reference to aiming high cited above, for example, is at once an introduction to further predictable examples of regal virtue (Moses, Cyrus, Romulus among them) and an incitement to the Medici to cultivate their *virtù* in the Machiavellian terms of energy, initiative, constitutional reform and armed force in whatever political context (Florence or elsewhere: it isn't clear) they operate. The point for them is to indulge the same kind of frankness in their approach to his text that Machiavelli argues is essential in their day-to-day dialogues with political counsellors at court.[12] The point for him is to use this freedom to convert humanist commonplaces into something else while retaining some contact with humanism via for instance the classical notion of *virtù* itself. Even were he capable of doing as much, it would be unfair and unrealistic to impose a totally new sense of political values and an entirely revised approach to political argument on the readership of *The Prince* that he envisages: Machiavelli is in dialogue with humanist culture, not simply bent on its destruction.

Hence the double structure of the text and its parallels. Just as, for example, the unfavourable situation of Moses' Israel or the disadvantages of Romulus' birth are seen as necessary challenges to their latent political energy (*virtù*), so the quoting of most eminent examples can act as inspiring inducements that the modern Medici reveal a similar quality. This last point is so important to Machiavelli's dialogue with his Medici readership that he remakes it in chapter XXVI using the same examples though in a mode of address coloured by prophetic fervour and flattering eulogy ('Nor can one see at this time where Italy might place higher hopes than in your illustrious house', p. 297). Here the common ground is a kind of patriotic rapture which defies the political difficulties previously analysed. In chapter VI, however, Machiavelli retains contact with effectual truth via the key local example (*'italiano e fresco'*, chapter XIII, p. 278) of Savonarola – a man who failed to see the need for force to back up his constitutional proposals (*'ordini nuovi'*, chapter VI, p. 265) once public opinion swayed against him. It requires political energy (*virtù*) to establish *'ordini nuovi'* in a corrupt state, but a further dimension of *virtù* – military force – to defend them once established by using necessary coercion.

The argument in chapter VI is coherent and relevant, recognisably political rather than ethical, possibly a reflection of Medici plans for Florence and at least to some extent guided by the dichotomies structuring chapter 1: Machiavelli is considering at this point kingdoms which are entirely new and acquired by *virtù*. At the same time we can scarcely call the argument deeply analytical, as the discussion of Savonarola is so fragmentary. The humanists could get away with perfunctory moral illustrations because they commanded a moral high ground to which it was an agreed religious duty of their pupils/readers to aspire: for them *exempla* merely illustrated tautologous and predictable moral lessons the value of which their interlocutor was in duty bound to appreciate. But a new political value system such as Machiavelli is specifically theorising in his assault on humanism in the first paragraph of chapter XV needs, in order to be convincing, more than a perfunctory set of historical illustrations of failures in recent history (here Savonarola. elsewhere Louis XII and Borgia). The other factors that he brings into the discussion – his attempts to analyse political facts as such, his extensions on the standard uses of rhetoric – in part respond to this need and serve to enrich and vary the dialogue with his potential employers, the Medici. What we have to consider, however, and again in part, since this is not the only function of such methods, is the extent to which they genuinely help to interrogate reality.

To begin with, quite detailed claims have been made for a scientific quality in Machiavelli's thought whereby within certain problem areas hypotheses are tested, objections considered and general rules of behaviour established, the dialogue here being reduced to simple exposition such as he affects in chapter 1.[13] But such claims may make too much of Machiavelli's often question-begging references to rules (*'regole'*: e.g. at the end of chapters III and XXIII) which often turn out to be little more than rules of thumb, aphoristic guide-lines such as *'he who thinks that recent favours cause the great to forget past wrongs is mistaken'* (chapter VIII, 269). Machiavelli calls such generalisation speaking broadly (*'parlare nel modo largo'*, chapter

XX, p. 289) and he can be both quite scathing on the subject, as when referring to the 'trite proverb' *'he who builds on the people builds on slime'* (chapter IX, p. 272), and quite reserved about his own use of it: for though some general rules (*'regole generali'*) allegedly never fail (e.g. *'an unwise prince can never be well advised'*, chapter XXIII, p. 294), in other contexts (e.g. chapter XX) Machiavelli argues that 'it is impossible to give a definite judgement of any of these things' (p. 289) and that 'of this matter one cannot speak broadly' (*largamente*: p. 290).

In fact Machiavelli's generalised judgements can be quite hesitant and a much more frequent procedure than their application is the more clearly dialogic structure whereby objections to the *'regole generali'* are countered by his introducing further distinctions which accommodate them. One such passage (on Caesar) is handled below, but the pattern can be observed and evaluated from the very beginning of the text. Chapter III, for instance, introduces the category of the new kingdom (*'principato nuovo'*, p. 259), the main subject of one of Machiavelli's continuing dialogues, and divides it on the basis of those which are entirely new and those which are annexations, the latter having either the same language as their conqueror or another, in which latter case they are to be pacified either by oneself or one's subjects, this second procedure being in turn effected by the establishment of either colonies or garrisons. If the effect here is one suggesting an infinite regress of dichotomies which undermine any simple political judgement, Machiavelli's common sense is summoned to break the chain at an appropriate point: a concession to the interlocutor as much as to the complexity of the subject.

The dialogic structure of the procedure is moreover rendered particularly apparent in chapter XII concerning mercenaries, which are divided up on the basis of their being skilled in arms or not. In the former case they risk harming you by going beyond their prerogative. 'And if it is replied that anyone under arms might do the same. I would answer, [*'replicherei'*] that armies fight either for republics or kings' (p. 275). The pattern of debate is clear and reveals an intention less to present reality scientifically than to equip a political figure with a set of categories with which to approach and argue about the problems facing him. The *'regole'* and the dichotomies belong less in a textbook analysis of history than alongside a stock of clever schemata, axioms, manipulated detail and classical topoi, supported by the application of an administrative rhetoric which belongs in the political negotiating room rather than the scholar's (or scientist's) study. So, for example, Machiavelli recalls himself countering Amboise's judgement whereby 'Italians are incompetent in war' with his own rejoinder 'Like Frenchmen in government' (chapter III, p. 262), a dialogic coup of which he is clearly proud although it hardly amounts to a scientific analysis of the two nations' potential.

What is more scientific is the conscious application of a theory to history in the first place, something which Machiavelli pursues at various points in all his works, but here via the comments on method which aim to situate *The Prince* in a contrasting dialogue less with other types of political agent (friendly or hostile) than with other types of political text. The alternative approach, to share the moral assumptions of all contemporary theories and to write harmoniously in accord with them, is to shun the struggle for theory vital to scientific work and resort to the literary panegyric of a shared religious system whereby, for instance, virtue brings its own reward, pride comes before a fall, two wrongs don't make a right, etc., all statements which Machiavelli would of course question if not refute. The dialogue of Machiavelli as scientist is thus with other theorists who are invited to respond to his approach by a revaluation of their own or by a more specific approach to experience on his alleged terms of *'verità effettuale'*. Machiavelli himself says 'the more one discusses things the better one understands them' and this phrase (from a despatch of 1499)[14] is emblematic of the dialogues which he is pursuing in his work on the philosophical level (presenting theories and rules about how reality might be better understood), on the technical level (considering specifics in his capacity as a commentator on detailed political issues) and on the personal level (recounting shared experiences for the purposes of mutual interest and satisfaction). Parallel to these again stands a further dialogue comprising a series of exhortations to the princes of Italy whereby they strengthen their ambition and realise their opportunities.

This latter culminates in chapter XXVI, frequently argued to have been composed at a later date than the remainder of the text. One reason for this distinction is the fact that the dialogue climaxing there (an impassioned address to Italians at large) is so unlike much of the textual patterning encountered elsewhere: 'Nor can I express with what love he [sc. the *'principe nuovo'*] would be received, with what thirst for revenge, with what persistent faith, with what piety, with what tears', (chapter XXVI, p. 298). Read objectively the text defies Machiavelli's sense of reality (not to say his affectations of cynicism), but an objective reading is not here appropriate. The dialogue evoked is with a subjectively predisposed supporter who will cheer on the author's points, converting the optimistic statements about Italy's readiness for rebirth into a self-fulfilling prophecy. It is not therefore one based on facts explained to a patient student, nor on distinctions generated to explain away objections, but on a virtuous circle wherein appeals for approval are both met with and precipitated by expressions of approval, all stimulated within a common ground of enthusiasm.

It follows that the notion of Machiavelli as objective political scientist in *The Prince* (or indeed elsewhere) is impossible to generalise. Scarcely ever in his published writings does he privilege historical reality as such, always transforming it either imaginatively or rhetorically to serve a greater good (here the reaffirmation of Italian national pride) or to fit it into preconceived categories such as the *virtù/fortuna* dichotomy, which is less a historical phenomenon than a piece of rhetorical mystification. This dichotomy has been rehearsed endlessly in studies of *The Prince*, often being seen as the key to Machiavelli's thinking in that the triumphant Prince must be a man of *virtù* (an exhortation to the Medici) whilst circumstance, via blind *fortuna*, will in the end bring about his failure (an implicit admonition made to Cesare Borgia). In fact the dichotomy is thus radically unstable, being at once a counsel of despair (unpredictable changes of circumstance will always in the end defeat one), a (somewhat glib) attempt to reconcile programmatic action with unpredictable outcomes (*fortuna* controls half the political world, *virtù* the remainder) and a political category appropriate to the vital question of how one gains power in the first place: 'Lands are acquired either by *fortuna* or by *virtù*' (chapter I, p. 258). Again, however, this category emerges more from an attempt to organise subject matter than from an objective appraisal of history. It is a moot point whether even chapter II ('Of hereditary kingdoms') relates to it: certainly chapter VIII (purportedly) falls right outside it: 'But because as a private citizen one becomes king in two further ways which cannot be entirely attributed either to *fortuna* or *virtù*, I think it inappropriate to neglect them' (p.269).

Why is there this confusion in the text, a confusion augmented by the following example of Agathocles, tyrant of Sicily, who clearly did become prince on the basis of *virtù*? Because Machiavelli has put forward these schemata only provisionally and in order to introduce the reader rapidly into his subject while giving the appearance of possessing a comprehensive command of it. Were the categories of chapter I truly scientific, then they would be tested assiduously and consistently by reference to the data following. They aren't. Acquisition via another's arms ('*armi d'altri*') as opposed to one's own ('*arme proprie*') is a dichotomy vaguely applied in chapters VI and VII but in a way very unsatisfactorily related to its sister categories, acquisition via *virtù* and via *fortuna*. Logically we should be dealing with four combinations: *arme proprie* + *virtù* (chapter VI), *arme proprie* + *fortuna* (–), *armi d 'altri* + *virtù* (–) *armi d'altri* + *fortuna* (chapter VII); however, only two of these are specifically covered and then with the curious anomaly whereby Cesare Borgia (the key example of princely *virtù*) appears under the fourth heading.

What do we conclude? That again the intended dialogue is most often with someone less concerned with the logic of Machiavelli's argument than with its persuasive force, this force helping him plaster over the gaps and inconsistencies in theoretical structure in favour perhaps of the political acumen with which Machiavelli maps out their real common ground: lived if not shared political experience; and a shared common goal: the establishment of a new kingdom ('*principato nuovo*'). It is thus only Machiavelli's allegation that the problem of acquiring and preserving states has been 'solved, in the rest of *The Prince*, through the topic of *virtù* and *fortuna*'.[15] If this were so, then the text would risk becoming very limited and allegorical.

In fact both more and less are involved: less in the sense that Machiavelli's central issue with the Medici readership is this topic of '*principato nuovo*' which he asserts more and more in the text, even at points where it seems marginally relevant; more in the sense that other readers are envisaged, for instance the classical historian who is sufficiently interested and well equipped to follow Machiavelli through all the detailed examples of plotting in imperial Rome which form the latter part of *Prince*, chapter XIX. Here indeed we see the results of Machiavelli's classical reading, nay enjoy a foretaste of the dialogues which would animate the chapters of the *Discorsi*[16] much as they enlivened Machiavelli's solitary evening studies. Now he speaks as a student of history to other students of history, hoping to nourish the kind of informed and delighted discussion that no doubt fermented later in the Orti Oricellari. But who among his political readership would have the forbearance to pursue all its subtle distinctions between the problems posed for the later Roman emperors by the people, the aristocracy and the army, for Machiavelli the three vital centres of power at that time? And does he not himself admit (mercifully dropping the discussion of Heliogabalus, Macrinus and Julian) that 'the princes of today are less afflicted by this problem' (chapter XIX, p. 288), and hence that for those specific readers the whole discussion has been off the point?

The common ground with these political readers is not a set of historical essays on Pertinax and Antoninus Caracalla, nor a series of imaginative metaphors concerning the river of *fortuna* and the dykes of *virtù* surrounding it (nor yet the kind of tavern quip that has *fortuna* a woman to be pummelled into obedience), but a conceptual space cleared by the author's force of argument (the metaphor is owed to T. M. Greene)[17] and then occupied by the dialogues which this argument presupposes all as a necessary preliminary to the Prince himself actually conquering a political space in Italy. What I would question is Greene's assertion that reading and action are inseparable and that 'The prince in other words should do what in fact Machiavelli is doing in the composition of this treatise'.[18] The whole text is much more provisional than that and the dialogues within it sketched out as dialogues rather than put forward in terms of objective achievements whose basis he and the reader then admire. Just as a prince has to think up new contingencies to accommodate the vagaries of circumstance (for 'it is a common defect of men not to anticipate storms during calm weather', chapter XIV, p. 295), so an adviser needs to respond with pragmatic flexibility in order to feed the ongoing dialogue which his public role comprises.

There are many examples of this procedure, but an especially patent one comes at the end of chapter XVI when Machiavelli has been considering largess and meanness, asserting with deliberate paradox that the latter is the better political quality. The opening paragraph, albeit abstract, is an interesting example of dialectical reasoning, with Machiavelli arguing that when applied in the political sphere both qualities turn into their opposites, the generous Prince being forced into miserly over-taxation, a practice which the parsimonious Prince will avoid, so revealing himself in the long term as the truly generous one: Julius II, Louis XII and Ferdinand V of Spain are current examples. The moral paradox is emphasised starkly: 'this [i.e. meanness] is one of those vices which make it possible for a prince to rule' (chapter XVI, p. 281); and thus far striking paradox, ingenious dialectics and contemporary examples have been the rhetorical tools constructing the argument.

Now, however, from being latent, the dialogue surfaces, Machiavelli (a playwright after all) even giving it a kind of dramatic form: 'And if someone should say' (*'Se alcuno dicessi …'*) that Caesar is an example of that type of prince who buys his way to power and uses generosity to sustain himself, I respond (*'respondo'*) that there is a further distinction between an established prince and one seeking power: the latter category applies to Caesar who would have lost power had he been as generous once emperor as he had been when bribing his way to the throne. But again a challenge is envisaged: 'And if someone were to reply' (*'Se alcuno replicassi …'*) 'What about all the generous princes who have survived and won wars?', 'I respond to you' (*'ti respondo'*) (so now the author, or his persona, is actually addressing his interlocutor directly) that it is a matter of whose wealth one is spending: if it is booty then he can afford to dispense it; if it is revenue (his own or his subjects') then he cannot (chapter XVI, p. 281). Further examples come, Caesar among them, but the pattern is already clear. Machiavelli anticipates objections, even using direct speech, and replies to them with further distinctions and examples confirming his initial points plus the consistent rider that above all else vice (*vizio*) which leads to hatred (*odio*) is to be avoided. Sarolli shows how Machiavelli used the same dialogic (he says inquisitorial)[19] procedures in his manuscript despatches, shifting from third to first person in precisely analogous ways. It is a professional compositional practice and the effect is not to establish an intellectual monopoly which leads the interlocutor (the *tu* of the dialogue) into inevitable defeat, but rather to encourage trust in the judgement of the persona (the *io* of the dialogue) who respects his opponent in discussion, has anticipated at least some of his objections and is able to present a meaningful if not exhaustive case, encouraging one to think that his command of the field of enquiry is respectably adequate if not in fact total. Others can then come into the discussion.

Indeed they did. It has been shown that from the start *The Prince* was read by some not as a didactic text in the mirror of the prince (*speculum principis*) tradition but as a set of comments on contemporary affairs.[20] Of course none of the examples is analysed with any reputable degree of historical precision (as we have seen, Savonarola is dismissed on the basis of the mere heading unarmed prophets ('*profeti disarmati*')), but time does not permit as much. Do we not see Machiavelli frequently avowing that he must not delay discussion?[21] What we have in chapter XVI is an excellent example of the kind of advice a political mentor (Niccolò Machiavelli by name) would give *viva voce* in the anterooms of the political headquarters where his prince was operating. Clear points unrestrained by deference, clever but not over-subtle distinctions, famous but relevant analogies (ancient and modern) applying a measure of both scholarly and practical expertise, an intelligently flexible rather than dogmatic confrontation of issues and a clear sense of priorities (politics before ethics): these are the components of Machiavelli's apparatus, rendered available to the Medici with the specific recommendation that a former opponent can be a more active supporter than those long-term servants who have grown complacent in their security,[22] and, this particular piece of special pleading apart, even at a distance of all but five centuries it is enough to convince one that a genuine political discussion is taking place.

The contours of this administrative rhetoric, what Langton has described as his 'issues-and-options style',[23] are for the reader to explore once the passages in which it operates have been identified. Listing of points, selection of telling narrative details cogently recounted, use of illustrative examples, establishment of significant dichotomies, emphasis of key terms in order to structure the argument in a preselected direction: all of these are apparent in the discussion, and the imagined interlocutor is the opponent in negotiation whom one has to influence in some way to accept the point one is proving, however transparent be the rhetorical subterfuges one employs. Two final points are worth making in the context of Machiavelli here and elsewhere. First, his freshness of approach, whereby we hear him say in effect 'I know that this question has been mishandled endlessly in previous discussions: let's talk turkey': this technique has a direct appeal in committee situations as any administrator knows. Second, one notes his skill in rendering points succinctly, compressing theories and explanations into a relatively short essay (similar to an administrative memorandum) which the interlocutor or reader can expand herself or himself if so inclined. The compositional skill of Machiavelli aims to secure the reader's attention, the brevity of *The Prince* as a whole (like that of the individual chapters of the *Discorsi*) aims to prevent his outstaying his welcome in the author/reader dialogue it stimulates.

In this regard one of the best narrative sections comes in chapter VII, which is concerned with the analysis of the career of Cesare Borgia under the not entirely satisfactory rubric of 'new kingdoms [i.e. the Romagna] acquired with the arms and *fortuna* of another' (i.e. the papacy, which one might argue owed to fortune its titular rights to that province). In fact notwithstanding this caveat the lengthy discussion of Borgia is justified by his relevance to the '*principe nuovo*' in general and by Machiavelli's privileged knowledge of the man. The discussion of the French invasion of 1499, incited by the Pope so as to buy French support for the Romagna policy, is a prelude to greater things, although significantly it defies the initial category by re-presenting Borgia as subject to the *armi* and *fortuna* of these allies, rather than of his father. What follows is a summary account of the Sinigaglia massacre and the pacification of the Romagna, which he achieved by scapegoating his lieutenant Ramiro de Lorqua, and again the narrative is brief, trenchant, delighting in lurid details and summary conclusions about the manipulation of alliances and public opinion.

'But let's get back to where we started', says Machiavelli (chapter VII, p. 267), confident that his descriptive energies have captivated his audience, which is frequently, indeed one might say nearly always, the case. What of the future? A key article of policy for Borgia was to extricate himself from the French alliance as it was an alliance of weak with strong (bad policy as we read in chapter III). A second was to guarantee a favourable papal succession, which he sought to ensure in four ways: (1) by wiping out the families of those he had dispossessed, so to rob a hostile Pope of potential allies; (2) by winning over the Roman grandees to his side so as to limit the Pope's influence; (3) by securing a majority faction within the college of cardinals; (4) by gaining sufficient power to be able to withstand a first strike by his opponents once the Pope had died.

The quality of the rhetoric is clear. It is based once again on the business of political meetings, points being listed in order of priority for discussion with influential and powerful interlocutors, Machiavelli meanwhile arming his persona (and alongside him the political leader that persona is imagined briefing) with sufficient information to create an aura of expertise and expressing himself with sufficient clarity to make it appear more reasonable to side with him than against him. The subordinate dialogues are once more with the Medici (e.g. chapter VII, pp. 267-8: 'this bit is to be noted and imitated by others' − i.e. Giuliano and/or Lorenzo), but also with Borgia himself. The confident projection of Borgia's future successes ('he was ready to pounce on Pisa. After this Lucca and Siena would immediately fall', p. 268) has been read as a piece of free indi-

rect speech where Machiavelli adopts the persona of Cesare in
a further variation on the dialogue of experienced diplomat
with emergent ruler,[24] whereupon in the next paragraph he
recounts in true indirect speech his own conversations with the
man where they discussed the mischance which laid him
mortally ill at the moment of his father's death, so rendering
void all the plans described above. Finally, can one not discern,
here and elsewhere in the work, a subdominant dialogue
between author and persona which helps to raise the text's
emotional tension? It arises from Machiavelli's onslaught on his
own self-doubt and aims to reassure himself that, despite his
disgrace, his political credentials remain valid.

The weaknesses of chapter VII have long been identified:
there is confusion over the exact reason for Borgia's downfall
(was it *fortuna* or a mistake over the papal election?) and his
account of the man's career is simplified to the point of distor-
tion. We can add further dislocations based on the confusion
generated within the rubric under which Machiavelli claims to
be writing (whose *fortuna* and whose arms are under discussion
– his own, those of the Pope or the French?).[25] Nevertheless,
confused and inconsistent though it be when viewed as a
historical account or as a piece of political philosophy, as an
incitement to ambition it is magnificent, and it is an incitement
legitimated by the infectious confidence which Machiavelli
portrays in his own powers of analysis. Do this, he says, using
my principles, and success is guaranteed.

One cannot therefore agree that this is a writer who leaves
little to the imagination.[26] On the contrary, an imaginative co-
operation by the reader is essential in order that his paradoxi-
cal theories and theoretical contradictions be lent coherence and
that the sketchy examples be filled out as historical facts. A
quite considerable degree of shared political experience is
assumed by the text and also a shared professional register; in
this context witness, for example, the virtual note-form references
to the college of cardinals facing Borgia in 1503: 'those whom
he had harmed were, among others, San Piero ad Vincula,
Colonna, San Giorgio, Ascanio: all the rest, once elected, had to
fear him, barring Rohan and the Spanish' (chapter VII, p. 269).
How much attention do we pay at such points either to the

abstract dichotomies of chapter 1 or to the chapter headings and
the moral dichotomies of chapters XV and following?
Abstraction and moral values set aside, the whole passage
advertises that sense of intimate discussion in small centres of
power located around detailed agendas and set to a limited time-
scale (as opposed to the more republican rhetoric of grandilo-
quence displayed before a large assembly).[27] It is for the reader
once more to grasp the quality of political debate, admire
Machiavelli's competence as analyst of circumstances, and
imagine how the argument about the exploitation of territorial
and financial opportunities can be pursued. After all, under
their kinsman Leo X the Medici lords have the good fortune to
re-enact his successes whilst using Machiavelli's (written or
verbal) advice to avoid his failures.

To re-enact them, yes, but in what context? It has never
been clear to scholars in what precise theatre Machiavelli was
imagining that the Medici would apply his recommendations,
be it Florence, the Romagna, or Italy at large. And if this vague-
ness has stimulated important disagreements it also has significant dialogic implications. In particular, it would seem
inappropriate to the dialogic structure of the text to point out
too specific a military or political project in any case; to do so
would be to occupy too much space in the dialogue the text
seeks to establish and maintain, and hence leave too little initiative for the interlocutor. The point is more to initiate a relationship than to present a theoretical *fait accompli*: meanwhile,
in terms of *'verità effettuale'*, it would be hopelessly inadequate
as hopelessly over-ambitious to detail every means by which
the Romagna could be conquered, every contingency by means
of which Florence could revitalised, every article of policy
fulfilling that grand triumphal march against the *barbari* infest-
ing Italy which is foreshadowed with such gusto at the end of
the work. Any ruler will have his own agenda and priorities
which one cannot pre-empt from a subordinate position: the
key aim at this stage of Italy's history (and of Machiavelli's
career) must be to prove what one has to offer, obtain appoint-
ment at almost whatever level, and then to work one's way into
a more significant and exclusively political dialogue in the real
chronotopes of governmental business.

If this approach to *The Prince* is accepted then it pre-empts,
and very significantly, the assertions of such as Russo, Busetto
and McCanles whereby (typically) Machiavelli's 'limpid affir-
mations and deductions do not require discussion'.[28] On the
contrary, they advertise the very discussions which they fore-
see, indeed depend on inciting. Some may read *The Prince* as a
'well-formed text immune to the embarrassment of contradiction':[29] so committed was Machiavelli to the thrust and counter-
thrust of political debate that I doubt he would himself be such
a reader. For though at times used for display, edification or
evaluation be it moral, logical or historical, his knowledge is
also seen as an instrument with which, however crudely and
against however many contradictions, to achieve power,
including that measure of political power he had enjoyed under
the republic. Above all, his knowledge is an incitement to
further dialogue. Hence if his rewritings of history (let us say
the career of Borgia) falsify and oversimplify, fitting brute facts
into predetermined categories like the heading of chapter VII,
this is deliberate. It facilitates the dialogue with the addressee
as prince (rather than as historian or philosopher of history),
making it easier for him to find a place in the text and analyse
its effects and advantages for him. And this process is in fact
what makes *The Prince* such an exciting text to read: it represents an intellectual assault by the author not on a real historical situation considered for its own sake but on such a situation
shot through with the author's own classical idealism, patrio-
tism, ambition and personal hopes, even if superficially these
hopes have now renounced the republican traditions of
Machiavelli's own immediate past.

This republican idealism will dominate the *Discorsi* when
they are written. It is at the same time quite wrong to see it as
entirely absent from *The Prince*. Just as Machiavelli's traditional
sense of morality fights back in chapter VIII against the examples (Agathocles, Oliverotto da Fermo, Cesare Borgia) which
have offended it, so chapter IX expresses a confidence in the
people ('*il populo*') apparently stifled when Machiavelli argues
elsewhere (e.g. chapter XVII) that people ('*gli uomini*') are
ungrateful, cowardly and selfish. In chapter IX Machiavelli's
respect for the people generates a new category of civil king-

ship (*'principato civile'*, in effect equatable with elective monarchy), but in doing so he once more once defies his own
dichotomy whereby all kings come to power either via *virtù* or
via *fortuna*. The civil monarch, Machiavelli says, owes his position either to the people or the aristocracy, but it is the former
who provide the more honest motive, as their aim in electing
him is freedom from oppression rather than an increase in aris-
tocratic power. So much is this the case that even a prince
created by the *grandi* should become the protector of the people
whose favour, respect and gratitude are political advantages to
be cultivated, points which rarely emerge in the exposition of
'principati nuovi' or the political morality devised in chapters
XV to XIX. What they reveal is again the subliminal dialogue
operating between Machiavelli's projected role in the Medici
principate and his service of the Florentine republic.

Given the radically complex nature of the work, the man
and the style (not to say the political context and the general
period in which he lived) it is thus odd that critics have so often
sought to idealise and unify aspects of Machiavelli's thought
and achievement rather than adopting the more obvious and in
fact juster approach to him by teasing out the contradictions
and oppositions which function in his text. Despite all the work
on Machiavelli's early texts, notably Chiappelli's analyses of his
diplomatic writings, one thus still hears that 'It was then [i.e.
autumn 1513] that ... the Florentine secretary began to transform himself into a man of letters'.[30] On the contrary he had
always been one, almost certainly as of his initial education.
Similarly, one hears of the key to the *'unité'* of Machiavelli's
thought,[31] of its *'monismo'* (a substitute for the church/state
dualism of medieval political philosophy);[32] and one reads of the
'intrinsic unity of the personality of the secretary'[33] which begs
the question whether, taken as a set of dialogic relations,
anyone's personality can possibly be reduced to a unitary
pattern; and of how *The Prince qua* text is 'ideologically closed',
probably a theoretical impossibility and certainly an unfair
comment in this case.[34]

It is then curious, but for our purposes vitally significant,
that a work which emerges from a thoroughly didactic tradition (humanist prince literature) in which the interlocutor occu-

pies an impregnable moral and intellectual position knowing all
the answers and disbursing his knowledge, tediously as so
predictably, to a passive recipient, should in fact be invigorated
with so many dialogic patterns. By contrast, when Machiavelli
chose, say, in the *Arte della guerra* some years later to adopt the
dialogue form, he produced a text which is much less dialogic
than *The Prince*. At the same time the various dialogic patterns
which I have outlined, from the most explicit direct addresses
of *'dico che'* and *'ti respondo'* to the most concealed self-questioning of a personality at which we can only guess, have surely
done more than many other aspects of this text to secure its
success, fame and stylistic appeal. To a remarkable extent it is
the unresolved dialogues within Machiavelli's *Prince* which
have generated the unending dialogue concerning it.

Notes

1 Cf. the task undertaken by A. H. Gilbert in *Machiavelli's Prince and its
   Forerunners* (Durham, NC: Duke University Press), 1938.

2 Cf. N. Rubinstein, 'Political Theories in the Renaissance', in *The
   Renaissance* (London: Methuen, 1982), pp. 153-200 (p. 167).

3 Cf. Machiavelli, *Lettere*, ed. F. Gaeta (Milan: Feltrinelli, 1981), p. 304: as
   in all other instances the translation is my own.

4 W. Gundersheimer, 'San Casciano, 1513: A Machiavellian Moment
   Reconsidered', *Journal of Medieval and Renaissance Studies*, 17 (1987), pp.
   41-58, (p. 55).

5 Cf. Machiavelli, *Lettere*, p. 304.

6 'He asks the questions and they respond. He does not truly participate
   in the give-and-take of dialogue. In the activity of language a step seems
   to be missing', S. De Grazia, *Machiavelli in Hell* (Princeton: Princeton
   University Press, 1989), p. 375.

7 Machiavelli, *Lettere*, p. 297.

8 Dedicatory letter, p. 257. This and all references to Machiavelli's works,
   unless otherwise indicated, are to the Martelli edition of his complete
   works (Florence: Sansoni, 1971).

9 The discussion refers to the peculiar situation of late medieval Italy and
   its military power-vacuum which mercenaries have been employed to
   fill.

10 Machiavelli's text *Dell'arte della guerra* which he published in Florence
    in 1521, having first read and then circulated it in manuscript among the
    very members of the scholarly group in which it is situated.

11 E. Garver, 'Machiavelli's *The Prince*: A Neglected Rhetorical Classic', *Philosophy and Rhetoric*, 13 (1980), pp. 99-120, (p. 99).

12 Cf. p. 182: 'the more freely one speaks, the better received one will be.'

13 Cf. A. Toscano, *Marsilio da Padova e Niccolò Machiavelli* (Ravenna: Longo, 1981), pp. 60-1.

14 See F. Chiappelli. *Nuovi studi sul linguaggio del Machiavelli* (Florence: Le Monnier, 1969), p. 157.

15 Garver, 'Machiavelli's *The Prince*', p. 103.

16 My feeling is that the majority of Machiavelli scholars now reject the traditional but abitrary notion whereby *The Prince* was somehow spawned out of *Discorsi*, I. 18, the latter's previous chapters being an unconscious lead up to it.

17 'The End of Discourse in Machiavelli's *Prince*', *Yale French Studies*, 67 (1984), pp. 57-71 (p. 59).

18 'The End of Discourse', p. 62.

19 'The Unpublished Machiavelli', *Review of National Literatures*, 1 (1970), pp. 78-92 (p. 91).

20 See J. N. Stephens and H. C. Butters, 'New light on Machiavelli', *EHR*, 97 (1982), pp. 54-69.

21 E.g. several times in chapter XIX alone: e.g. 'I wish to discuss briefly ...', 'to abbreviate matters ..., etc.

22 See p. 290: 'Princes, and especially new princes, have found more faithful and useful those men who at the beginning of their reign were suspect to them.'

23 J Langton, 'Machiavelli's Paradox', *American Political Science Review*, 81.4 (1987), pp. 1277-83 (p. 1278).

24 See M. McCanles, *The Discourse of 'Il Principe'* (Malibu: Udena, 1983), pp. 78ff.

25 In this context there is a confusing but instructive disrepancy between the Latin and Italian chapter headings.

26 See J. J. Marchand, 'Le discours paradoxal dans le *Prince* de Machiavel', *Colloquium Helveticum*, 5 (1987), pp. 29-41 (p. 29).

27 Cf. certain of Machiavelli's earlier writings: see W. E. Wiethoff, 'Machiavelli's "Heroic" Political Oratory', *Southern Speech Communication Journal*, 47 (1981), pp. 10-22.

28 See McCanles, *The Discourse of 'Il Principe'*, p. 26.

29 *The Discourse of 'Il Principe'*, p. 26.

30 W. Gundersheimer, 'San Casciano, 1513', p. 41.

31 A. Michel, 'Machiavel lecteur de Tite-live', in G. Barthouil (ed.), *Machiavelli attuale* (Ravenna: Longo), 1982, pp. 139-48, (p. 140).

32 Toscano, *Marsilio da Padova*, p. 150.

33 'L'intrinseca unità della personalità del segretario'; see L. Caretti, 'Machia-
    velli scrittore', in *Machiavelli* (Bologna: Boni, 1973), pp. 31-42 (p. 33).

34 N. S. Struever, 'Machiavelli, Montaigne, and the Problem of External
    Address in Renaissance Ethics", in K. Brownlee (ed.), *Discourses of Authority
    in Medieval and Renaissance Literature*, (London: University Press of New
    England, 1989), pp. 236-53 (p. 239).

5

Language and *The Prince*[1]

JOHN M. NAJEMY

The Prince has a reputation, one that Machiavelli himself did his best to promote, for successfully escaping the ambiguities and superfluous ornaments of language, or rhetoric, and thus making possible, and bringing to the centre of its purposes, direct contact with things themselves. Machiavelli announces this as a fundamental aim and feature of the book in the dedicatory letter where he claims to distance himself from the classical traditions of rhetorical *amplificatio*: 'I have not embellished or inflated this work with abundant rhythmical cadences or with turgid and grandiloquent words; neither are there any other blandishments and irrelevant decorations with which many authors usually describe and bedeck their writings' ('La quale opera io non ho ornata né ripiena di clausule ample, o di parole ampullose e magnifiche, o di qualunque altro lenocinio o ornamento estrinseco, con li quali molti sogliono le loro cose descrivere e ornare').[2] As students of Renaissance rhetoric would be quick to point out, Machiavelli here uses terms that echo the technical language of the rhetorical arts: *ornata*, *ornamento*, *ornare*, *ample* and *ampullose*. The term *ornamento* itself points to a particularly Renaissance notion of the power of language. 'Figures and tropes', as Brian Vickers notes, 'were sometimes described as "the ornaments of rhetoric", a term frequently misunderstood in the modern sense of a decoration not functional to the overall aim.... [T]he ornaments were associated with *amplificatio*, not in the medieval sense of expanding discourse but in the classical-Renaissance sense of making it more intense and effective.'[3]

However conversant Machiavelli may have been with the terms and doctrines of professional rhetoric,[4] it is none the less clear that in this passage from the dedicatory letter of *The Prince* he quite deliberately and polemically shares in, and contributes to, what Vickers calls the modern misunderstanding of *ornamentum* as a purely decorative and thus dispensable aspect of language. Machiavelli's assumption is precisely that *ornamento* is 'estrinseco' – on the outside, marginal, and, in one sense of the Latin word from which this usage derives, irrelevant. Even more damning are the overtones of his characterisation of rhetoric as a matter of 'lenocinio', whose figurative meaning of 'artifice' or 'excessive ornament' depends on the Latin *lenocinium*, which means pimping, pandering and thus, in speech, meretricious ornament. The dedicatory letter rejects the techniques of rhetoric (even as it demonstrates Machiavelli's knowledge of this skill so central to Renaissance humanism and education) because he wants whatever 'honour' his work earns to emerge from the content itself: from the *varietà* – usually taken to mean 'newness' or 'originality', the way in which the book varies or differs from the conventions that usually dominate in such writing – and from the *gravità* – the seriousness and importance – of, respectively, the *materia* and the *subietto*, two terms that can be translated together as the 'subject matter'. Any honour his book earns should be a function, or so he hopes, not of its language but of its success in putting readers into direct contact with things themselves, with a *materia* and a *subietto* whose newness and importance do not need to be enhanced by artful, and inevitably artificial, uses of language.

In the dedicatory letter Machiavelli implicitly repudiates the entire tradition, central to Renaissance humanism, that had accepted the beneficent power and the utility of language and eloquence in politics and political discourse. This notion was embedded in assumptions that stretched back to Brunetto Latini in the thirteenth century, who had proclaimed that the 'science of speaking well and of governing people is the noblest art in the world',[5] and it found its most confident expression among the Florentine civic humanists, several of whom, including Coluccio Salutati, Leonardo Bruni and Poggio Bracciolini, had preceded Machiavelli in the Florentine chancery. The rhetorical arts had also benefited from an assumed compatibility with the aims of politics among the professional theorists of rhetoric. George of Trebizond, author of the influential *Rhetoricorum libri V*, wrote an oration in praise of eloquence in the 1430s in which he declared that the ancients were certainly right to name rhetoric the 'art of humanity', 'the most important part of the civil science which is the mistress and lord of all human affairs', and 'the most noble instrument of politics'.[6] Even Angelo Poliziano, the classical scholar and poet who became a central figure in the depoliticised Medicean cultural circles at the end of the fifteenth century, accepted the idea that language and speech were the foundation of politics, asserting that 'there is nothing more fertile and useful than to persuade one's fellow citizens by means of words, so that they perform actions advantageous to the state and refrain from those that are damaging'.[7] In polemical opposition to this tradition, *The Prince* announces its intention to establish a discourse of politics independent of rhetoric and eloquence.

The mistrust of rhetoric and its meretricious ornament that Machiavelli displays in the dedicatory letter reflects a still more fundamental worry about language itself, evident both in the body of *The Prince* and in the letters that Machiavelli wrote to Francesco Vettori in the months preceding the composition of the treatise. The locus of this worry is an awareness of a certain indeterminacy or inexactness of language, which Machiavelli only occasionally acknowledges and never openly theorises in the letters or in *The Prince*. One notable expression of this worry is the letter to Vettori of 9 April 1513, in which Machiavelli (responding to similar doubts expressed by Vettori himself) asserts that 'if it has become bothersome to you to discuss things [i.e. politics], because many times you see events taking place apart from the discourses and concepts that one forms about them ["per vedere molte volte succedere e casi fuora de' discorsi et concetti che si fanno"], you are right, for a similar thing has happened to me'.[8] The background to these worries lies in the events of 1512-13 that had brought about the fall of the republic, the return of the Medici, the sacking of Machiavelli and his arrest, imprisonment, torture, and exclusion from political work. Since Machiavelli had been an envoy and highly placed secretary and adviser to the republican government, that work had been predicated on the assumption of a verifiable 'riscontro' or correspondence between 'cose' and 'discorsi', between things – political events, the purposes and actions of princes, and their results – and the language employed to describe, represent, analyse and understand such things. As he told his superiors on one occasion in 1502, 'things can't just be guessed at ... and if one doesn't wish to write fantasies and dreams ["ghiribizzi e sogni"], one has to verify matters ["bisogna che riscontri le cose"]'.[9] The letter of 9 April 1513 shows Machiavelli in some doubt and anxiety about the nature, or even the possibility, of this correspondence of 'cose' and 'discorsi'. Things, he now admits, have happened apart from (literally 'outside of' – *fuora*) the 'discourses and concepts' one forms about them. This admission brought close to the surface some troubling, though unspoken, questions. Do 'things' always go their own way, oblivious of the efforts of language to understand them? Is the desired 'riscontro' ever possible, and, if so, how? Or is it frequently, or always, merely an illusion? Is language always missing the mark? And what relationship actually exists, or can exist, between 'discourses and concepts' and 'things' outside language?

The Prince wants to provide answers to these questions, and it does so, as I shall try to suggest, in practice if not in theory and in a way that aims to subordinate language, with all its potential indeterminacies and ambiguities, to the discipline and purposes of a discourse that does not depend on common usage. Before we examine passages that place this aim in evidence and seek to implement it, it is essential to realise that the aim itself of liberating discourse from the pitfalls of common usage implicitly rejects another notion central to Renaissance theorising about language, a notion that may be the most important and revolutionary development in the philosophy of language in the century before Machiavelli. As many scholars, and recently Richard Waswo,[10] have argued, the historically grounded linguistics of Lorenzo Valla (d. 1457) was the spearhead of an attack on the prevailing theory of language that had assumed its essentially representational, or referential, function. In that traditional view, words represent, or stand for, things because of some connection or identity that is necessary and inherent in the relationship between word and thing, and which is thus neither random nor contingent. Waswo speculates (along lines that seem particularly appropriate for understanding Machiavelli in 1513) that the wish to harness language to this mimetic, representational function emerges from 'the incredulity, distrust, and ambivalence we feel toward the power of words',[11] and that the various theories of referential or representational semantics constitute an 'effort to make language a more perfect mirror of the wholly separate object-world'.[12]

Valla sought to overturn this whole way of thinking about language. Two principal notions governed his approach: first, that any language changes with time, as his studies of the history of the Latin language revealed, with the addition not only of new words but of new meanings for old words; and, second, almost as a corollary to the first point, that the meanings of terms are thus determined by usage and convention, or, as Waswo nicely puts it, by 'the company a word keeps – that is, its total context: use in relation to other terms, grammatical form, historical circumstances'.[13] Within the framework of these assumptions, apparently obvious and simple but in fact far-reaching in their implications, 'knowledge and truth are functions of the "common use" of language'.[14] 'Knowledge' of the world is a consequence of how humans use language and can never be independent of it. As Valla says, 'Words uttered by men are indeed natural, but their meaning is determined by conventions ... Sounds indeed exist in nature, but words and meanings are fashioned' ('Vox humana naturalis illa quidem est, sed eius significatio ab institutione descendit. ... Ut soni quidem sint a natura, voces autem et significationes ab artifice').[15] The last word of this sentence is particularly intriguing. Valla's first purpose in using it must be, as Waswo's translation suggests, to affirm that meaning belongs to the realm of things made by human effort – to *ars* or *arte*, and thus to the *artifex* – and not to the realm of nature. But *artifex* also meant one who practises a trade or skill, and thus an artisan or a guildsman, and the political overtones of this second and socially more specific sense of the phrase 'ab artifice' link the passage to Valla's polemical argument that it is the usage of ordinary persons, not that of intellectuals or of the socially powerful, that constitutes the meaning of terms and, consequently, the world as we are able to know it. 'Thus', says Valla, 'housewives sometimes have a better sense of the meaning of words than the greatest philosophers. For the former employ words for a purpose, the latter for a game' ('Itaque melius de intellectu verborum mulierculae nonnumquam sentiunt, quam summi philosophi. Illae enim verba ad usum trahunt: isti ad lusum').[16] Valla's approach to language began to stimulate significant interest and application among humanists toward the end of the fifteenth century and the beginning of the sixteenth (the best-known chapter of this story being the powerful influence that his philological method of reading texts exerted on Erasmus), and it was a major influence on discussions of rhetoric and poetics when Machiavelli faced his own dilemma of language in *The Prince*.[17]

Machiavelli's response to this dilemma ignored or contradicted the crucial ideas that emerged from Valla's linguistic revolution: the historical and social processes by which words become invested with meaning. *The Prince*'s mistrust of the temporal and collective dimensions of language is especially evident in passages in which Machiavelli attempts to stabilise and control the meaning of words. Wherever the text encounters a potential slipperiness or uncertainty in the terms it employs, Machiavelli intervenes swiftly to contain and stabilise this polysemous tendency – what we might call the 'spillover' effect that produces a multiplicity of meanings for any term. This strategy is implicit in one of *The Prince*'s best-known features: its almost obsessive reliance on differential pairs, or binary oppositions, whose appeal for Machiavelli must have been their capacity to generate the impression that the meaning of each term is determined and stabilised by its apparently necessary oppositional relationship to its paired other.[18] The famous opening sentence of the first chapter imposes this technique peremptorily: 'All states and all dominions that have had or now have authority over men have been and now are either republics or princedoms' ('Tutti gli stati, tutti e' dominii che hanno avuto e hanno imperio sopra gli uomini, sono stati e sono o republiche o principati').[19] Without explanation, examples,

survey of usage, or historical background, the text simply
asserts the equation of 'stati' with 'dominii' and limits the
species of this genus to only two possibilities – 'republiche' and
'principati'. The absence, indeed the implicit denial, of any
notion that usage, context, and time can change the meanings
of words and thus affect the stability of analytical categories
emerges from the repeated combination in this sentence of the
present perfect and present tenses ('hanno avuto e hanno', 'sono
stati e sono'), which underscores the sense of the timeless validity of its definitions and categories. The differential pairs that
structure the rest of the introductory chapter, similarly
presented without explanation or justification, create the
analytical framework for the next ten chapters, which deal with
the different kinds of principalities listed (as well as a few not
listed) in chapter I: the division of principalities into hereditary
and new; new principalities into completely new ones or ones
grafted on to a hereditary principality; the distinction, assumed
to be valid for both kinds of acquired states, between those that
were previously independent and those that lived under a
prince; and, finally, the distinction between new principalities
acquired with the arms of others and those acquired with one's
own arms, alternatives that the text immediately conflates with
the most famous of Machiavelli's differential pairs, *fortuna* and
virtù. The force of this procedure in chapter I is to produce the
impression, by the end of this paragraph of apparently logical
entailments, that the locked opposition of *fortuna* and *virtù*
must lie in the very structure of things.

If the strategy of preemptive stabilisation of language is
implicit and taken for granted in the first half of *The Prince*, it
becomes explicit and a more open locus of worry beginning
with chapter XV, 'Concerning matters for which men, and
particularly princes, are praised or blamed' (p. 280).[20] This is
the first time in the book that a chapter title openly refers to
things predicated of princes by others. The chief purpose of the
chapter is to assess the way people use language to make judgments about princes, and it is no coincidence that a more direct
concern with controlling and containing the threat posed by
the slipperiness of language should appear at the point where
the text takes up the problem of how people look at, evaluate

and say things about princes. But why, we might ask, does a chapter that proposes to examine the criteria for praising and blaming princes – a topic that will quickly translate itself into a discussion of linguistic usage and meaning – begin with Machiavelli's bold pronouncement that, because it is his 'intention to write something useful to those who can understand it' ('sendo l'intento mio scrivere cosa utile a chi la intende'), he believes it (I give a clumsily literal translation for the purposes of the analysis that follows) 'more worthwhile to go behind to the effectual truth of the thing than to the imagination of it' ('più conveniente andare drieto alla verità effettuale della cosa, che alla imaginazione di essa') (chapter XV, p. 280)? One reason for this beginning is that the ensuing discussion will claim that accurate and true judgements about princes are indeed possible. The ability to write 'useful' and 'true' things about princes requires the notions of utility and truth to be themselves stabilised. Machiavelli is evidently not satisfied to say, simply and tautologically, that he will write truth where others have written falsehood. Instead he combines 'truth' and 'utility' into 'effectual truth', and, according to his usual method of defining terms by differentiating them from their paired others, he opposes this 'effectual truth' to 'imaginazione'.

But why did Machiavelli choose 'imaginazione' as the assumed opposite of 'effectual truth'? And what indeed is the sense of 'imaginazione' in this passage? Typically, the text pretends that the opposition is both self-evident and reflective of relationships outside the linguistic realm. But a reading of the letters that Machiavelli and Vettori exchanged during the summer of 1513 – just months or even weeks before the composition of *The Prince* – reveals that it was Vettori who introduced into their dialogue the verb 'immaginare' as part of his critique of Machiavelli's claims to be able to interpret, accurately and effectively, the words, purposes and actions of princes. Vettori had suggested that such interpretation was inevitably a matter of approximation and guesswork: 'We must believe that each of these princes of ours has some purpose, and because it is impossible for us to know their secrets, we have to guess at it from their words and actions, and some of it we just imagine' ('Noi abbiamo a pensare che ciascuno di questi nostri principi habbia un fine, et perché a noi è impossibile sapere il segreto loro, bisogna lo stimiamo dalle parole, dalle dimostrazioni, et qualche parte ne immaginiamo').[21] Vettori's scepticism is grounded in the idea that any discourse about princes is necessarily a matter of reading and interpreting, or weighing ('bisogna lo stimiamo'), the words and actions that stand between the purposes and secrets of princes and those who would know these secrets. That the purpose ('fine') of a prince is implicitly a 'secret' suggests that his words and actions may function less as signs pointing to that purpose than as screens intended to keep it a secret. The 'parole' and 'dimostrazioni' of a prince may therefore be frequently and deliberately unreliable. But this passage also implies that the observer has nothing else on which to base an interpretation and that the relationship established between a prince's words and actions and his secrets and purposes is, as far as one can ever tell, little more than an approximate and imperfect correspondence inferred but never known for certain. And whenever even this risky process of reading the signs proves unsatisfactory, the alternative, says Vettori, is to 'immaginare' what cannot be interpreted.

Vettori was comparing the interpretation of princely actions and policies to the reading of texts, and the unspoken assumption in this implied comparison is that the best readers can do is to interpret the signs provided by the text. Any claim to knowing the purposes and intentions behind the signs is illusory. Chapter XV of *The Prince* shows Machiavelli wrestling with Vettori's notion of an inevitable structural indeterminacy in any discourse about princes. The first step in containing this threat is to oppose 'verità effettuale' to 'imaginazione', which allows Machiavelli to assert that 'true' knowledge about princes is indeed possible and that he can structure such a discourse, as he says in the chapter's second paragraph, by 'leaving behind things imagined about princes and discussing those that are true ('Lasciando, adunque, indrieto le cose circa uno principe imaginate, e discorrendo quelle che sono vere') (chapter XV, p. 280).

But there is another and more subtle step contained in Machiavelli's declaration that he has found it more profitable to 'go behind to the effectual truth of the thing *than to the imagination of it*'. The emphasised words in this phrase ('che alla imaginazione di essa') say that the 'imaginazione' belongs to, or is a property of, 'essa' ('it'). But to what does 'essa' refer? Grammatically, there are two possibilities: 'essa' could be either the 'verità effettuale' or the 'cosa', both of which are feminine, and it is intriguing that Machiavelli creates and leaves this ambiguity unresolved in a passage whose ostensible purpose is to proclaim the possibility and desirability of precision in language and thus of 'effectual truth'. In fact, the more likely of the choices would seem to be 'cosa', chiefly because the structure of the sentence contrasts one property or feature of 'cosa' with another. What this sentence implies is that the 'cosa' (events, princes, their actions, policies, etc.) is there in any case, and that one can either get 'behind' it and seize its 'effectual truth' or – such would seem to be the logic of the sentence – remain in front of it and see only *its* 'imaginazione'. The 'imaginazione' of the 'cosa' is thus the appearance it has, or gives, to someone who does not get 'behind' it to see its true nature. In using the term this way, as I have speculated elsewhere, Machiavelli may have been thinking of, or was perhaps influenced by, Lucretius's notion of the *imago*, the film or membrane which, he says in the *De rerum natura*, is given off by all objects and causes vision.[22] As we know, Machiavelli copied the entire poem sometime in his youth and presumably knew it well.[23]

But this was not at all the meaning of 'immaginare' for Vettori, who had used the word to denote a kind of supplement to the process of interpretation, something akin to the creative infusion of intuitions or hunches not directly warranted by the signs available for interpretation. For Vettori all political discourse begins with the interpretation of appearances; and when this fails or falters, as he seems to assume it must, we can only 'immaginare'. Machiavelli redefines 'imaginazione' to mean precisely those sometimes misleading appearances which, for Vettori, are in most cases the only material available for interpretation. Machiavelli thus contains 'imaginazione' by (1) restricting its meaning to the appearances of things; and (2) contrasting a discourse limited by appearances with one that gets behind the appearances to the essence of things. That at least seems to be the intention. But did he notice that in the next sentence he uses the same word in a very different sense

in saying that 'many have imagined ["si sono imaginati"]
republics and principalities that have never been seen or known
to exist in reality ["essere in vero"]' (chapter XV, p. 280)? This
'imaginazione' seems to be the pure invention of worlds that
exist only in the mind, not the perception of appearances
suggested by the phrase 'imaginazione di essa'.

The opposition between appearances and essences directs
the rest of chapter XV to the issue of language and generates
the long list of paired 'qualities' that Machiavelli says are generally used to praise or blame princes. The crux of the matter is
the necessity of distinguishing between, on the one hand, the
inevitably misleading impressions created by the everyday,
ordinary use of language and, on the other, what Machiavelli
believes he can identify as the *actual* consequences of the 'modi
e governi', the methods and conduct, of princes. His attention
goes first to the structure of common speech about princes: 'I
say that all people, when they are spoken of ["quando se ne
parla"], and especially princes because they are in a higher position, are designated ["notati"] by some or the other of those
qualities that bring them either blame or praise' (chapter XV,
p.280). This is the continuation of the sentence that begins with
Machiavelli's declaration that he will 'leave aside things *imaginate* about princes', and his point is surely that the habits of
everyday speech that result in the attribution to princes of these
qualities, thus producing their blameworthy or praiseworthy
reputations, are themselves among the 'things *imaginate* about
princes'. They belong, in other words, to the realm of misleading appearances. But Machiavelli's next sentence reveals his
entrapment in the fundamental contradiction of *The Prince*'s
notions of language. Wishing simultaneously to give his first
example of this structure of common speech and to explain and
justify his own choice of terms with which to provide this
example, Machiavelli writes: 'Thus it is that one person is held
to be *liberale* [generous], and another *misero* (to use the Tuscan
term, since "avaro" in our language is more one who desires to
possess by means of theft, and we call "misero" the person who
refrains excessively from using what is his own)' (chapter XV,
p. 280). Machiavelli's larger argument asserts the imprecise and
misleading quality of the habits of speech involved in the

conventional use of the pairs of terms he is about to list, and the *liberale*/*misero* pair is presumably the first bit of evidence adduced in support of this contention. But his parenthetical aside concerning the choice of *misero* over *avaro* − his belief that *misero* is the 'correct' opposite for *liberale* − reveals his own need to stabilise language, to make each term mean this and not that, and thus his conviction that in *his* use of language terms can indeed stand for the correct things. The odd aspect of the aside is that this assertion of precise and correct meanings claims dependence on common usage 'in our language' ('in nostra lingua'): an approach to the problem of meaning that might remind us of Lorenzo Valla − were it not for the absence in chapter XV of anything like supporting evidence from texts or actual usage.

The full list of paired terms that Machiavelli offers in chapter XV as examples of the kind of language commonly used to praise or blame princes is as follows (and in this order):

liberale (generous)	*misero* (miserly)
donatore (giver)	*rapace* (rapacious)
crudele (cruel)	*pietoso* (merciful)
fedifrago (treacherous)	*fedele* (faithful)
effeminato, pusillanime (effeminate, cowardly)	*feroce, animoso* (bold, courageous)
umano (humane)	*superbo* (haughty)
lascivo (lascivious)	*casto* (chaste)
intero (trustworthy)	*astuto* (cunning)
duro (harsh)	*facile* (lenient)
grave (serious)	*leggieri* (frivolous)
religioso (religious)	*incredulo* (unbelieving)

Machiavelli obviously makes no effort to list the 'quality' bringing blame or praise consistently in the same position within each pair. Almost as a gesture to the strength of common usage, he must have assumed that it would be self-evident that in the first, second, sixth, eighth, tenth and eleventh (and last) of the pairs the term bringing praise in common usage is listed first, whereas in the third, fourth, fifth, and seventh pairs it is listed second. He must have made a similar trusting assumption about the ninth pair that opposes *duro* to *facile*, but was it − or is it – clear which of these terms denoted praise and which blame? If *duro* meant tough, it presumably would have brought praise; if it meant harsh, it could have brought blame. Similarly, if *facile* meant lenient in the sense of tolerant, praise could presumably have resulted; but if it meant permissive, or yielding, one imagines that it would have generated blame. The example of Scipio in chapter XVII (p. 283) will reveal Machiavelli's opinion that the commander who is 'facile' damages his army and, ultimately, his own reputation. Because he claims to be overturning the conventional understanding of these terms, it may be inferred that Machiavelli assumes that common usage praises (wrongly, in his view) the prince who is 'facile'. But the story he tells about Scipio highlights the criticism that the commander received from the Senate for his excessive leniency, which suggests that, among the Romans at least, common usage did not differ from Machiavelli's own sense of the matter. The impression grows that Machiavelli too easily assumed, without a careful examination of actual usage, that the conventional meanings of terms were somehow inevitably the opposite of his own.

Apparently not noticing this difficulty, Machiavelli continues chapter XV by saying that he 'knows' that 'everyone professes that it would be a most praiseworthy thing for a prince to have, of all the qualities listed above, those that are held to be good ones' (p. 280). But he insists that this entire way of speaking about princes is flawed. The first of the two reasons he gives is about human nature: 'the human condition does not permit' anyone to have or be all those good things. And, because a prince must choose for which of these 'good' qualities he wishes to be known, the criterion governing his choice should be that of survival in power. He must be 'sufficiently prudent to escape the infamy of those vices [i.e. those of the aforementioned qualities that are not held to be good] that would deprive him of his power' (p. 280), and do his best with regard to the others but without excessive scruples.

The second reason why this common usage is so flawed, according to Machiavelli, concerns language itself. He contends that the meanings and judgments normally attaching to these terms simply do not correspond to the *real* effects or results of the modes of conduct that the terms presume to represent and evaluate: 'if one considers the entire matter correctly' ('se si considerrà bene tutto'), he writes, 'one will find that some things that appear to be virtues ["che parrà virtù"] would, if followed, lead to [a prince's] ruin; and some others that seem to be vices ["che parrà vizio"] would, if followed, result in his security and well-being' (chapter XV, p. 280). The problem lies in the conventional understanding of these alleged 'virtues' and 'vices'. Common speech is ignorant of what Machiavelli claims to know: namely, that some modes of conduct usually called virtues are in fact damaging to a prince, while others commonly called vices strengthen him. Implicitly, Machiavelli faults common speech for not knowing, or obscuring, the real meanings of these qualities, which he claims to know by seeing, and speaking, beyond the misleading appearances of conventional speech to the actual effects of a given mode of conduct – to what he takes to be the thing itself and its consequences, quite apart from the labels that ordinary speech attaches to it. In *his* language, and the Prince's, 'discorsi et concetti' can indeed correspond, accurately and precisely, to 'cose'.

The Prince that Machiavelli invents is a master of this distinction between conventional speech, trapped in its ambiguities, imprecision and misleading appearances, and the higher and purified discourse hypothesised by Machiavelli, in which words mean only what they ought to mean, language faithfully reflects and represents an extralinguistic reality, and the 'effectual truth' of things luminously emerges. *The Prince*'s need to make language do these things is, I think, at the centre of what Fredi Chiappelli called its 'tecnificazione' of language, the impulse to assign 'absolute value and stable meaning' to the terms that shoulder the burden of demonstrating the necessity, systematicity, and predictability of the structural verities that the text promotes.[24] This was no doubt the impression Machiavelli wished to create, but the impulse behind the process of 'tecnificazione' – the need that pushed him in this direction – would seem to be anything but technical or scientific.

Chapters XVI to XIX are devoted to explicating the difference between the conventional usage surrounding the pairs of terms listed in chapter XV and the meanings, judgements and truths that come to light if the habits of everyday speech are replaced by a different set of practices. In each case Machiavelli shows the inadequacy of the commonly accepted understanding of the 'qualities' used to judge princes, and the heart of these demonstrations is, in the words of chapter XVIII, that whereas 'everyone sees what you [the prince] appear to be, few feel what you are' ('Ognuno vede quello che tu pari, pochi sentono quello che tu se'') (p. 284). The Prince, unlike the people he rules, speaks and acts in a linguistic realm of pure and exact signification in which words can convey precisely what things 'are' and not what they seem to be.

The mistrust and rejection of ordinary speech implicit in these chapters become explicit in the advice Machiavelli offers in chapters XXII and XXIII concerning the Prince's choice of ministers and the need to avoid flatterers. As Michael McCanles has remarked, in chapter XXII 'The prince's counselors ... are ... signs evoking the discourses of others'.[25] To this we might add that, because the discourses of others in *The Prince* always belong to the lower order of language dominated by indeterminacy, imprecision and mere appearance, counsellors inevitably represent the dangerous intrusion of an extraneous discourse that the Prince must control. One aspect of this danger is that princes are usually judged by the company they keep. Machiavelli writes in chapter XXII that 'The first estimation ["coniettura"] people make of a ruler's brain is to look at the men he has around him' (p. 293), an idea that echoes the concern of chapter XV about the judgements that conventional speech imposes, often wrongly, on a prince. And this leads Machiavelli to repeat the old classification, proverbial in antiquity,[26] of the 'three kinds of brains: the first understands on its own ["intende da sé"], the second discerns what others understand, the third understands neither itself nor others' (p. 293). The last of these Machiavelli obviously dismisses as 'inutile', but the essence of his growing fantasy of the Prince's pure, unmediated discourse that needs no dialogue, no exchange and no mixing of voices is contained in the judgement that the first kind of intelligence is 'eccellentissimo' and the second – the kind that hears and understands what others say – is inferior to it.

In chapter XXIII Machiavelli attempts to translate this radical distinction between the Prince's own discourse and that of the world around him into a set of coherent recommendations for dealing with advisers and avoiding flatterers. About the latter, he says that the only way to 'guard oneself against flattery' is to make people understand that they do not offend you in telling you the truth', except that 'if everyone can tell you the truth, you lose respect' ('ma quando ciascuno può dirti el vero, ti manca la reverenzia') (chapter XXIII, p. 293). (Machiavelli passes over this moment rather quickly, without explaining just why his Prince loses respect if 'ciascuno' can speak frankly to him. The passage does not even say that this respect diminishes when uncontrolled numbers of people actually do speak to the Prince; the loss of respect is already a consequence of the fact that they are able to do so. Perhaps the unspoken thought in this sentence goes back to the worries expressed in chapters XV and XXII, namely, that the lower order of language, which is by definition all that 'ciascuno' can speak, will weaken the Prince with inevitably flawed judgements about him. In any case, here again is the recurring mistrust of everyday speech.)

So Machiavelli recommends a 'terzo modo' that consists in limiting the speech that reaches the Prince to that of certain 'wise men' ('uomini savi') to whom 'alone he must give free rein to speak the truth to him, and only on those things about which he asks and not about anything else' ('solo a quelli debbe dare libero arbitrio a parlargli la verità, e di quelle cose sole che lui domanda, e non d'altro') (chapter XXIII, p. 293). Machiavelli must have noticed the gap between the 'libero arbitrio' that the Prince should give to his wise men and the simultaneous restriction of that freedom to 'only those things about which he asks', since he immediately closes the gap by recommending that the Prince must of course 'ask them about everything and hear their opinions', generally conducting himself with his advisers in such a way that each may understand that 'the more freely they speak, the more it will please him' ('quanto più liberamente si parlerà, tanto più li fia accetto'). But 'apart from these advisers, he should not want to hear anyone else' ('fuora di quelli, non volere udire alcuno') (chapter XXIII, pp. 293-4).

The chapter's last paragraph repeats these oscillating contradictions by concluding that 'a prince should, therefore, always seek advice, but when *he* wants it, and not when others wish [to give it]'. Machiavelli's anxiety about uncontrolled and unauthorised speech reaching the Prince is so acute that he actually suggests that the Prince 'must remove the idea [literally, take away the intention: *torre animo*] of advising him from the mind of any person unless he requests it'. But the always present counter-anxiety of an isolated, almost autistic, Prince instantly leads his argument back yet again to the seemingly reassuring recommendation, presented here too with an overtone in which one can almost hear the missing 'of course', that the Prince must be a 'great inquirer' ('largo domandatore') and 'a patient hearer of the truth ["paziente auditore del vero"] concerning those things about which he has asked; indeed he should be angry if he discovers that anyone is not telling him [the truth] out of some fear' (chapter XXIII, p. 294).

It seems impossible to imagine that any aspiring adviser of such a prince, facing this self-cancelling set of rules about when to speak and when to be silent, would not throw up his hands in despair and look for another line of work. And such a response could only have found confirmation in the conclusion that chapter XXIII adopts in order to find some way out of this labyrinth of contradictions, namely, that 'good advice, from whomever it comes, must arise from the prudence of the prince, and not the prince's prudence from good advice' (chapter XXIII, p. 294). Thus, even when advisers speak some good advice, it is the prince's prudence that controls their speech, which, despite all the insistence on the necessity of advisers, implies that ultimately they do little more than reflect, ratify, and echo what the Prince already 'intende da sé'.

The origin of the difficulties Machiavelli encounters in chapter XXIII lies in the presupposition that the truth sought by his Prince must be distinct from, even opposed to and threatened by, ordinary speech and language. The problem of advising the Prince becomes one of isolating him from this common speech, and thus of controlling language and speakers, in a word, a matter of censorship. The Prince must prevent most people even from speaking to him, and he must allow the chosen few to speak only when he so authorises them. Only by knowing already and on his own where and on what subjects he is likely to hear the truth should a prince permit even his selected wise men to speak, which brings Machiavelli close to saying that the Prince himself is the arbiter of truth, the guarantor of the necessary demarcation between the misleading conventions of common language and the truth of his own uncontaminated discourse. The Prince's greatest power is his extraordinary (literally, beyond the ordinary and conventional) ability to use, hear and interpret language in such a way as to filter out appearances and ambiguities, to define and control a superior form of language use on the basis of that ability, and thus to know and speak a truth inaccessible to other forms of speech. It was, to use the terms Hanna Pitkin has applied to other aspects of Machiavelli's thought,[27] a fantasy of autonomy. Machiavelli wants his Prince not to have to depend on what others say or perceive. The Prince's knowledge and language stand apart from the collective dialogue, remote from the mixing of voices and from the process by which, among ordinary speakers, the always tentative, uncertain and shifting meanings of words emerge from exchanges of speech and writing. In the intention of *The Prince*, the Prince's discourse comes closer to truth – and to power – the less it depends on, and the more it is isolated from, the common dialogue. This is indeed a fantasy of linguistic and epistemological autonomy, one to which *The Prince* is tempted both by the desire to preserve the accessibility and intelligibility of the extralinguistic realm, and also by the troubling awareness that language, as commonly practised, never yields that perfect intelligibility, that unambiguous correspondence between words and things that Machiavelli thirsted for. So *The Prince* 'imagines' a language practice 'never seen' – I use the words Machiavelli himself uses about those who imagine republics and principalities (chapter XV, p. 280) – 'or known to exist in reality'.

The Prince's notions of language betray a pervasive theoretical contradiction that the text pretends not to notice by assigning one sense of how language works (and one side of the contradiction) to people in general and the other to the Prince (and his inventor). In this book, quite unlike much of what he wrote in subsequent years, Machiavelli simultaneously acknowledges and rejects what Renaissance reflections on language had taught him: that language is continuously made, constructed, revised, refashioned, unsettled and destabilised by collective usage. In *The Prince* he wants to believe that, although this was *generally* so, for certain purposes and in certain hands – those of the Prince and of the few who touch, perceive and feel what he really is – another kind of language practice is both possible and necessary for survival in power.

But, as always, *The Prince* is not the whole of Machiavelli. Very different ideas about language inform the works that came later, and what separates *The Prince* from them may be, more than anything else, the process by which Machiavelli dismantled the linguistic fantasy contained in the work for which he is (rightly or wrongly) best known to us, but which remained relatively unnoticed, perhaps even ignored, by his contemporaries. At some point he seems to have realised that he needed to revise his working assumptions about language in order to write about politics in ways that would permit others to respond and to engage him in dialogue.

This different approach to language is already apparent in the opening pages of the *Discourses on Livy*. One example must suffice here.[28] In the second paragraph of the second chapter of the first book,[29] 'wishing to discuss what the *ordini* of the city of Rome were and what events led to its perfection', Machiavelli addresses the question of the classification of constitutional systems. 'I say', he begins, 'that some who have written about republics say that in [each of] them is [found] one of the three kinds of regime, which they call Principate, Aristocracy and Popular [government]' ('dico come alcuni che hanno scritto delle republiche dicono essere in quelle uno de' tre stati, chiamati da loro Principato, Ottimati, e Popolare'). In this sentence it is worth noting that, whatever Machiavelli means by 'republiche', the term represents a genus one of whose three species, called 'stati', is the 'Principato'. This is not the same relationship established among these terms in the opening sentence of the first chapter of *The Prince*, where 'republiche' and 'principati' are presented as alternative species of the genus 'stati'. But, of course, in *Discourses*, I.2 Machiavelli does not claim to be giving his own view of the matter; he is reporting the view of 'some who have written about republics', on which he then casts some doubt by contrasting it with the different 'opinion' of still other writers ('Alcuni altri') who are judged to be wiser 'according to the opinion of many' ('secondo la opinione di molti'). Neither here nor in the rest of the paragraph does Machiavelli explicitly state a view of his own concerning the correct system for the classification of political regimes. We get the impression that he prefers the opinion of the second group, largely because he says that 'many' prefer it and because he devotes more space to it. But at no point in the paragraph does he announce that he has finished summarising the views of others and is ready to render his own judgement. Whatever opinions, views and definitions are contained in this passage emerge from the representation of the linguistic usage of others, and Machiavelli's own opinion is never formally distinguished from these representations. The procedure, and the assumptions behind it, could hardly be in starker contrast to those of *The Prince*. In these few sentences Machiavelli overturns the definitions of key terms in *The Prince* and apparently has no use for its persistent distinction between what it claims is the misleading usage of others and the alleged exactitude and accuracy of its own use of language.

The second opinion reported by Machiavelli in *Discourses*, I.2 is that there are six, instead of three, kinds of government, three of which are very bad ('pessimi') and three 'good in themselves, but so easily corrupted that even they turn out to be pernicious'. The three good ones are those already mentioned in his summary of the first view. The other three are described as follows:

> The bad ['rei'] ones are three others which depend on the first three; and each of them is so similar to the one that is closest to it that they easily jump from the one to the other: thus a Principate easily becomes tyrannical; Aristocracy easily becomes an oligarchic regime; Popular government converts itself without difficulty into anarchy. Thus if the founder of a republic establishes one of the three [good] regimes in a city, he does so for a brief time only, because he is unable to apply any remedy to prevent it from slipping into its contrary, on account of the similarity of the virtue and the vice in such cases.[30]

Machiavelli here mocks the very notion, so crucial to *The Prince*, of the stability of categories, terms and definitions. As is well known, the substance of the theory spelled out in the rest of the chapter concerning the cyclical mutability of constitutions and the advantages of a mixed constitution comes mostly from Polybius and Aristotle, and also, as recently argued, from the medieval traditions of the mixed constitution.[31] But when Machiavelli adds to this theory his comments about the similarity and proximity of the opposing terms of the differential pairs that structure the argument ('Principato'/'tirannico'; 'Ottimati'/'stato di pochi'; 'Popolare'/'licenzioso'), and how this similarity causes the 'good' kinds of government to 'jump' and 'slide' into the opposing but corresponding 'bad' kinds, he is quite deliberately (even if playfully) signalling his abandonment of the assumptions about language that underlie *The Prince*. Here he no longer assumes that differential pairs generate stable meanings or even that they define oppositions. And in this jumping and sliding of categories into one another, time plays a role that it had not had in the pages of *The Prince*.

These sentences merit a closer look for yet another reason which takes us back to issues of rhetoric. The idea that constitutional forms 'slide' into their contraries because 'each of them is so similar to the one that is closest to it that they easily jump from the one to the other' ('ciascuno di essi è in modo simile a quello che gli è propinquo, che facilmente saltano dall'uno all'altro'), and that no constitution can last for very long because there is no 'remedy to prevent it from slipping into its contrary, on account of the similarity of the virtue and the vice in such cases' ('nessuno rimedio può farvi, a fare che non sdruccioli nel suo contrario, per la similitudine che ha in questo caso la virtute ed il vizio'), point to Machiavelli's familiarity with, and deliberate invocation of, a tradition of commentary, recently illuminated in a groundbreaking essay by Quentin Skinner, on the rhetorical technique of paradiastole – the figure of speech by which virtues are redescribed as vices, and vices as virtues, and which was, according to Skinner, 'the main device employed by practitioners of the *Ars rhetorica* to indicate the shifting and ambiguous character of virtue and vice'.[32] In his wide-ranging discussion of the analyses of, and comments on, paradiastole by ancient and Renaissance rhetoricians, historians and poets, Skinner calls attention to two passages that seem particularly relevant for a reading of *Discourses*, I.2: Livy's description in the *History of Rome* (XXII.xii.12) of the rhetorical technique employed by the angry subordinate who tried to ruin the reputation of Quintus Fabius Maximus by 'falsely inventing faults that were close to his virtues' ('adfingens vicina virtutibus vitia'); and Ovid's advice to lovers in the *Ars amatoria* that, by applying the right words, one can mitigate the most unfortunate aspects of any situation ('Nominibus mollire licet mala', II.657) and thus 'let defects remain hidden through their similarity to merits' ('lateat vitium proximitate boni') (II.662).[33] The sentences in *Discourses*, I.2 about the proximity and similarity of virtues to vices very likely allude to one and perhaps both of these passages, but with an important difference of tone and implication. Livy denounces the 'false invention' of faults and describes it as an 'infamous practice'; Ovid recommends the reclothing of defects, or vices, as merits, but he does not pretend that this is anything other than a hiding of what he knows are defects. Both Livy and Ovid refer to the rhetorical technique of trying to make one thing appear another as a deliberate deception, in the one case reprehensible and in the other useful. But in *Discourses*, I.2 the slippage from one constitutional form to another is not presented as a way of making one thing *seem* like its assumed opposite, of making 'Principato' seem like 'tirannico', or 'Popolare' seem like 'licenzioso'. The blurring of 'virtue' and 'vice' and of the good and bad forms of government is, so Machiavelli seems to be saying, inherent in the life itself of those forms and thus in history, in the natural evolution and change of human communities, in 'things' themselves.

Or does *Discourses*, I.2 artfully call into question the old distinction between words and things? On the one hand, Machiavelli appears to be offering a theory about the extralinguistic realm: about how states and constitutions proceed through the cycle that determines their character and form at different historical moments. At the same time, however, as we become aware of the intricate links between this chapter and its sources, we see that it consists largely of the texts and voices

of those – Polybius, Aristotle, Livy, Ovid, Lucretius – who have
already written about these matters. Machiavelli's refusal to
distinguish his own voice from theirs thus functions as an
acknowledgement of the impossibility of separating the knowledge of anything from the texts and voices of those whose
utterances simultaneously constitute and decompose the terms
in which the thing is known. The structure of *Discourses*, I.2
points to the extent to which any discourse of politics – including that most authoritative of discourses, the words of one who
founds a republic ('uno ordinatore di republica') – is inevitably
implicated in the ambiguities and instability, not only of
conventional speech but of all the categories and definitions on
which any discourse of politics needs to be based, and thus
dependent on the whole community of discourse in which the
knowledge of anything must consist. In *Discourses*, I.2 it is not
at all clear what distinction remains between words and things,
between history and politics as objects of knowledge and as
'discourses and concepts' invented and transmitted by one's
predecessors. The carefully constructed intertextuality of this
passage – its dialogue with so many texts and even with an
aspect of the history of rhetoric that must cause the reader to
worry about any claim to distinctions between what is and
what seems to be – highlights its inconclusive character. Even
the best theories are approximate and leave much unexplained.
The next paragraph begins in fact with the assertion that 'these
variations of governments occur by chance' – which is to say
that, despite the alleged explanatory power of the theory of the
cycle of constitutions, it is impossible to know actually why
these changes happen. There are no claims here to a realm of
perception and speech transcending usage, context and tradition. The language of this book depends on, and is part of,
social and historical communities of discourse from which there
is no appeal to the kind of higher tribunal that Machiavelli had
imagined in *The Prince*.

Notes

1 This chapter is adapted from some pages of the discussion of *The Prince* in chapter five of my *Between Friends: Discourses of Power and Desire in the Machiavelli-Vettori Letters of 1513-1515* (Princeton: Princeton University Press, 1993), esp. pp. 185-97.

2 For the text of *The Prince* and Machiavelli's other works, I quote from Niccolò Machiavelli, *Tutte le opere*, ed. Mario Martelli (Florence: Sansoni, 1971), henceforth cited as *Opere*. Where none is specified, English translations are my own. However, for the passage quoted above from the dedicatory letter, I have used the translation of James B. Atkinson in Niccolò Machiavelli, *The Prince* (Indianapolis: Bobbs-Merrill, 1976). I have generally consulted Atkinson's translation in doing my own.

3 Brian Vickers, 'Rhetoric and Poetics', in Charles B. Schmitt and Quentin Skinner (eds), *The Cambridge History of Renaissance Philosophy* (Cambridge: Cambridge University Press, 1988), p. 743.

4 For an important contribution on this point, see Quentin Skinner, 'Thomas Hobbes: Rhetoric and the Construction of Morality', *Proceedings -of the British Academy*, 76 (1990), pp. 1-61, 23-5 and 44. See below, note 33, for some comments on Skinner's approach to rhetoric in *The Prince*.

5 Brunetto Latini, *Li livres dou tresor*, ed. F. Carmody (Berkeley: University of California Press, 1948), p. 17.

6 Vickers, 'Rhetoric and Poetics', p. 729, quoted from John Monfasani, *George of Trebizond: A Biography and a Study of his Rhetoric and Logic* (Leiden: Brill, 1976), pp. 259-60, 366-7.

7 Also in Vickers, 'Rhetoric and Poetics', p. 730, quoted from Eugenio Garin, *L'umanesimo italiano*, 2nd edition (Bari: Laterza, 1958), pp. 83-4.

8 *Opere*, p. 1131

9 *Opere*, p. 443. I have briefly discussed this letter to the Ten in the context of the criticisms directed at Machiavelli during his chancery years in 'The Controversy surrounding Machiavelli's Service to the Republic', in G. Bock, Q. Skinner and M. Viroli (eds), *Machiavelli and Republicanism* (Cambridge: Cambridge University Press, 1990), pp. 105-6.

10 Richard Waswo, *Language and Meaning in the Renaissance* (Princeton: Princeton University Press, 1987).

11 Waswo, *Language and Meaning*, p. 28.

12 *Language and Meaning*, p. 34.

13 *Language and Meaning*, p. 92.

14 *Language and Meaning*, p. 102.

15 Quoted and translated by Waswo, *Language and Meaning*, pp. 105-6.

16 *Language and Meaning*, pp. 95-6. The Latin contains a nice play on 'usum' and 'lusum' that does not come through in the translation.

17 For other important studies of theories of language in the Renaissance, and in particular of Valla, see Salvatore Camporeale, *Lorenzo Valla*,

umanesimo e teologia (Florence: Istituto Nazionale di Studi sul Rinascimento, 1972); Franco Gaeta, *Lorenzo Valla: filologia e storia nell'umanesimo italiano* (Naples: Istituto italiano per gli studi storici, 1955); Donald R. Kelley, *Foundations of Modern Historical Scholarship: Language, Law and History in the French Renaissance* (New York: Columbia University Press, 1970), chapter 1; Lisa Jardine, 'Lorenzo Valla and the Intellectual Origins of Humanist Dialectic', *Journal of the History of Philosophy*, 15 (1977), pp. 143-64; and Jerry H. Bentley, *Humanists and Holy Writ: New Testament Scholarship in the Renaissance* (Princeton: Princeton University Press, 1983), pp. 32-69.

18 For an excellent analysis of *The Prince*'s use of these differential pairs, see Michael McCanles, *The Discourse of 'Il Principe'* (Malibu: Undena, 1983), pp. 15-17 and *passim*.

19 Translation from Atkinson, p. 97. Text in *Opere*, p. 258. All references to *Il Principe* are to Martelli's edition in *Opere* and will henceforth be given by chapter (unless the chapter number is already provided nearby) and page number within parentheses following the quoted passages in the body of the chapter.

20 *The Prince*'s chapter titles are in Latin; this chapter is called 'De his rebus quibus homines et praesertim principes laudantur aut vituperantur'. The translation of the title is from Atkinson, p. 255.

21 *Opere*, p. 1143, letter of 12 July 1513 (my translation).

22 *De rerum natura* IV. 51-2, in the Loeb edition, trans. W. H. D. Rouse (New York: G. P. Putnam's Sons, 1924), pp. 250-1.

23 For the discovery and identification of the manuscript, see Sergio Bertelli and Franco Gaeta, 'Noterelle machiavelliane: un codice di Lucrezio e di Terenzio', *Rivista storica italiana*, 73 (1961), pp. 544-53; also Bertelli, 'Noterelle machiavelliane – ancora su Lucrezio e Machiavelli', *Rivista storica italiana*, 76 (1964), pp. 774-90. On Machiavelli's use of Lucretius, see Gennaro Sasso, 'De Aeternitate mundi ("Discorsi", II 5)', in Sasso, *Machiavelli e gli antichi e altri saggi*, vol. I (Milan and Naples: Riccardo Ricciardi, 1987), pp. 167-399, especially 202-16.

24 Fredi Chiappelli, *Studi sul linguaggio del Machiavelli* (Florence: Felice Le Monnier, 1952), pp. 48-9 and *passim*. According to Chiappelli, however, when the text passes from the delineation of its necessary rules, ensconced in a lexicon of fixed and absolute meanings, to the task of providing examples with which to support this structure, a different tendency comes into play that he sometimes calls 'personal' and sometimes 'artistic'; pp. 84ff. Chiappelli contributed two other books to the study of Machiavelli's language: *Nuovi studi sul linguaggio del Machiavelli* (Florence: Felice Le Monnier, 1969), which analyses the writings from the first three years of Machiavelli's career in the chancery; and *Machiavelli e la 'Lingua fiorentina'* (Bologna: Massimiliano Boni, 1974), which enters into the much disputed question of the date and attribution of the *Discorso o dialogo intorno alla nostra lingua*.

25 McCanles, *The Discourse of 'Il Principe'*, p. 95.

26 Atkinson so characterises it in his edition of *The Prince*, p. 342, where he gives examples of it from Livy, Hesiod and Cicero.

27 Hanna Fenichel Pitkin, *Fortune Is a Woman: Gender and Politics in the Thought of Niccolò Machiavelli* (Berkeley: University of California Press, 1984), especially chapters 1 and 12, pp. 3-22, 307-27.

28 I have tried to provide a couple of others in the epilogue of *Between Friends*, pp. 335-49.

29 The text of *Discourses*, I.2, discussed in the rest of this chapter, is quoted from *Opere*, p. 79. The translation is mine.

30 *Opere*, p. 79; my translation.

31 On this last point, see James M. Blythe, *Ideal Government and the Mixed Constitution in the Middle Ages* (Princeton: Princeton University Press, 1992), pp. 293-95. Gennaro Sasso provides the essential reading of *Discourses*, I.2 and its ancient sources, chiefly the sixth book of Polybius, in 'Machiavelli e la teoria dell' "Anacyclosis"', in *Machiavelli e gli antichi*, vol. I, pp. 3-65, an earlier version of which appeared in his *Studi su Machiavelli* (Naples: Morano, 1967), pp. 161-222. In another essay Sasso discusses the presence in *Discourses*, I.2 of traces of Machiavelli's reading of Lucretius; see 'Machiavelli e i detrattori, antichi e nuovi, di Roma', in *Machiavelli e gli antichi*, vol. I, pp. 401-536, esp. 467-79.

32 Skinner, 'Thomas Hobbes: Rhetoric and the Construction of Morality', p. 4. The full citation of Skinner's essay is in note 4, above.

33 Skinner, 'Thomas Hobbes', p. 9. Skinner does not connect these passages or the technique of paradiastolic redescription to the *Discourses*. In the few pages devoted to Machiavelli in an essay that recreates a whole chapter in the history of rhetoric and whose principal objective is a reading of Hobbes, it is in *The Prince* and its 'notorious central chapters' (XVI to XVIII) that Skinner finds 'the most sensational use' of paradiastole 'among all those who published such handbooks of "counsel" in the course of the sixteenth century' (pp. 23-5). But if paradiastole, when used as a consciously applied technique, was understood as a means of calling into question and blurring the lines of demarcation between virtue and vice (or between the opposing terms of any differential pair), then I think that what Machiavelli is trying to do in these chapters of *The Prince* is not paradiastolic, at least in intention. Far from calling into question the validity of rigidly demarcated distinctions, *The Prince* seeks to find, not to obscure, the *true* relationship (and the distance) between the understanding of virtue and vice in common language and the actual effects of the modes of conduct that give rise to reputations for virtue or vice. *The Prince*'s insistence that conventional speech fails to define and describe this relationship accurately does not mean that (for the Prince) there need be anything ambiguous about the correct definitions. This is precisely what Machiavelli wants to teach the Prince. It is, I think, in the *Discourses* that Machiavelli applies the technique of paradiastolic redescription with the intention of underscoring, in Skinner's words, the 'shifting and ambiguous character of virtue and vice'.

6

The end justifies the means: end-orientation and the discourses of power[1]

MAGGIE GÜNSBERG

Introduction

This study of Machiavelli's *The Prince* takes as its starting-point the notion of the 'end', using this as a means of entry into the text which allows access to a specific series of interacting narrative and discursive processes. It is hoped that an outline of these processes will be of particular interest in the context of contemporary debates both within and between the two sets of heterogeneous arguments grouped together under the headings of feminism and postmodernism respectively. While a relationship of interdependency clearly obtains between the textual processes of *The Prince*, linked as they are by the cardinal feature of end-orientation, my analysis of them will broadly speaking follow two lines of investigation.

In the first of two sections, entitled 'Narrative', Machiavelli's text will be examined precisely from the point of view of narrative, as questions are posed concerning the textual typologies of *The Prince*. Attention will be focused primarily on the text as an end-oriented, product-led narrative showing an allegiance to linearity and cohesion. In this context, features characterising the goal-orientation of quest/conquest/achievement narrative will come into play, centring on the Prince-as-hero or, more interestingly, would-be hero. With action man as its main protagonist, the narrative embodies stereotypical masculine values and positions the reader accordingly. Reader-positioning is then examined in the text read as realist narrative. Informing these narrative considerations is a set of assumptions concerning the processes and effects of power relations in inter-connecting areas, particularly those of gender and class.

Under the heading 'Discourses of Power', the second section examines the more obvious manifestations of power concerns in the text, as well as those which are less immediately apparent. *The Prince* clearly deals on an overt level with issues of power, not only as regards its subject-matter but in the use to be made of the text itself (the primary purpose of the text in its materi-ality being to reinstate Machiavelli in public life). The text is thus also end-oriented in its very functionality. An exploration of the subject-matter of *The Prince* leads to a discussion of a more covert aspect of the text featuring underlying discourses of power and the assumptions which contribute to their forma-tion (e.g. dominance/sovereignty as a self-evident feature of inter-state, now international, relations, particularly as put forward in *realpolitik* texts).

This area raises epistemological questions currently under discussion in the feminism/postmodernism debate. The use in the text of dichotomy or binarism in a transhistorical fashion is one such question. Another example is the public–private oppo-sition invoked by *The Prince*, with the automatic cultural priv-ileging of the former, together with an alignment of public/ masculine and private/feminine. Machiavelli's text will be examined for allegiance to dichotomy and transhistoricism, as well as essentialism and universalism. Attention will also be paid to his generalisations, his cause and effect mode of argu-mentation, and his recourse to the 'natural' as a basic justifica-tory category. Similarly open to critique is Machiavelli's use of history as a storehouse of facts, proofs and certainties, a use which is also end-oriented and reveals how discourse-formation always ends up serving a purpose. Throughout this second section we shall also examine the specific types of power rela-tion which his discourses, both overt and covert, set up, and between whom (e.g. between monolithic social groupings or differentiated ones). The particular relevance for feminist theory here lies in the implications of Machiavelli's discourses of power for the other discourses they subjugate (namely, the discourses of groups/classes/genders subordinated in the forever ongoing processes constituting power relations).

It will already be apparent that the focus of this study of *The Prince* is ideological in nature. Ideology does not, of course, operate in isolation from economic and historical processes and, in the light of postmodernism's warnings against universalisation, can be properly accessed only in its specific historical manifestations. In our case, this would entail a study of the economic and historical processes which gave rise to the particular forms taken by the ideological workings of *The Prince*. It is unfortunately, however, not within the scope of this chapter to proceed in this direction with anything resembling the requisite degree of thoroughness. Instead, there follows an all-too cursory overview which, it is hoped, will at least suggest a vital further dimension to the subsequent two sections.

The economic and historical processes specific to fifteenth- and sixteenth-century Florence are those of early capitalism and an emerging state identity. In this context, the complex and changing patterns of, to cite just one area, women's work in both urban and rural Florence, is of relevance. A study by Brown outlines the increasing confinement of Florentine women in particular in the home from the thirteenth century onwards, with the result that, by 1610, it was reported that 'in Florence women are more enclosed than in any other part of Italy; they see the world only from the small openings in their windows'.[2] As Brown points out, issues as varied as changes in inheritance systems and family structures, in conjunction with the classic primary female role of reproduction, need to be examined in order to account for factors such as confinement to the private area, and 'the high concentration of women in relatively low-skill jobs and their absence in others'.[3] It is in this specific context that indications in *The Prince* of the low status of women are to be considered.

A variety of historical processes and events inform the assumptions, ends and very existence of *The Prince*. In the first place, the return of the Medici family to power in Florence in 1512 meant that the Florentine state reverted from republic to principality, with a concomitant emphasis on the role of the individual ruler, or Prince-as-hero figure. This in turn invoked the traditional stereotypes of masculinity involving heroism in the form of those brave and belligerent actions which are advocated by the text. Second, the text itself was a direct result of the Medici's return to Florence, which signalled the end of Machiavelli' s career in the service of the Republic, and his writing of a work which he hoped would further his ambition to be reinstated in public office. A third important factor concerns the overall situation of the fragmented and war-torn set of states which made up Renaissance Italy, together with Machiavelli's genuine view that Italy's only hope was to unite, possibly under one leader, in order to prevent the continuing exploitation by foreign powers of a situation of inter-state hostilities. The particularly destructive Wars of Italy (1494-1559), which had been raging throughout the nineteen years preceding the writing of *The Prince,* and which were to continue well after Machiavelli's death, saw the mostly pernicious interventions of France, Spain, Germany and Switzerland in the Italian peninsula. Given such a context of conflict, it is not difficult to account for the persistence of the underlying dominance–subordination dynamic which informs Machiavelli's view of inter-, and intra-, state relations.

With regard to the genre of Machiavelli's text, Foucault reminds us of the preceding tradition:

> Throughout the Middle Ages and classical antiquity, we find a multitude of treatises presented as 'advice to the prince', concerning his proper conduct, the exercise of power, the means of securing the acceptance and respect of his subjects, the love of God and obedience to him, the application of divine law to the cities of men, etc.[4]

The sixteenth century, however, saw a shift in perspective in this genre. Foucault continues:

> But a more striking fact is that, from the middle of the sixteenth century to the end of the eighteenth, there develops and flourishes a notable series of political treatises that are no longer exactly 'advice to the prince', and not yet treatises of political science, but are instead presented as works on the 'art of government'. Government as a general problem seems to me to explode in the sixteenth century, posed by discussions of quite diverse questions.[5]

Once again, historical processes are implicated in this change of focus. Of specific relevance to our text is the demise of feudalism, the consequent rise of large states and, in particular, the drive for a united Italy: 'the sixteenth century ... lies, to put it schematically, at the crossroads of two processes: the one which, shattering the structures of feudalism, leads to the establishment of the great territorial, administrative and colonial states.'[6] Of special importance is the development of 'the administrative state, born in the territoriality of national boundaries in the fifteenth and sixteenth centuries and corresponding to a society of regulation and discipline'.[7] Not to be overlooked, then, are Machiavelli's own personal experiences of these particular processes, not least his role in the field of administration.

Narrative

Textual Typologies

As a text, *The Prince* is commonly classified as political theory. On closer inspection, however, it also bears examination as narrative. This is because, far from merely arguing abstract issues, it can also be seen to describe a succession of events; in other words, it tells a story, or stories.[8] Awareness of the fact that story-telling is not exclusive to fictional texts opens up the possibility of a productive interdisciplinary approach. Haraway offers a timely reminder of the 'fruitfulness of paying close attention to stories in biology and anthropology, to the common structures of myths and scientific stories and political theories'.[9] Her comment that 'there would be no stories, no questions, without the complex webs of power' points, moreover, to the interlinking of narrative and discourses of power.[10]

An examination of *The Prince* from the point of view of story-telling reveals a main story together with what we might call a set of sub-stories. The protagonist of the main story is the Prince, whose assumed role and desire is to gain power and maintain it, and who faces various obstacles in this quest. In narrative terms, this story fulfils the requirements of what has been termed the 'general matrix' of narrative. In other words, it contains at least 'two attributes – related but different' (e.g. desiring power and gaining it) 'of at least one agent' (i.e. the

Prince) 'and a process of transformation or mediation, which allows passage from one attribute to the other' (e.g. the process of overcoming obstacles on the path to gaining power).[11] In plot terms, this main story can be described as combining at least two discernible types of plot. The first is a variant of the plot of fortune, namely the action plot. This is organised around a problem, and its solution, in particular, by means of action. The second is a variant of the plot of character, the maturing plot, which features an 'inexperienced or naive' protagonist who needs to be educated.[12] As regards the identity of the protagonist, the Prince of the title could be, and often is, interpreted generically. However, it is also of interest, in the context of this second plot variant, to note the historically specific individuals to whom the work was dedicated. Machiavelli was nine years older than the original Prince to whom the work was addressed, namely the 'politically inexperienced and easily compliant' Giuliano de' Medici. Upon the removal from Florence of the latter by Pope Leo X, who replaced him in 1515 with his nephew, Lorenzo, Machiavelli changed the identity of the addressee, this time twenty-three years his junior.[13]

Feeding into this main story is a set of sub-stories. Each of these narrates a series of events illustrating how either to succeed or to fail in achieving the desired goal of the main story. These stories function rather like *exempla,* the moral tales told not for their own sake but within the context of the medieval sermon. Machiavelli in fact refers to his sub-stories as examples.[14] These sub-stories differ from the main story in terms of time and mood, in that they narrate events which have already taken place (whether in the recent or the distant past). In so doing, moreover, these sub-stories make frequent use of historical material, thereby illustrating the common ground of history and narrative in 'referential (representational) discourse'.[15]

The main story, on the other hand, consists of the projection of a possible future and ultimately hypothetical scenario. It does not, that is, recount what has actually happened, in the form of a narration of past events, but what could happen. This brings us to the question of end-orientation which, it will be recalled, provides our primary focus. Having established the textual typologies of *The Prince* as narrative, the following discussion of end-orientation and closure in narrative structure will lead to a consideration of end-, or goal-, orientation in terms of the Prince-as-hero. One major observation which will be made at this point is that an identical ideology of end-orientation, of emphasis on product and achievement, rather than process, can be seen to inform the narrative in more than one of its aspects.

End-orientation and closure are characteristics of the sub-stories in two senses. In the first place, each story sets out a causally and temporally ordered series of events which have a goal and which lead to a resolution, or closure, in relation to that goal. These events may either culminate in a desired end or lead to failure in achieving the proposed goal. One story which illustrates a set of events leading to, for example, the desired acquisition of power, is that of Agathocles (chapter VIII). The story concerning Commodus, on the other hand, shows how a series of misguided actions culminates in disaster (chapter XIX). Secondly, the sub-stories are end-oriented in that they are told for a certain purpose, namely that of building up, or feeding into, the main story. The main story itself is very interesting in this context. We have already noted its hypothetical mood, in that it tells the story, not of a prince but of a would-be prince; rather than narrating events in the past tense, it projects a variety of possible events along the path to the desired goal, which is to gain power and maintain it. This story therefore differs radically from the sub-stories in that, although it is still end-oriented, in effect it lacks closure. We do not know, within the bounds of the narrative, whether the Prince heeds the instructions at the end of each sub-story, or whether he succeeds in his goal. (Nor do we discover, again within the realms of the text itself, whether the ultimate goal of the sub-text of *The Prince*, which is to reinstate Machiavelli in public office, is achieved.) In terms of narrative end-orientation and closure, then, *The Prince* can be described as consisting of a goal-oriented but open-ended main story, together with a set of sub-stories which are also goal-oriented, but which feature multiple closures.

In relation to closure and end-orientation, *The Prince* is also interesting in the context of an erotics of narrative. The presence or absence of closure is linked to the notion of reader desire in the sense that a desire to know is stimulated in the reader not just at ·the outset of the narrative but by the very existence of the narrative itself. This desire is then maintained throughout the text by various means, to be either satisfied (by the closed text) or left unsatisfied (by the open-ended text).[16] The key element in the stimulation of this desire to know is that of suspense, or a slowing down of comprehension, achieved by delays and gaps in imparting information.[17]

We have already discussed the lack of closure in the main story of *The Prince* and its sub-text. In another sense, however, it is true to say that we do not really expect to know an outcome, although the narrative does beg the question to a certain extent. (It is possible for reader curiosity to be sufficiently stimulated to encourage further research outside the text in order to discover, first, whether Lorenzo became a successful prince, and second, whether he reinstated Machiavelli in public office.) In terms of delays and gaps in the main story which, as we recall, features a maturing plot, or plot of character, as one of its strands, the education of the protagonist by means of instruction, or pronouncements on correct and incorrect ways of proceeding, can be seen to be interrupted by the sub-stories used to illustrate the pronouncements themselves. In other words, instead of moving from one instruction to the next, the main story is delayed each time a sub-story is told by means of example. The action plot of the main story, which also concentrates on correct or incorrect ways of proceeding, is similarly delayed by these sub-stories. Within the sub-stories themselves, delays and gaps in information function to postpone closure until the last possible moment.[18] Finally, from a wider perspective, both main and sub-stories are informed by a fundamentally closed set of assumptions and values which ultimately allow for no open-endedness. As a prelude to an examination of these in the second section, we shall now explore end-orientation in the Prince-as-hero on the basis that the epic qualities of the narrative reinforce a particular set of values which are both gender- and class-specific.

Epic heroism

We have seen how the sub-stories feature both end-orientation

and closure, and how the main story, with the Prince as protagonist, while remaining open-ended in terms of resolution, or
final outcome, is nevertheless oriented towards a specific goal.
The narrative is therefore product-led rather than process-led,
with the goal itself giving the narrative an allegiance to linearity
and cohesion. In our text, linearity is provided by the aim of the
Prince to get from A (a position of not ruling) to B (ruling and
maintaining this power position). The goal takes the form of an
achievement, the fulfilment of a task, with the protagonist-
Prince as a hero on a quest. His quest, as we have noted, is to
gain power and then retain it. However, the ultimate goal, not just
of the Prince but of his lineage, goes beyond individual ambition
to encompass the wider, epic scheme of uniting and saving
Italy:

> See how Italy beseeches God to send someone to save her from
> those barbarous cruelties and outrages; see how eager and will-
> ing the country is to follow a banner, if only someone will raise
> it. And at the present time it is impossible to see in what she can
> place more hope than in your illustrious House, which ... can lead
> Italy to her salvation.   chapter XXVI, pp. 134-5[19]

In this context the Prince is even hailed in divine terms as a
saviour (chapter XXVI, p. 138; 'redentore', p. 97).

The path to fulfilling this grandiose quest is by means of
conquest by the Prince, whether of a state of his own (if his
principality is not hereditary) or of other states (in order to
ensure that he maintains his rule). One essential part of conquest
is that of action, the main ingredient of traditional epic narrative.
Once educated and instructed in the ways of princehood, the
protagonist must be able not simply to theorise but to act. The
emphasis is on action from the very beginning of *The Prince*. In
the dedication Machiavelli says 'I have not found among my
belongings anything as dear to me or that I value as much as
my understanding of the deeds of great men' (dedication, p. 29).
The text continues to prioritise action along with both a specific
gender (man), and social status ('great') evaluated in terms of
deeds.

Moreover, as the above quotation shows, the author himself
has access to these 'deeds of great men', access which he gains
through his cognitive faculties ('la *cognizione* delle azioni delli

uomini grandi', p. 13, my italics). His protagonist must likewise enter the world of male valour, in his case by following the footsteps of other 'great men' in acting as they have done: 'So a prudent man should always follow in the footsteps of great men ["uomini grandi"] and imitate those who have been outstanding. If his own prowess ["virtù"] fails to compare with theirs, at least it has an air of greatness about it' (chapter VI, p. 49). This point is repeated as the moral end-point of a sub-story about to be recounted narrating the rise of Cesare Borgia to power: 'So if we consider the duke's career as a whole, we find that he laid strong foundations for the future. And I do not consider it superfluous to discuss these, because I know no better precepts to give a new prince than ones derived from Cesare's actions' (chapter VII, pp. 54-5).

The end of this sub-story reiterates the centrality of the duke's actions, which should be emulated by the Prince: 'So having summed up all that the duke did ["Raccolte io adunque *tutte le azioni* del duca"] ... So a new prince cannot find more recent examples than those set by the duke ["che *le azioni* di costui"]' (chapter VII, p. 60, my italics). Notably, these actions are primarily combative in nature: 'The Prince should read history, studying the actions of eminent men ["*le azioni* delli uomini *eccellenti*"] to see how they conducted themselves during war and to discover the reasons for their victories or their defeats, so that he can avoid the latter and imitate the former' (chapter XIV, pp. 89-90, my italics). The text ends with an exhortation to the Prince and his lineage to imitate such actions which, in particular, determine social greatness: 'Therefore if your illustrious House wants to emulate those eminent men ["quelli *eccellenti* uomini"] who saved their countries ...' (chapter XXVI, pp. 136-7, my italics).

With references to the Prince's lineage, or progeny, and past and present examples of 'eminent men', a historical brotherhood of heroic action-men is established. The sub-stories play a major part in cataloguing this brotherhood. The story of Ferdinand of Aragon is another example which depicts, hyperbolically, the series of actions of yet another role model: 'If you study his achievements ["le *azioni* sua"], you will find that they were all magnificent and some of them unparalleled' (chapter

XXI, p. 119). If we follow these actions we see that they are, once again, combative in nature: Ferdinand attacked Granada, assaulted Africa, and attacked France. In the introduction to this sub-story we are once again instructed as to the moral to be gleaned by the end of its narration: ' Nothing brings a prince more prestige than great campaigns and striking demonstration of his personal abilities' (chapter XXI, p. 119). We can conclude, then, that in the central expression 'great man', 'great' indicates the high social status acquired by the 'man' who fulfils the masculine stereotype of combat-based action. The identity of the 'great man'/the Prince, is dominated by his military activity. In other words, the Prince is the embodiment of traditional heroic action.

The characteristics of the Prince which we have just outlined (goal-orientation, action/armed combat, nationwide impact, quasi-divine status), situate this area of the text in one of the oldest narrative traditions, namely that of the epic. Definitions of this genre appear in great part to match aspects of our narrative, and provide a useful framework.[20] The prime ingredient of the epic formula is that of action, as the titles of some classic epics indicate (for example, the *Gesta Romanorum* and the *Chansons de geste,* with the Latin 'gesta' meaning 'deeds, actions'). These epic qualities place *The Prince* in a narrative tradition informed by stereotypical masculine values, within a culture based on a dichotomous splitting and evaluation of gender attributes. Action, conquest and domination in the public arena, together with freedom of movement, are some of the characteristics of the masculine side of the binary divide inherent in Western systems of thought at least as far back as the Greeks.[21] We shall deal with binarism as an epistemological concern in the next section. For the moment we shall focus on the exclusively masculine ethos informing *The Prince* at the level of the main epic story which we have identified. This set of values, moreover, is also implicated in the work as a piece of *realpolitik*. Elshtain describes the 'realist refrain' in terms of the presumption of 'a world of sovereign and suspicious states', a presumption which excludes 'possibilities ... for a politics not reducible to who controls or coerces whom'.[22]

Confrontation and conflict, in other words, the absolute

necessity for war, is the primary axis around which the Prince's actions are structured: 'A prince, therefore, should have no other object or thought, nor acquire skill in anything, except war, its organization, and its discipline. The art of war is all that is expected from a ruler ... The first way to lose your state is to neglect the art of war; the first way to win a state is to be skilled in the art of war' (chapter XIV, p. 87). Even the legal system is made subservient to military considerations: 'The main foundations of every state ... are good laws and good arms; and because you cannot have good laws without good arms, good laws inevitably follow. I shall not discuss laws but give my attention to arms' (chapter XII, p. 77). Elshtain reminds us of the roots of this cultural prioritisation of masculinity/ confrontationality, particularly by the epic genre:

> For the Greeks, war was a natural state and the basis of society. Manly valour was shown by the spirit with which men pursued honour and fame. The great epics of war and tragedy and triumph constructed, in and through figurations which have lost none of their power to evoke and provoke, the centrality of war-making and its glories and necessities and terrible triumphs. Heraclitus deemed war the 'father of all things', arguing that it is only through strife as a natural law of being that anything is brought *into* being.[23]

The way in which epics delineate the founding of states on masculine ur-beginnings is also in evidence in the exhortation to the Prince to save and reconstitute Italy by means of con/quest, genealogy and war. Machiavelli himself provides us with a binary checklist consisting, on the one side, of positive values which will bring the Prince praise and, on the other, of negative values which will invite blame. The particular opposition which is relevant at this point, and which throws the entire list into gender relief, refers to 'one man effeminate and cowardly, another fierce and courageous' (chapter XXV, p. 91).

It is not only the protagonist-Prince, moreover, who is to be seen conquering. The author himself is at pains to display, in this work, his own 'understanding of the deeds of great men, won by me ...' (dedication, p. 29). The conquering of knowledge, the dominance of mind over matter, recalls the master– slave metaphor of dominance with which the Greeks articulated their understanding of knowledge, namely by conquering, or transcending, matter with reason.[24] The conquest of matter by form appears in chapter VI in a set of short sub-stories narrating 'the actions and lives' of 'the most outstanding ["eccellenti"] men' who came to power as a result of their own actions, or prowess, rather than by Fortune. This discussion again posits a dichotomous set of binary opposites which is based on the domination of one side of the divide by the other, and which again builds in a stereotypical gender specificity.

The first of these dualities, the form–matter opposition, appears in conjunction with that of prowess–Fortune/opportunity (the famous *'virtù–fortuna'* pair which has been the focus of much debate): 'Fortune, as it were, provided the matter but they gave it its form; without opportunity their prowess would have been extinguished, and without such prowess the opportunity would have come in vain' (chapter VI, p. 50).[25] Form and prowess (*virtù* here being defined as heroic, military action) are seen to conquer matter and Fortune. The associative chain of binary oppositions is further built up as Moses is placed on the side of form and prowess, and the Israelites on that of matter and Fortune, namely in a position of needing to be liberated and so providing Moses with both opportunity/Fortune and matter: 'Thus for the Israelites to be ready to follow Moses, in order to escape from servitude, it was necessary for him to find them, in Egypt, enslaved and oppressed by the Egyptians' (chapter VI, p. 50).

A subsequent gender duality fixes the entire set of oppositions in a gender-specific mode, as the feminine is associated with matter, Fortune, weakness and peace: 'Cyrus needed to find the Persians rebellious against the empire of the Medes, and the Medes grown soft and effeminate through the long years of peace' (chapter VI, p. 51). The positioning of peace as the negative Other of heroic, masculine war further reiterates the war/action ethos which runs through the text.[26] Once again, the heroes of these sub-stories, together with the protagonist of the main story, the Prince, are not alone on the positively valued side of this binary divide. A continuous thread in our argument is the way in which the author can be seen to occupy certain positions in the text, and here Machiavelli clearly places himself alongside the heroes on the side of form, in his case exemplified as mind, through his heroic conquest of matter.

Along with author-positioning, that of the reader is also of relevance in a narrative informed by stereotypical masculine values: end-orientation, quest, conquest, action, war. This orientation has clear implications for reader-positioning which go well beyond the work's specific addressee. It is not only Giuliano, or Lorenzo, who are in a position of alignment with the protagonist-Prince. The values and assumptions of the text go beyond these individuals, or even any would-be prince. In the words of Althusser, the ideological bent of the text 'hails or interpellates concrete individuals [in our case, readers] as concrete subjects'.[27] However, it is not simply a matter of the reading individual being, as it were, 'loud-hailed' as a specific kind of reading subject. More interestingly, and more insidiously, it is the covert rather than the overt features of *The Prince* which, almost imperceptibly, give focus to a reader position. These will in the main be dealt with in the next section. For the moment we shall confine our attention to a particular narrative facet of this more covert form of 'hailing', namely that of realism.

In one respect the text effaces its own workings in the manner of many literary texts, especially those of the realist genre. In effect *The Prince* operates as a realist text not only in the sense that it is an example of *realpolitik,* with 'realism' operating in opposition to idealism, or Utopianism. It is also a realist work in the sense of realism as a narrative mode of representation. This mode has as its key feature the illusion of mirroring 'reality', of depicting the 'truth' by means of the unquestionable discourses of rationality and causality.[28] In the hierarchy of discourses which go to make up *The Prince,* we can identify, in a position of privilege, discourses of con/quest, war, and stereotypical masculinity, while those of co-operation, peace and stereotypical femininity are subordinated. Also discernible, as we have seen, is the assumed association of certain of these discourses with each other, together with their splitting into two opposing groups, by the epistemological process of binary contrast, a process which allows only for (opposing) dualities rather than a series of differences.

The Prince, then, has a realist, cause-and-effect foundation, informed by certain 'facts' and leading inexorably to certain 'truths'.[29] We shall now proceed to an exploration of the specific epistemological processes whereby certain value-laden 'truths' and assumptions come to form such an integral, and thus insidious, presence in the narrative workings we have just examined, processes which contribute to the formation of particular end-oriented discourses of power.

Discourses of power

Informing the narrative processes examined in the last section in terms of end- or goal-orientation, and con/quest via action, is a set of discursive processes. These will be referred to as 'discourses of power' in as much as, in their formation, they reinforce particular hierarchies of power. This section will move from an exploration of overt discourses of power to those which are covert, to those discursive processes which are not immediately obvious but which underlie, or are embedded in, other processes, such as those of narrative, from which they have been, as it were, separated out.

The most covert discursive processes structure thought according to a specific power-related epistemology which contributes to the formation of a set of uncontested assumptions presented as 'truth' in the form of overt subject matter. This subject matter deals in an obvious way with power, but in such a way as to exclude any value-systems other than those inherent in the set of assumptions brought into play. In the first section it has hopefully been shown how the narrative formulation of this subject matter also functions towards a given end in the context of a specific set of power relations.

This second section begins with a closer look at the text in its obvious material functionality, followed by an appraisal of the (overt) subject matter in order to identify more clearly the precise nature of the power relations posited by the text. This leads to a focus on the set of assumptions which informs these power relations, and the epistemological processes which lie at the heart of their value systems.

Overt–covert: functionality, subject matter and assumptions
The Prince deals on an overt level with issues of power in terms
of the use to which the text itself, in its materiality, is to be
put. In other words, the main function of the text is in its capacity as a 'thing' ('cosa'). Machiavelli himself describes it so in his
dedication:

> Men who are anxious to win the favour of a Prince nearly always
> follow the custom of presenting themselves to him with the
> possessions ['cose'] they value most, or with things they know
> especially please him. ... I have not found among my belongings
> anything ['cosa'] as dear to me or that I value as much as my
> understanding of the deeds of great men.   p. 29

The materiality of this gift, of this 'little book', is underlined
by its position along a paradigm of other material gifts ('horses,
weapons, cloth of gold, precious stones, and similar ornaments
worthy of a high position'). In its material functionality, then,
The Prince is intended, in the first instance, to persuade its
addressee to take a certain course of action (in itself one definition of power), that is, reinstate its author in public life in the
service of the state. In the second instance, it is intended to
produce what is perceived as the re-empowerment of its author
by means of such a reinstatement, with the concomitant implication of the private sphere as low in status. (Machiavelli was
Secretary and Second Chancellor of the Florentine republic from
1498 until 1512, when the Medici returned to power. *The Prince*
was begun during the following year, after Machiavelli's release
from prison and his withdrawal to the family property at San
Casciano.)

Furthermore, with Machiavelli's reference to his 'little book',
which he considers ' unworthy' of its addressee, we are not solely
in the realms of self-abasement as a (meaningless) rhetorical
device. The register used to address the Prince is in itself obviously structured by hierarchical power relations. In relation to
the Prince, Machiavelli is in a position of servitude: 'I am anxious
to offer myself to Your Magnificence with some token of my
devotion ["servitù"] to you'. He speaks from the standpoint of
'a man of low and humble status', using an extended spatial
simile of low-lying land as opposed to mountains, in order to
emphasise his lowness, and that of the people and ordinary citi-

zens with whom he identifies, in relation to the 'loftiness' of the Prince. This hierarchical structure is extended to the subject matter of the text, which he describes using the term 'gravity' ('gravità'), a term with positive connotations. This not only conforms to the division in Renaissance rhetoric (derived from antiquity) of style, on the basis of subject matter, into grand or grave, middle and low, with corresponding value associations; it also argues a higher status for his chosen subject in relation to other, by implication, peripheral and lower-status topics.

In the short dedication to *The Prince*, then, we can already see how hierarchy as a basic structure shapes and defines power relations as founded on difference evaluated in terms of dominance and subordination rather than, say, in terms of equal validity and power distribution. This relationship of dominance and subordination is vindicated and 'naturalised' by the application of imagery from the natural world (high mountains and low plains) to the sphere of the social, here epitomised in expressions of class difference. Thus, while the Prince is automatically accorded a high, privileged status, the people, or ordinary citizens ('populi', 'populare') are the lowest of the low.

Proceeding now with our examination of the overt subject matter of the text, we see that interlinking with the hierarchy of class in the network of power relations is that of gender. This becomes particularly interesting when we learn that women are not classed as citizens or subjects but are listed alongside the property of their husbands: 'The prince can always avoid hatred if he abstains from the property of his subjects and citizens and from their women' (chapter XVII, p. 97). This piece of advice to the Prince harbours many assumptions: that women are regarded exclusively in terms of their relationship to men (as wives, daughters and sisters); that they do not own property in their own right (as, in reality, did widows); that their not being subjects or citizens is a normal and acceptable state of affairs; and, finally, that within the social framework as it stands, women by implication have no actual right to protection as individuals in their own right, but only inasmuch as they have male relatives.

A repetition of this advice to the Prince adds a further

definition of the position of women in society, namely their function as the repositories of male honour: 'He will be hated above all if, as I said, he is rapacious and aggressive with regard to the property and the women of his subjects. He should refrain from these. As long as he does not rob the great majority of their property or their honour, they remain content' (chapter XIX, p. 102). The low status of women in class terms is compounded by the ranking of stereotypical femininity as the negative Other of stereotypical masculinity (as we saw in the previous section). 'Effeminacy' is included in the list of negative characteristics which the Prince must avoid in order not to be despised: he should not be fickle, frivolous, effeminate, cowardly, or irresolute. On the contrary, he must show, in his actions. grandeur, courage, sobriety and strength (chapter XIX, p. 102).

Starkly opposed binarisms of this kind are an inevitable component of power relations based on dominance and subordination, an organisation of power relations which necessitates two separate groups, each sharply defined and differentiated from the other. It is the constant dynamic at work between these two groups as opposites which forges the system of power relations invoked by the text. As a result, two opposing sets of gender attributes must be culturally defined so as to (1) be stereotyped, (2) be kept separate from each other in the categories of feminine and masculine, and (3) remain associated exclusively with their appropriate biological partners (masculine/male and feminine/female).[30] The final turn of the screw as far as women are concerned is the overt, albeit metaphorical, suggestion that physical coercion is advisable in order to subjugate women, treatment which, furthermore, is portrayed as welcomed by women themselves:

> Fortune is a woman, and if she is to be submissive it is necessary to beat and coerce her. Experience shows that she is more often subdued by men who do this than by those who act coldly. Always, being a woman, she favours young men, because they are less circumspect and more ardent, and because they command her with greater audacity.   chapter XXV, p. 133

This passage, of course, also contains concomitant assumptions about masculinity. Not only does it assume that men would

actually consider beating women; it also posits age as a problematic social category which stereotypes men into becoming
inherently less masculine as they get older. Overall, the passage
locks both masculinity and femininity into a confrontational
relationship with each other, in accordance with the hierarchical structure of power relations as constituted by the conflict-
ual dynamic of dominance and subordination.

Hierarchies of gender, class and even subject matter, are
discernible, then, in the advice given by the text to the Prince.
In the previous section we examined the interlocking hierarchical dichotomies of form–matter, prowess or action (*virtù*)–
Fortune, war–peace, strength–weakness, and masculinity–
femininity/effeminacy. All of these dichotomies interweave in
the context of the broader social complex of the state; or rather,
these culturally determined hierarchies appear to exist in the
shadow of a state conceptualised as necessarily subtended by
power relations of dominance and subordination. In reality, the
way in which hierarchies of class and gender are actually
played out contributes in large part to the formulation of the
state, all based on the assumption that power relations are
necessarily of the confrontational dominance–subordination
variety.[31]

Other alternatives, such as co-operation rather than conflict,
are either not included or dismissed obliquely. (The Medes, for
instance, are criticised for their love of peace which, according
to the assumptions underlying *The Prince*, has made them pejo-
ratively 'effeminate'.) Dominance, or sovereignty, is taken to be
a self-evident feature of inter-state relations (just as it is
assumed to be the hallmark of gender and class relations, as we
have seen). This is held by Machiavelli to be a universal truth:
'and the people are *everywhere* anxious not to be dominated or
oppressed by the nobles, and the nobles are out to dominate
and oppress the people. These opposed ambitions …' (chapter
IX, p. 67, my italics). Once again stereotyping is taking place,
this time in terms of class. It is an assumption to say that all
nobles wish to dominate and oppress the people. This being the
case, the people are not everywhere filled with anxiety.
Universalisation, or generalisation, as we shall see later, is one
of the ways in which Machiavelli 'proves' his points.

With these assumptions, we are back in the realm of realism, this time in the context of *realpolitik*. Elshtain situates Machiavelli in the realist tradition of international relations:

> Realism's bracing promise is to spring politics free from the constraints of moral judgment and limitation, thereby assuring its autonomy as historic force and discursive subject-matter, and to offer a picture of the world of people and states as they really are rather than as we might yearn for them to be. ... The genealogy of realism as international relations, although acknowledging antecedents, gets down to serious business with Machiavelli, moving on to theorists of sovereignty and apologists for *raison d'état*.[32]

The cardinal presumption made by this particular discourse of international relations as expressed by *The Prince* concerns the concept of the state. Elshtain again:

> We are familiar with what modern realism presumes: a world of sovereign states as preposited ontological entities, each seeking either to enhance or to secure its own power. State sovereignty is the motor that moves the realist system as well as its (nearly) immutable object. Struggle is endemic to the system and force is the court of last resort. It cannot be otherwise, for states exist in a condition of anarchy in relation to one another ... the realist refrain: a world of sovereign and suspicious states.[33]

One direct consequence of this which we can see at work in Machiavelli's text is, as Pocock points out, his automatic association of the civic with the martial, and, indeed, Pocock calls Machiavelli's '"militarization of citizenship" a potent legacy that subverts ... consideration of alternatives that do not bind civic and martial virtue together'.[34] Machiavelli himself states that he does not intend to deal with laws in *The Prince* because these are inoperative without strong arms to back them up:

> The main foundations of every state, new states as well as ancient or composite ones, are good laws and good arms; and because you cannot have good laws without good arms, and where there are good arms, good laws inevitably follow, I shall not discuss laws but give my attention to arms.   chapter XII, p. 77

From a feminist perspective which embraces co-operation, this basic martial assumption means that 'possibilities for reciprocity between men and women, or for a politics not reducible to who controls or coerces whom, are denied'.[35] In other words, assumptions about the nature of the state are relevant not only as regards inter-state relations; these assumptions, as indicated earlier, are also crucial in their structuring of intra-state power relations as hierarchical and inherently confrontational. As Elshtain puts it: 'Historic realism involves a way of thinking – a set of presumptions about the human condition that secretes images of men and women and the parts they play in the human drama'.[36] Opposition and conflict, then, are ontologically built into the inner workings of such a state in the areas of gender, class, race and age.

Covert: epistemological processes

The historical and economic dimension outlined in the first part of this chapter permeates, or rather allows for, the continuing use of certain epistemological structures (simple binary opposi-tions, universalisation, etc.) to maintain the dominance–subordination hierarchy of power relations. Generalisation, universalisation and over-simplification are all at work as covert tactics which serve to reinforce the overt values of The Prince. Some of the major forms taken by these tactics are as follows: (1) generalisations (particularly about human nature and social groupings), (2) binary oppositions (e.g. true–false, public–private, war–peace), (3) cause-and-effect mode of argumentation based on logocentrism, (4) analogy via metaphors and similes (particularly using the category of the ' natural' as a self-evident means of justification and normalisation) and (5) the use of other discourses, especially those of history and myth, as an uncon-testable, ready-made source of facts, proofs and certainties.

It will be immediately apparent that these forms, as well as expressing certain epistemological basics, belong also to the tradition of classical rhetoric still current during the Renaissance. Whether or not we assume, along with Pocock, that Machiavelli was 'using a language of whose full burden of implication he could not have been aware', there can be no doubt that he was consciously writing within this rhetorical tradition and, moreover, was doing so during a period which abounded in treatises on the subject.[37] Machiavelli's awareness of rhetorical matters is apparent in the dedication to *The Prince*, where he claims that he has not 'embellished or crammed this book with rounded periods or big, impressive words, or with any blandishment or superfluous decoration of the kind which many are in the habit of using to describe or adorn what they have produced' (pp. 29-30).

Machiavelli's emphasis in the text is not on style but on 'the variety of its contents and the seriousness of its subject matter' (p. 30). Nevertheless, rhetorical forms are employed throughout the work, whose aim is aligned to an above-average degree with that of rhetoric, namely to persuade. It is through the filter of these traditional forms that the basic epistemological tendencies with which we are concerned take shape. The above five forms all belong to the interlinking areas of *inventio* (the exploration of material to discover arguments in support of a proposition) and *elocutio* (the figures of speech and thought, and the grand, middle or low register through which the arguments are expressed).[38] In the analysis which follows, the forms will be described in their rhetorical context. However, the main focus remains on the epistemological tendencies which they convey and, in particular, on the specific end to which these tendencies are oriented. The forms can also be seen to interlock with each other in varying combinations (for instance, the example which concludes the first part of this section is a generalisation (1), using the cause-and-effect mode of argumentation (3), and expressed in binary oppositions (2).

Generalisation. Generalisation or universalisation in *The Prince*, especially about human nature and social groups, plays a central role in working to over-simplify, and thereby obscure, actual differences and complexities. The employment of such a 'falsely universalizing perspective' is instrumental in structuring reality along the lines of the confrontational dominance–subordination hierarchy, the end being to promote the hegemony of the dominant group: 'Perhaps reality can have "a" structure only from the falsely universalizing perspective of the dominant group. That is, only to the extent that one person or group can dominate the whole, will reality appear to be governed by one set of rules'.[39] As Elshtain argues, this mechanism is to be found in the 'realist' way in which Machiavelli's text deals with human nature, in that his 'realism exaggerates certain features of the human condition and ignores others'.[40]

Generalisation about human nature and social groups occurs in a variety of ways in the text. In addition to overt references to the general and to generalisation, the use of 'always' is very common, as in the statements 'the prince is always compelled to injure those who have made the new ruler', and 'For always, no matter ... one needs the goodwill of the inhabitants' (chapter III, p. 35). Also leading to generalisation is the use of 'whoever', as in 'Whoever does not attend carefully to these points will quickly lose what he has acquired' (chapter III, p. 391). In terms of rhetoric, these generalisations follow the pattern of the common topics of invention, namely the maxim, 'a short, pithy statement of a general truth', or the commonplace, 'a general argument, observation or description'.[41] Maxims are recommended by Aristotle in his *Rhetoric*: 'They serve for speeches because audiences are commonplace. People are pleased when a speaker hits on a wide, general statement of opinions that they hold in some partial or fragmentary form.'[42] The status of the addressee of Machiavelli's text, which is full of maxims, might even be called into question at this point. Although the dedication makes much of the Prince's lofty position in relation to the lowly author, the rhetorical technique employed might be taken to imply quite the opposite in its appeal to commonly held, rather than exceptional, views.

Machiavelli's generalisations about human nature leave no room for exceptions: 'The populace is by nature fickle'(chapter VI, p. 52), 'men always dislike enterprises where the snags are evident' (chapter X, p. 72), 'One can make this generalization ["dire questo generalmente"] about men: they are ungrateful, fickle, liars and deceivers, they shun danger and are greedy for profit; while you treat them well they are yours' (chapter VII, p. 96), 'men in general ["in universali"] judge by their eyes rather than by their hands', and 'the common people are always impressed by appearances and results' (chapter XVIII, p. 101). In all these examples, human nature is illustrated by generic references to 'the people' and 'men' ('populo', 'uomini') as opposed to the Prince. The behaviour of classes other than the populace also appears as generalised (for example, the nature of the nobles ('grandi')). All these generalisations rest on the assumption of a polarisation of the Prince versus the rest; in other words, the basis of these generalisations is one of dominance–subordination. In the terminology of Foucault, the Prince is posited as being in a relation of 'transcendental singularity' to the rest of the population.[43]

This fundamental over-simplification of the complex and multifarious workings of the state is evident not only in Machiavelli's generalisations about human nature but also in the monolithic character of his references to the Prince's subjects and 'their women'. No distinction, for instance, is made between all the different classes of Florentine women in existence at the time, nor is there any recognition of their varying circumstances (working or non-working, married, single or widowed, etc.). Cases of differentiation amongst 'the people' in terms of employment, for example, are the exception rather than the rule (e.g. his reference to 'trade, agriculture or any other profession' and to guilds in chapter XXI). The overriding lack of differentiation in the monolithic group 'the people' works to suppress particularity in favour of the general and effectively silences subordinate groups in their differentiation.[44]

Machiavelli is quite open about generalising: 'From this we can deduce a general rule, which never or rarely fails to apply: that whoever is responsible for another's becoming powerful ruins himself' (chapter III, p. 44). Significantly, he also recognises the need to consider the particular: 'It is impossible to give a final verdict on any of these policies unless one examines the particular circumstances ["particulari"] of the states in which such decisions have to be taken' (chapter XX, p. 114). Nevertheless, he continues by generalising: 'None the less, I shall as far as possible discuss the matter in generalizations' ('in quel modo largo') (chapter XX, p. 114). Later he even goes so far as to say 'But here generalization ["parlare largamente"] is impossible, because circumstances vary', but resorts irresistibly to the general once again: 'I shall say just this: a prince will never have any difficulty' (chapter XX, p. 117).

Towards the end of *The Prince* Machiavelli emphasises the need to adapt to the times and the circumstances, which can be taken as another recognition of the importance of the particular and the historically specific: ' I also believe that the one who adapts his policy to the times prospers, and likewise that the one whose policy clashes with the demands of the times does not' (chapter XXV, p. 131). However, correct policy is inevitably based on fixed generalisations and assumptions about human nature and social groupings, universalisations which are founded on the dominance–subordination dynamic of power relations. Universalisation appears to have been a characteristic feature of the workings of the Renaissance intellect. According to Pocock:

> late scholastic thought was very well equipped with concepts dealing with universals, not too badly off for concepts relating the particular to the universal, but far from well supplied with concepts for understanding the relation, notably the succession or sequential relation, of one particular to another ... 'reason', as they understood the term, was concerned with universal, abstract, and timeless categories.[45]

Generalising from the particular was one of the standard topics of invention recommended in Aristotle's *Rhetoric* (for example, 'in arguing individual motive, point to general motives').[46] Conversely, one of the invalid topics or fallacies of argument was to 'make a statement about the whole, true only of individual parts'.[47] We might venture to conclude, in the terms of classical rhetoric itself, that Machiavelli's use of generalisation often amounts, in effect, to an invalid topic.[48]

Generalisations do not always stand on their own in *The Prince*, but may be found interlocking with other epistemological forms and tendencies. For instance, the generalisation 'men must be either pampered or crushed, because they can get revenge for small injuries but not for grievous ones' (chapter III, p. 37) also makes use of the cause-and-effect mode of argumentation, and two binary oppositions.

Binary oppositions. Manichean, dichotomous oppositions are used in *The Prince* to posit two contrasting alternatives. This position ignores other possibilities, such as various combinations of the two, or the gradations in the interlying area.[49] It also suppresses the mutual embeddedness of the two sides. Jay points out that this structure orders reality in a way which distorts difference and that, furthermore, it is 'in the interest of certain social groups to understand gender distinctions in that way'.[50]

Of the binary opposites used by Machiavelli in *The Prince,* one of the most fundamental is the assumption that it is exclusively the dominance–subordination dichotomy which orders power relations. This is, however, only one way of conceptualising power. Foucault makes this point in his writings on power: 'One should not assume a massive and primal condition of domination, a binary structure with "dominators" on one side and "dominated" on the other, but rather a multiform production of relations of domination which are partially susceptible of integration into overall strategies'.[51] *The Prince* also relies heavily on the true–false dichotomy. This overtly abstract and 'empty' dichotomy or paradigm is, however, very much tied, in its syntagmatic manifestations, to the specific power relations within which it is utilised, and which it helps to re/produce.[52]

The form taken by the contrasting dichotomy in *The Prince* is frequently that of the 'either … or' construction; for example, 'men do you harm either because they fear you or because they hate you' (chapter VII, p. 61). In this case other, alternative reasons are ignored, such as the possibility that men may be paid to 'do you harm', and thus be motivated neither by fear nor by hate, but occupy a position of indifference to their victim. There are many other binary oppositions in the text in addition to the dominance–subordination, true–false, fear–hate dichotomies mentioned here. In the first section we discussed the series mind–matter, *virtù–fortuna*, war–peace, masculine–feminine. Other important dichotomies are public–private, good–bad, and also Machiavelli's use of *potentia–podestà* (two terms for power with different connotations). Our purpose here is to draw attention to the fundamental epistemological tendencies expressed by this basic structure and to examine how the specific forms it takes in *The Prince* are governed by the end to which they are oriented.

At this point, it is worth noting that non-oppositional binaries are also in evidence in our text as a means of argumentation (for example, 'All he has to watch is that they do not build up *too much strength and too much authority,* and with *his own strength and their support,* chapter III, pp. 38-9, my italics). The simplistic and over-simplifying nature of the binary structure, whether oppositional or not, may owe its existence at least in part to the need for rhythm and balance in oratory, the oral means of persuasion from which the precepts of rhetoric were derived. Machiavelli would have been well aware of the fact that dichotomous structures were an important part of rhetoric, both as a topic of argument under *inventio* and as a figure of speech or thought under *elocutio* (for example, antithesis, *oppositio*, etc.).[53] This was the case in visual as well as verbal expression during the Renaissance. Lazzaro comments 'The dialogue, or balance of opposites, or pairing of complementaries, is a basic mode of verbal and visual expression in the Renaissance'.[54]

The domination of *The Prince* by the binary opposition would seem to indicate that Machiavelli found this structure particularly compelling as a rhetorical device. At any rate, it functions here as a powerful vehicle for ineluctably propelling the text, at all levels, towards an end pre-set by dominant values based on a simple system of A/Not-A choices.

Cause and effect. This mode of argumentation has as its end the provision of the 'truth' part of the true–false opposition, an end achieved by means of structuring reality as a continuous, linear chain of events following a pattern of progression from cause to effect. The cause-and-effect formulation is in itself another binary opposition which, like all dichotomies, belies the mutual embeddedness or 'co-presence' which actually obtains between these artificially separated parts. An effect, says Deleuze, 'is strictly co-present to, and co-extensive with, its own cause, and determines this cause as an immanent cause, inseparable from its effects, pure *nihil* or x, outside of the effects themselves'.[55]

Under the 'veil of objectivity', the cause and effect rationale appropriates and engineers 'truth' by, once again, (over)simplifying relationships between real events; in other words, by omitting and belying the actual complexity of these relationships, which would be less tendentiously represented by other, more comprehensive forms of conceptualisation, and particularly by 'an interactive model that eschews the dichotomy'.[56]

For Machiavelli, the cause-and-effect mode of argumentation was a respectable rhetorical technique listed by Aristotle as a valid topic under invention, which aimed to 'Prove an effect by showing the presence of its cause, or vice versa'.[57]

Machiavelli's use of this particular mode of argumentation takes the form of the 'if ... then' construction (chapter II, p. 34), the frequent use of 'because', and phrases such as 'it was for those reasons' (chapter II, p. 35), 'it is reasonable that' (chapter II, p. 34), etc. Appeals to reason punctuate the text. The following example links reason to the commonplace and the ordinary, to the effect that it does not have to be explained or justified but is itself automatically used to justify another term: 'There is nothing fantastic about this, it is very commonplace and reasonable' (chapter III, p. 43). Linked to this are claims to 'real truth'; for example, 'so leaving aside imaginary things, and referring only to those which truly exist' ('quelle che sono vere') (chapter XV, p. 9), and 'I have thought it proper to represent things as they are in real truth ["alla verità effettuale delle cose"], rather than as they are imagined' (chapter XV, p. 90). Furthermore, it is particularly in the ways in which it appeals to reason and to the truth that *The Prince* belongs to the realist tradition of both political writing and realist narrative.

Analogy. Certain epistemological and rhetorical devices structure reality in such a way as to make the resulting order appear the only one possible; in other words, they normalise what is in effect not necessarily normal. Analogy is another device which can be seen to work in this way. The particular type of analogy referred to here derives rules for the social sphere from that of the 'natural' by the use of metaphor or simile. This ideological slippage from the natural (which cannot be changed) to the social (which can be changed and which it is therefore in the interests of hegemonic groups to police) is a form of epistemological tendentiousness which varies its face according to the historical period in which it is re/produced. The metaphor is classed under *elocutio* as a trope or an ornament, and despite Machiavelli's (rhetorical) claim in the dedication that he will avoid such embellishment, strategic use of this figure is made in *The Prince*.

Given the rhetorical awareness of the Renaissance, it would indeed have been unusual for the metaphor or simile to be absent from *The Prince*. Aristotle attached great significance to the use of metaphor, particularly as a necessary part of the enthymeme (the form of proof which differentiated rhetoric from logic in that it focused on the concrete, namely on public questions, rather than on the abstract). Metaphor, in its capacity of substituted rather than literal name, was instrumental in providing 'descriptive vividness of the concrete'.[58]

For the social state, then, Machiavelli substitutes the 'natural' phenomenon of the body, with the Prince as doctor:

> As the doctors say of a wasting disease, to start with it is easy to cure but difficult to diagnose; after a time, unless it has been diagnosed and treated at the outset, it becomes easy to diagnose but difficult to cure. So it is in politics. Political disorders can be quickly healed if they are seen well in advance (and only a prudent ruler has such foresight).   chapter III, p. 39

He similarly substitutes simple plant-life for the complex social mechanism of the state, this time with the Prince as gardener: 'Then again, governments set up overnight, like everything in nature whose growth is forced, lack strong roots and ramifications. So they are destroyed in the first bad spell' (chapter VII, p. 54). With the Prince as doctor or gardener, power is once again assumed to operate from the top downwards. This assumption is naturalised in its expression by means of a metaphor or simile which relies on the 'indisputable' factual basis of nature itself. However, as feminist scientists are careful to point out, 'Facts are theory-laden; theories are value-laden'.[59] The word 'natural' recurs throughout the text to explain and justify selected types of social behaviour; for example, 'The wish to acquire more is admittedly a very *natural* and common thing' (chapter III, p. 42, my italics), and 'disorder arises chiefly because of one *natural* difficulty always encountered in new principalities' (chapter III, p. 34, my italics).

The tendentiousness of anthropomorphism is also in evidence in Machiavelli's advice to the Prince to 'act like a beast', and to 'learn from the fox and the lion' (chapter XVIII, p. 99). The argument that human/male behaviour should copy animal behaviour is clearly tautologous, in that animal behaviour itself is already codified and rationalized along anthropomorphic lines by those who seem to be merely describing it.[60] Once again, Machiavelli's use of analogy, and in particular his references to the natural as a viable parallel to the social, is not in itself exceptional, and can be seen to recur during other periods (for example, Pirandello's play *L'Innesto*, (*The Grafting*) of 1921 presents a botanical metaphor as a euphemism for rape), while the state as body is a familiar metaphor.

The integration of the discourse of the natural world with the discourse of the social and political in *The Prince* leads us to our final epistemological section.

Use of other discourses. Different discourses are imported and interwoven as a means to persuade the addressee of *The Prince* of the inevitability of a certain, predetermined end. Discourses pertaining to the natural world, myth, the Bible and above all history (both past and present) are utilised as a ready-made source of uncontestable facts. In his dedication, Machiavelli cites his own study of history as the basis of *The Prince* and throughout the text he emphasises the need for the Prince likewise to acquaint himself with the 'deeds of eminent men'. This use of history as an ultimate model enabling the Prince himself to make history ('so that he can do what eminent men have done before him') assumes a particular definition of history. According to this assumption, history is a linear chain of events which can be controlled by a few (men) in terms of actions geared to a confrontational mode of interrelation ('As for intellectual training, the Prince should read history, study the actions of eminent men to see how they conducted themselves during war', chapter XIV, p. 89). History is also, furthermore, interpreted as a storehouse of proofs and certainties: by studying the 'actions of eminent men' during war, the Prince may 'discover the reasons for their victories and defeats' (chapter XIV, p. 89).[61]

Machiavelli's use of elements of historical and other discourses, like the sub-stories used to convey them in the manner of religious *exempla*, again fits into the rhetorical tradition of his time. Expressed by means of figures of thought, these other discourses form one type of inductive proof whereby only selected instances are cited (the other type being scientific proof, where all instances are given).[62] These discourses appear in the form of figures such as analogy ('reasoning or arguing from parallel cases'), anamnesis ('recalling matters of the past'), chriae ('a short exposition of a deed of a person whose name is mentioned') and example ('an example cited, either feigned or true; an illustrative story').[63]

In his use of examples from history, Machiavelli himself hints at the way in which recourse to this discourse is end-oriented, in other words partial and tendentious: 'Many who have studied the lives and deaths of certain Roman emperors may perhaps believe that they provide examples contradicting my opinion' (chapter XIX, p. 106). However, his recognition does not prevent him from proceeding in like manner: 'As I wish to answer these objections, I shall discuss the characters of some of the emperors, showing that the reasons for their downfall are not different from those I have adduced' (chapter XIX, p. 106). The open-endedness of history is therefore posited rhetorically, as it were – it is introduced only to be negated. What remains is the use of history for the predetermined ends of the text.

Conclusion

It is specifically through their tendency towards end-orientation that discourses of power, both overt and covert, can be seen to enmesh with narrative processes in *The Prince*. The epistemological and rhetorical structures, and realist epic features, which characterise Machiavelli's text place him within certain traditions of philosophy, rhetoric, political writing and narrative. These traditions show the continued influence of classical authority, as well as that of the medieval sermon, in the use made of *exempla* and its effects on early developments in prose narrative and the writing of history. To a certain extent, then, this critique clearly has as its subject not only *The Prince* itself but also the traditions within which Machiavelli was writing.

Nevertheless, the way in which these traditions come together in his text are of special interest in the light of recent

developments in postmodernist feminism. Examined from this
point of view, *The Prince* can be seen to be structured around
end-orientation in all of its aspects, from that of its material
functionality as a piece of rhetoric aiming to persuade, to the
closures of each of its sub-stories or *exempla*. Founded on a fixed
set of ideologically slanted epistemological assumptions, the text
is characterised by its use of particularly oversimplifying forms
of rhetoric to suppress complexity and the pluralism of equally
valid differences. In all its narrative and discursive practices,
then, *The Prince* works, ultimately, to exclude open-ended
possibility in favour of the predetermined certainty of dominant, stereotypical values.

Notes

1 I am grateful to the following for their helpful comments on the first
   draft of this chapter: Martin Coyle, Giulio Lepschy, William Outhwaite
   and Darrow Schecter.

2 Grangier de Liverdes, quoted by Judith C. Brown, 'A Woman's Place
   was in the Home: Women's Work in Renaissance Tuscany', in Margaret
   W. Ferguson, Maureen Quilligan and Nancy J. Vickers (eds), *Rewriting
   the Renaissance: The Discourses of Sexual Difference in Early Modern
   Europe* (Chicago: University of Chicago Press, 1986), pp. 206-26 (p. 215).
   Enclosure of women continued well after the Renaissance. For the depic-
   tion of enclosure in, for example, the plays of Pirandello, see Maggie
   Günsberg, *Patriarchal Representations: Gender and Discourse in
   Pirandello's Theatre* (Oxford: Berg, 1994), ch. 3.

3 Brown, 'A Woman's Place', p. 215.

4 Michel Foucault, 'Governmentality', in Graham Burchell, Colin Gordon
   and Peter Miller (eds), *The Foucault Effect: Studies in Governmentality*
   (London: Harvester Wheatsheaf, 1991), pp. 87-104 (p. 87).

5 'Governmentality', p. 87.

6 'Governmentality', pp. 87-8.

7 'Governmentality', p. 104.

8 Shlomith Rimmon-Kenan, *Narrative Fiction: Contemporary Poetics* (London:
   Methuen, 1983), p. 3; Oswald Ducrot and Tzvetan Todorov, *Encyclopedic
   Dictionary of the Sciences of Language* (Oxford: Blackwell, 1981), p. 297.

9 Donna J. Haraway, *Simians, Cyborgs and Women: The Reinvention of
   Nature* (London: Free Association Books, 1991), p. 82.

10 Donna J. Haraway, 'Primatology is Politics by Other Means', in Ruth
   Bleier (ed.), *Feminist Approaches to Science* (New York: Pergamon Press,

1986), pp. 77-118 (p. 80).

11   Ducrot and Todorov, *Sciences of Language*, p. 297. This is, of course, only one of several ways of analysing narrative. The reader is referred to Ducrot and Todorov, *Sciences of Language* and Rimmon-Kenan, *Narrative Fiction*, for references to other methods.

12   Norman Friedman, *Form and Meaning in Fiction* (Athens: Ga, University of Georgia Press, 1975) in Ducrot and Todorov, *Sciences of Language*, pp. 298-9.

13   Felix Gilbert, *Machiavelli and Guicciardini: Politics and History in Sixteenth- Century Florence* (Princeton: Princeton University Press, 1965), pp. 131, 135.

14   The original Italian text uses the word 'esemplo', or 'exemplo', derived from the Latin 'exemplum', which, as well as denoting 'example', also refers to 'a short narrative used to illustrate a moral'. See J. A. Cuddon, *A Dictionary of Literary Terms* (Harmondsworth: Penguin, 1979) p. 250.

15   Ducrot and Todorov, *Sciences of Language*, p. 296.

16   For the distinction of open versus closed as applied to texts, see Umberto Eco, *Opera aperta* (Milan: Bompiani, 1976).

17   For a full examination of these narrative features, see Rimmon-Kenan, *Narrative Fiction*, ch. 9.

18   The lengthy story of Cesare Borgia, for instance, is interrupted by a digression on Remirro de Orco in chapter VII.

19   *The Prince,* translated by George Bull (Harmondsworth: Penguin, 1975). The original Italian is given when relevant and is taken from *Il Principe e altre opere politiche*, ed. Stefano Andretta (Milan: Garzanti, 1982).

20   Abrams describes the epic as 'centered on a heroic or quasi divine figure on whose actions depends the fate of a tribe, a nation, or the human race'. He goes on to isolate the following features: 'The hero is a figure of great national ... importance' (the Prince must save Italy), 'The setting ... is ample in scale' (the goal of the Prince exceeds individual attainments as well as single states), 'The action involves superhuman deeds in battle ... accomplished despite the opposition of some of the gods' (the Prince must show prowess in his military exploits as one manifestation of his *virtù*, despite the occasional opposition of Fortune) and finally 'In these great actions the gods or other supernatural beings take an interest or an active part' (the Prince cannot act without taking into account Fortune, which either aids or obstructs his actions) (Meyer H. Abrams, *A Glossary of Literary Terms* (London: Holt, Rinehart & Winston, 1981), pp. 50-1).

21   Ian Maclean, *The Renaissance Notion of Woman: A Study in the Fortunes of Scholasticism and Medical Science in European Intellectual Life* (Cambridge: Cambridge University Press, 1985); G. E. R. Lloyd, *Polarity and Analogy: Two Types of Argumentation in Early Greek Thought* (Cambridge, 1971).

22 Jean Bethke Elshtain, 'Realism, Just War, and Feminism in a Nuclear Age', *Political Theory*, 13,1 (1985), pp. 39-57 (pp. 40, 42).

23 Jean Bethke Elshtain, 'The Problem with Peace', *Millennium*, 17,3 (1988), pp. 441-51 (p. 441).

24 Geneviève Lloyd, *The Man of Reason: 'Male' and 'Female' in Western Philosophy* (London: Methuen, 1984).

25 The term *virtù* has various meanings, depending on context. The particular association I have concentrated on is that of 'action'. See Russell Price, 'The Senses of *Virtù* in Machiavelli', *European Studies Review*, 3,4 (1973), pp. 315-45.

26 In this connection see Elshtain, 'The Problem with Peace'.

27 Louis Althusser, 'Ideology and Ideological State Apparatuses', in *Essays on Ideology* (London: Verso, 1984). Eco's semiotic equivalent of Althusser's ideologically-interpellated subject is the Model Reader, whose 'creation' is likewise determined by a set of assumptions presented by the text (Umberto Eco, *The Role of the Reader: Explorations in the Semiotics of Texts* (London: Hutchinson, 1981), p. 7).

28 Belsey provides a useful definition of this type of representation: 'Classic realism is characterized by "illusionism", narrative which leads to "closure" and a "hierarchy of discourses"which establishes the "truth" of the story... [A] high degree of intelligibility is sustained throughout the narrative as a result of the hierarchy of discourses in the text. The hierarchy works above all by means of a privileged discourse which places as subordinate all the discourses that are literally or figuratively between inverted commas... To the extent that the story first constructs, and then depends for its intelligibility, on a set of assumptions shared between narrator and reader, it confirms both the transcendent knowingness of the reader-as-subject and the "obviousness" of the shared truths in question' (Catherine Belsey, 'Constructing the Subject: Deconstructing the Text', in Judith Newton and Deborah Rosenfelt (eds), *Feminist Criticism and Social Change* (London: Methuen, 1985), pp. 45-64 (p. 53)).

29 However, as Haraway succinctly points out: '"facts" depend on the interpretive framework of theory, and ... theories are loaded with the explicit and implicit values of the theorizers and their cultures. Thus, all facts are laced with values. ... Facts are theory-laden; theories are value-laden; values are story-laden. Therefore, facts are meaningful within stories' (Haraway, 'Primatology is Politics', p. 79).

30 For a discussion of gender stereotyping in Italian epic poetry of the Renaissance, see Maggie Günsberg, '*Donna Liberata*? The Portrayal of Women in the Italian Renaissance Epic', in Zygmunt G. Barański and Shirley W. Vinall (eds), *Women and Italy: Essays on Gender, Culture & History* (London: Macmillan, 1991), pp. 173-208.

31 Foucault distinguishes between the 'transcendental singularity of Machiavelli's prince' and the actual playing out of social hierarchies which go

to make up the State on the basis that power does not simply work from the top downwards, but operates at the level of a society's extremities and particularities: 'We have seen, however, that practices of government are, on the one hand, multifarious and concern many kinds of people: the head of a family, the superior of a convent, the teacher or tutor of a child or pupil; so that there are several forms of government among which the prince's relation to his state is only one particular mode; while, on the other hand, all these other kinds of government are internal to the state or society. It is within the state that the father will rule the family, the superior the convent, etc. Thus we find at once a plurality of forms of government and their immanence to the state' (Foucault, 'Governmentality', p. 91).

32 Elshtain, 'Reflections on War', p. 39.

33 Elshtain, 'Reflections on War', p. 39.

34 Elshtain, 'Reflections on War', p, 42.

35 Elshtain, 'Reflections on War', p. 42.

36 Elshtain, 'Reflections on War', p. 40.

37 John G. A. Pocock, ' Custom and Grace, Form and Matter: An approach to Machiavelli's Concept of Innovation', in Martin Fleischer (ed.), *Machiavelli and the Nature of Political Thought* (London: Croom Helm, 1973), pp. 153-74 (p. 155); Bernard Weinberg (ed.), *Trattati di poetica e retorica del Cinquecento* (Bari: Laterza, 1970-74).

38 The other three rhetorical areas are *dispositio, memoria* and *pronuntiatio*. See Charles S. Baldwin, *Ancient Rhetoric and Poetic* (Gloucester, Mass: Peter Smith, 1959); Donald L. Clark, *Rhetoric and Poetry in the Renaissance* (New York: Columbia Press, 1922); Weinberg, *Trattati di poetica*.

39 Jane Flax, quoted by Linda J. Nicholson (ed.), *Feminism/Postmoderism* (London: Routledge, 1990), p. 6.

40 Elshtain, 'Reflections on War', p. 40.

41 Richard A. Lanham, *A Handlist of Rhetorical Terms* (Berkeley: University of California Press, 1969), pp. 64, 100.

42 *Rhetoric*, 1395b, quoted by Baldwin, *Ancient Rhetoric*, p. 20.

43 See note 31.

44 In relation to silenced or 'muted' groups, see Edwin Ardener, 'Belief and the Problem of Women' and 'The Problem Revisited', in Shirley Ardener (ed.), *Perceiving Women* (London: Dent, 1975), pp. 1-17, 19-27; see also Gayatri C. Spivak, 'Can the Subaltern Speak?', in Cary Nelson and Lawrence Grossberg (eds), *Márxism and the Interpretation of Culture* (Urbana, Ill.: University of Illinois Press, 1988), pp. 271-316.

45 John G. A. Pocock, *The Machiavellian Moment* (Princeton: Princeton University Press, 1975), p. 156.

46 Quoted by Lanham, *A Handlist*, p. 109.

47 *A Handlist*, p. 109.

48 For a discussion of Renaissance views on the particular, see Pocock, 'Custom and Grace'.

49 Jay calls this area the 'excluded middle'. She explains: 'In A/Not-A dichotomies only one term has a positive reality; Not-A is only the privation or absence of A. A/B distinctions are necessarily limited; in themselves they do not encompass C, D, and so forth. But there is nothing about them that necessarily prevents also considering C (a third possibility), and then the distinction becomes A/B/C. In other words, mere contrary distinctions are not eternally tied to dichotomous structure, and *as* dichotomies they are limited in scope' (Nancy Jay, 'Gender and dichotomy', *Feminist Studies*, 7,1 (spring 1981), pp. 38-56 (pp. 42-3).

50 Jay, 'Gender and Dichotomy', p. 38.

51 Michel Foucault, *Power/Knowledge: Selected Interviews and Other Writings 1972-1977* (Brighton: Harvester Press, 1980), p. 142.

52 Foucault's notion of the 'effects of power' (rather than its imposition from above) is useful in this context, and in particular his description of 'the ensemble of rules according to which the true and the false are separated and specific effects of power attached to the true'. He goes on to discuss the problems of 'detaching the power of truth from the forms of hegemony, social, economic and cultural, within which it operates at the present time' (*Power/Knowledge*, pp. 132-3).

53 Lanham, *A Handlist*, pp. 109-10.

54 Claudia Lazzaro, 'The Visual Language of Gender in Sixteenth-Century Garden Sculpture', in Marilyn Migiel and Juliana Schiesari (eds), *Refiguring Woman: Perspectives on Gender and the Italian Renaissance* (Ithaca: Cornell University Press, 1991), pp. 71-113, p. 77.

55 Gilles Deleuze, quoted by Burchell, *The Foucault Effect*, p. ix.

56 Lynda Birke, summarised in Susan J. Hekman, *Gender and Knowledge: Elements of a Postmodern Feminism* (Cambridge: Polity Press, 1990), p. 125.

57 Lanham, *A Handlist*, p. 109.

58 Clark, *Rhetoric and Poetry*, p. 29; Baldwin, *Ancient Rhetoric*, pp. 7, 24.

59 Haraway, 'Primatology is Politics', p. 79.

60 See Ruth Bleier, *Science and Gender: A Critique of Biology and Its Theories on Women* (New York: Pergamon Press, 1984) and *Feminist Approaches*.

61 See Edward H. Carr, 'Causation in History', in *What is History?* (Harmondsworth: Penguin, 1987), pp. 81-102.

62 Lanham, *A Handlist*, p. 132.

63 Lanham, *A Handlist*, p. 122.

7

The Prince and textual politics

ANDREW MOUSLEY

Machiavelli's prince never creases to be a political figure; he is, in Burd's phrase, 'a force, an embodied idea, almost as impersonal as the state itself'; in his dealings he shapes and touches the lives of his subjects at every point. Yet in all this, questions and answers regarding human conduct are to be framed in terms of the political science which Machiavelli may be said to have founded. Nothing as amorphous or irrelevant as Christian faith or ethics is to be allowed to intrude. God, in short, is banished not only from the state but from history and human experience.[1]

Machiavellism came into being only after the death of its eponym. That is not to say that it was not inherent in the *modus operandi* of fifteenth-century Italian politics with its firm grounding in *ragione di stato*, but only when the amorphous assumptions of the quattrocento were given coherent and aphoristic expression in the writings of Machiavelli could a conscious concept develop. Even that was not enough, for Machiavelli did not create Machiavellism. Rather it was a developing and changing doctrine … which grew from the embryo of his writings.[2]

The above quotations point to what seems to me to be a characteristic dilemma for readers of Machiavelli: on the one hand, there has been and still is a tendency to assign Machiavelli a definite position in cultural history, as founder of modern 'politics', a politics without faith or ethics; on the other, a recognition of the elusive character of Machiavelli's writings, of their resistance to any single, identifiable 'Machiavellism'.[3] Machiavelli's displacement of ethical and religious categories raises a further problem: certainty about the existence of such a displacement is countered by uncertainty as to its significance, with critics variously identifying cynicism, realism, power politics, political science and historical consciousness amongst the outcomes of Machiavelli's banishment of God. Symptomatic of the tendency to read both doctrinal clarity and diversity of perspective into Machiavelli is the attempt made by J. N. Stephens to pinpoint the fluctuations of stance in *The Prince*: 'The amoral sentiments lie in the first eighteen chapters, the immoral ones in chapters 15 to 19 and the moral exhortations in chapters 21–6.'[4] The desire to designate precisely the shifts in point of view is suggestive of the way Machiavelli, and by extension Machiavelli's treatment of politics, are at once susceptible and resistant to confident categorisation.

The *Prince* itself lends some support to the view of its author's canonical status as founder of a new mode of political praxis and enquiry. Machiavelli does see himself in the text as an innovator and systematiser. In terms of Raymond Williams's useful distinction between archaic, residual, dominant and emergent ideologies, Machiavelli might be seen as attempting to locate 'God' as an archaic and the art of practical politics as an emergent discourse, ready (because Machiavelli has made it 'ready') to become dominant. However, as Williams points out, in understanding innovatory or emergent forms, 'what we have to observe is in effect a pre-emergence, active and pressing but not yet fully articulated, rather than the evident emergence which could be more confidently named'.[5] Despite Machiavelli's efforts, then, to make the practice of politics available to power through the confident naming of its object of knowledge, 'politics' does not emerge as a fully coherent domain in *The Prince*. Neither will ethical perspectives consign themselves totally to the past. It is the problem the text has in constituting politics as an autonomous and easily accessed practice that the present chapter seeks to explore.

Machiavelli originally dedicated *The Prince* to Giuliano de' Medici, but after Giuliano's death in 1516 the text's dedicatee instead became Lorenzo de' Medici. Offsetting the implication that the book might be continually re-dedicated to anyone interested in power (its maintenance, its acquisition or even its

subversion) is the reassuring sense of the book having a definite destination (in the shape of the Medici family) and, consequently, a definite purpose. The content of the dedicatory letter
offers further reassurance about the text's exclusivity of readership and function by clearly announcing the way the book is
to be read and used. The letter establishes a position of confidence
for the reader, a position from which the advice to be offered
may be easily assimilated, the strategies of 'princely government' authoritatively mastered.[6] Given the precarious situation
of *The Prince*'s immediate readership (in 1512, after eighteen
years of exile, the Medici family had been reinstated and the
Florentine republic dissolved), it is perhaps not surprising that
an ex-public servant, himself looking to be reinstated, should
attempt to transmit both for his own and for his dedicatee's
benefit a compensatory sense of control, a promise to reduce to
textual order the difficult art of maintaining one's position. The
urgently needed answer to the high mortality rate of governments and government officers will be this readable manual,
this text ready for the reader's immediate use. 'It is not in my
power', Machiavelli writes, 'to offer a greater gift than one which
in a very short time will enable you to understand all that I have
learned in so many years, and with much difficulty and danger'
(p. 3). The writer may have spent time and trouble acquiring a
difficult knowledge but the reader is spared these labours. He
is instead the beneficiary of an achieved knowledge, an at least
temporarily completed examination of past texts and modern
events. The digest of Machiavelli's 'knowledge of the conduct
of great men' acquired through 'long experience of modern
affairs and continual study of ancient history' is this single
'small volume' (p. 3) promising a methodical summary, a convenient reduction of past and present affairs and writings to their
essentials. The proposed relationship of reader to text is thus
one of easy consumption; the knowledge it offers is made
(partly) equivalent with such other immediately usable or reas-
suringly status-conferring objects as 'horses, weapons, a cloth
of gold' (p. 3). One of the implications of comparing a text with
such objects is that it will prove as tangible and as serviceable
as them, by clearly defining and giving substance to what becomes an increasingly elusive subject – the subject of politics.

In its preoccupation with the use-value and practical application of both itself and other texts, *The Prince* resembles many another humanist handbook. To cite just one indicative example written or compiled out of a similar sense of urgency as Machiavelli's work: Erasmus' preface to his *Apophthegmes* (1542) similarly appeals to the immediate benefit of those 'universal sorte of wrytinges ... as doo comprehend proverbes, sage sentencies, and notable saiynges or actes' since these forms of discourse are 'most fitte for Princes & noble mene' engaged in 'urgente causes and busie maters of the commonweale'.[7] A comparison between the Machiavellian and Erasmian responses to 'urgente causes and busie maters' is suggestive in that different kinds of usefulness and readerly involvement are implied by each. With Erasmus' diverse assortment of *sententiae*, it is for the reader to arrange and find uses for the multiplicity of verbal resources placed at her or his disposal. The 'wisdom' imparted by a commonplace collection like Erasmus' is piecemeal, makeshift, requiring the reader to process materials which do not themselves form a synthesis. By contrast, *The Prince* promises to offer more of a finished product, a systematic treatment of its subject. In this respect Machiavelli's text reflects a trajectory of humanism towards the efficient methodisation of discrete bodies of (practical) knowledge.[8] There will be no need for the reader to deliberate over the use(s) of the text, it is implied, for this will be made self-evident through the efficient methodisation of the art of princely government. That Machiavelli seems to be writing confidentially, for the sole benefit of a single reader/ruling elite, has the effect of further channelling potentially diverse readings and uses of the text towards a single reading, a single use. It is 'princely government' (p. 4) rather than any other form of government which is ostensibly the subject of Machiavelli's text.

The determination to pare down the text's subject matter to its essentials, and in doing so methodically to re-constitute that subject, informs other aspects of the dedicatory letter. The sense of a subject being newly (and correctly) constituted through reduction to its essentials is in fact strong throughout the text. The appeals to innovation and to greater veracity made in chapter XV, for example – 'what I have to say differs from the precepts offered by others ... it seems to me better to concentrate on what really happens rather than on theories and speculations' (p. 54) – is first made in the dedicatory letter with similar demarcations between the ideal and the real, speculation and actuality:

> I have not embellished this work by filling it with rounded periods, with high-sounding words or fine phrases, or with any of the other beguiling artifices of apparent beauty which most writers employ to describe and embellish their subject-matter; for my wish is that, if it is to be honoured at all, only its originality and the importance of the subject should make it acceptable.   p. 3

Appeals of this kind have the effect of constituting *The Prince* as a realist text: rather than constructing its object of knowledge, Machiavelli's text purports to describe that object as it exists already. This objectivity is to be consolidated by streamlining the art of politics, that is by excluding and marginalising those aspects of the subject that have conventionally been seen as integral parts of it. The idealism conveyed through 'high-sounding words or fine phrases' is perceived as alien to the 'true' matter of politics; so, too, is that relativising form of linguistic embellishment which would give Machiavelli's otherwise definitive, realist treatment a distinctly rhetorical flavour. Machiavelli's much-vaunted realism at this point seems to be working together with his emphases upon the speed and efficiency of the text's transmission of knowledge, to render the art of practical politics as transparently and unproblematically as possible.

It is this attempt to 'de-rhetoricise' or 'de-textualise' the art and study of politics, to transfer it from the uncertain realm of language and language use to the more certain, extra-discursive realm of 'things', which has contributed to Machiavelli's reputation as a founding father of political science.[9] Likewise, the constitution of politics as an autonomous realm with discoverable laws and rules of its own has been seen, as I noted at the beginning of the chapter, as part of an originating, 'scientific' project. And *The Prince* is not entirely innocent of the characteristics which justify this view of it. As already suggested, Machiavelli himself claims to be doing something new, and not in an exploratory but a methodical way: 'I hope it will not be considered presumptuous', he writes, 'for a man of very low and humble condition to dare to discuss princely government, and to lay down rules about it' (p. 4). This is not the language of a provisional advice book. The aim, clearly, is to be indispensable, to offer more than just advice. It is on the basis of such appeals that the reader might be encouraged to attempt to find in *The Prince* a single, definitive explanation of the laws of statecraft.

So far I have been describing *The Prince* as a monolithic text. Although a text's position in culture is never fixed, it can nevertheless attempt to fix its own position, to establish the way it should be read and used. The appeal to the text as object of immediate consumption; the removal of its subject matter from the subjective realm of language; the attempt properly to constitute the subject of politics for the sole benefit of its (princely) reader by reducing it to its essentials: these are some of the ways in which Machiavelli's dedicatory letter attempts to chart a definite position for his text. Written in exile for a recent exile, *The Prince* is in one sense a book for the temporarily dispossessed, a reliable manual mapping the way back to power and authority in a world where authority cannot afford to be complacent for fear of once again being displaced.

In the main bulk of the text, accordingly, Machiavelli attempts to 'centre' his hypothetical ruler or 'principe', otherwise in danger of being displaced, by outlining a number of scenarios and showing how they can be brought under his control. Much of the advice seems straightforward, with Machiavelli elaborating, but careful not to over-elaborate, one aspect of statecraft after another, and drawing neat cause-and-effect conclusions from the illustrative examples cited. The use made of Cesare Borgia in the chapter on 'Auxiliaries, mixed troops and native troops' is characteristic:

> I never hesitate to cite Cesare Borgia and his actions. This Duke invaded the Romagna using auxiliaries (and all his troops being French), and with them he captured Imola and Forlì. But since he distrusted them, he then used mercenaries, which he thought less dangerous, employing the Orsini and Vitelli troops. When he later

found them to be of doubtful value and loyalty, and therefore dangerous, he disbanded them and formed an army composed of his own men. And the difference between these kinds of army is very obvious if one compares the reputation of the Duke when he used only French troops or when he used the Orsini and Vitelli troops, and when he possessed his own soldiers, and was self-sufficient militarily. Then it became much greater, and he was never more esteemed than when everyone saw that he was the complete master of his own forces.   chapter XIII, p. 49

Military matters are of particular importance in Machiavelli's re-constituted art of government: 'A ruler ... should have no other objective and no other concern, nor occupy himself with anything else except war and its methods and practices' (chapter XIV, pp. 51–2). In terms of the Machiavellian distinction between the ideal and the real, war can clearly be situated on the side of the 'real'. It is a solid, tangible practice about which a solid, tangible knowledge can be produced; and it displaces ethical discourse as the prime constituent or foundation of authority.[10] The 'efficacy' (p. 52) of war in maintaining or acquiring power sharply contrasts with the inefficiency of that outmoded form of authority embodied by the morally upright leader who 'does not do what is generally done, but persists in doing what ought to be done' (chapter XV, p. 54). Machiavelli's demystification of statecraft thus seems to be serving the exclusive purpose of re-consolidating power at a more tangible, practical level than the idealism which has conventionally under-pinned it. Grounded in actual praxis and experience, power can be rebuilt upon sure foundations. Military strength is one such indispensable foundation.

The art of war is also reducible to an easily mastered tech-nique, generating precisely the kind of cut-and-dried statement – 'A ruler ... should have no other objective' – cited above. In the chapters on military matters, Machiavelli's advice book is arguably at its most assertive and methodical. Chapter XIII, on 'Auxiliaries, mixed and native troops', for example, concludes briskly, giving the impression of having successfully limited the topic to teachable proportions: 'The right way to organise one's forces will be easily grasped, if the methods used by the four men I have cited above are examined' (p. 51). As this refer-ence to Machiavelli's use of illustrative material suggests,

examples and citations are efficiently slotted into the narrative
as conclusive concrete evidence. The example of Cesare Borgia
given above bears this out. It functions as a proof, a way of
clinching a point which thereby becomes indisputable. Whereas on other occasions Machiavelli has to work hard to derive
general principles from particular circumstances or examples,
here there is no question as to the conclusion to be drawn: military self-sufficiency leads to the highly desirable Machiavellian
goals of independence and mastery.

These goals are achieved precisely through the ability to
extract general principles from experience. The ideal Machiavellian ruler will be able to place himself in a position of autonomy because he has partially abstracted himself from particular
practices and circumstances, and understood others as general
types rather than as individuals. The achievement of the Prince
will thus be to constitute himself as an all-powerful subject
through the reduction of others to manipulable objects.[11] He
will be one step ahead of others because Machiavelli's text will
have taught him how to assign roles to others, how to reduce
others to pawns in his own master-plan or master-narrative. It
will have done so by offering a series of character profiles of
the typical mercenary and typical auxiliary in the identifying,
authoritative language of the 'expert' statesman: 'In short, with
mercenaries, their cowardice or reluctance to fight is more
dangerous; with auxiliaries their skill and courage' (chapter
XIII, p. 49). 'Statesmen ... teach how to tie / The sinews of a
city's mystic body' wrote John Donne.[12] Machiavelli's text on
statecraft might usefully be thought of as teaching the Prince
how to tie the sinews of a state's 'mystic body', how to convert
a potentially unknowable, heterogeneous entity into a know-
able, homogeneous one. The statesman's identification of those
who pose a threat to the state's homogeneity forms part of that
expertise which will render the principality obedient to its prince.

The positioning of *The Prince* within the unitary framework
suggested by Machiavelli himself in his dedicatory letter is thus
encouraged by various strategies and characteristics of the main
bulk of the text. The chapter headings alone – 'How the strength
of all principalities should be measured' (chapter X, p. 37),

'How flatterers should be shunned' (chapter XXIII, p. 81) – seem
to fulfil the letter's promise to provide a short, readable manual;
and the chapters themselves, on first impression at least, likewise seem to stay within the boundaries of their terse, encap-
sulating headings. And yet there are at the same time various
levels of resistance in Machiavelli's text to the kind of systematising thought which would reduce 'Machiavelli' himself to
some unequivocally identifiable 'Machiavellism'. The possibility
of the text serving more than one purpose, and more than one
reader, is recognisable, though perhaps only retrospectively,
from the initial assurances of the dedicatory letter onwards. In
the letter itself Machiavelli makes use of a metaphor which
bifurcates as much as it clarifies the purpose of the text:

> I hope it will not be considered presumptuous for a man of very
> low and humble condition to dare to discuss princely govern-
> ment, and to lay down rules about it. For those who draw maps
> place themselves on low ground, in order to understand the char-
> acter of the mountains and other high points, and climb higher
> in order to understand the character of the plains. Likewise, one
> needs to be a ruler to understand properly the character of the
> people, and to be a man of the people to understand properly the
> character of rulers.   chapter I, p. 4

While the map-making image promises to make of statecraft a
clearly defined terrain, it is also an image of carnivalesque
inversion, with ruler and ruled exchanging positions or at least
points of view: the ruler can properly know himself and what
it means to rule only by adopting the perspective of the people
and vice versa. The aim of this exchange, for the ruler, is to
return him to his superior position with a greater knowledge
of, and control over, his subjects' view of power. The apprentice ruler, like Shakespeare's Machiavellian Prince Hal, will
familiarise himself with low-life culture in order to contain it
more effectively. Just as Machiavelli's unembellished, demysti-
fied view of statecraft promises to consolidate the ruler's position, so too does this similarly demystifying 'view from below'.
Yet there is no guarantee that this double way of seeing will
have so simple or single an effect. The metaphor might suggest
a stable correspondence between a hierarchical order of society
and a hierarchical order of nature but it simultaneously

unleashes a series of destabilising alternative perspectives: what if the elevation of the people has the effect of enabling them to understand better their subjugation? What if bringing the ruler down to the level of the people has the effect of permanently undermining his authority?

Further difficulties and equivocations lie in wait for the reader in the main part of the text, as the elaboration of each topic often extends beyond any simple programmatic advice. Chapter 1, for example, begins with a confident, controlling act of classification: 'All the states, all the dominions that have held sway over men, have been either republics or principalities' (p. 5). As Thomas Greene has suggested, 'We appear to enter upon a total system, a Thomism of statecraft'.[13] But a number of qualificatory, antithetical divisions and sub-divisions then immediately follow:

> Principalities are either hereditary (their rulers having been for a long time from the same family) or they are new. The new ones are either completely new (as was Milan to Francesco Sforza) or they are like limbs joined to the hereditary state of the ruler who annexes them (as is the Kingdom of Naples to the King of Spain). States thus acquired are either used to living under a prince or used to being free; and they are acquired either with the arms of others or with one's own, either through luck or favour or else through ability.   chapter I, p. 5

While these divisions serve the merely functional purpose of introducing the topics to be dealt with in subsequent chapters, they point at the same time to that confrontation which we have already seen emerge elsewhere in the text between the general and the particular. The assertive pronouncement on the (limited) nature of human governments almost immediately threatens to dissolve under pressure of those potentially endless permutations which defy the totalising overview of the schematiser. If the reader had been expecting statecraft to be made instantly available in the form of generalisable techniques, then this opening summary might prove disappointing, for in Machiavelli's emphasis, here and in subsequent chapters, upon the different ways of acquiring different kinds of state, he is effectively refusing the reader access to any single, totalising technique.[14] The variety of governments cannot be easily homogenised; the 'principato' is not merely an extension of its 'principe'. It is instead the site of continual struggle between competing conceptions of government.

Machiavelli's commitment to flexible methods appropriate to changing circumstances – 'if it were possible to change one's character to suit the times and circumstances, one would always be successful' (chapter XXV, p. 86) – militates against the attempt to lay down anything other than provisional rules. Particular circumstances will always be tantalisingly beyond the grasp of the systematically deployable rule or general principle. And yet not to have some answer to the unpredictable goddess Fortune is to risk emasculation:

> I conclude, then, that since circumstances vary and men when acting lack flexibility, they are successful if their methods match the circumstances and unsuccessful if they do not. I certainly think that it is better to be impetuous than cautious, because fortune is a woman, and if you want to control her, it is necessary to treat her roughly. chapter XXV, p. 87

Here, as on other occasions, a general rule is difficult to recover from the contradictory messages Machiavelli gives: it seems that rough, manly treatment of Fortune is being recommended as a substitute for the ideally responsive, flexible relationship to Fortune which elsewhere in the text seems possible. Yet too much responsiveness and not enough shaping of events would according to the above quotation be unmanly. Perhaps the 'final' position Machiavelli wants his reader/ruler to reach is to see that he must master different circumstances through a variety of different methods. Although this is impossible because 'men' are insufficiently flexible, Machiavelli, apparently not conforming to this general law himself, persists in outlining diverse methods with which to master (or be responsive to) the times. Ironically, Machiavelli's final position on Fortune proves to be opaque, and resistant to any neat formula.

The text's refusal to totalise is also bound up with its refusal to provide a universalising rationale for any one form of government. The established, hereditary principality is no more 'natural' or part of an eternal scheme of things than any other form of government. All governments are the result of secular forces and human innovation, rather than divine decree.

Machiavelli has been described by J. G. A. Pocock as a 'student of delegitimized politics'.[15] According to Pocock, Machiavelli's republican consciousness is largely responsible for his secularised view of politics:

> The republic was not timeless, because it did not reflect by simple correspondence the eternal order of nature; it was differently organized, and a mind which accepted republic and citizenship as prime realities might be committed to implicitly separating the political from the natural order.[16]

Florentine republicanism is contrasted by Pocock with its imperialist counterpart: 'Affiliation with the empire ... like affiliation with monarchy generally, was affiliation with the timeless.'[17] *The Prince* is from this angle a covertly republican text, in which no ruler is granted access to the timeless or universal.

Rather, the legitimacy of principalities is, in Pocock's terms, continually being cast into doubt by a republicanist perspective which effectively deconstructs the mystery or mystique of statecraft. Although this stripping away of illusions is partly compensated for by supplying the ruler with a reliable manual on the secularised art of government, uncertainties linger as to the implications of *The Prince*'s delegitimization of politics: is Machiavelli's demystification of statecraft merely a by-product of his attempt to reconstitute it on a surer foundation? Or are power and the state irredeemably damaged? The realist project of *The Prince*, in other words, points in conflicting directions.

Against the view of *The Prince* as an example of 'apparatus' writing, a specialising, expert manual produced solely for the benefit of the apprentice statesman, we should therefore set an alternative perspective. Intended as a way of helping its author back inside a reconsolidated state, the text simultaneously retains an outsider's view, a position from which authority is presumptuously subjected to the humbling perspective of the people. This double view of authority, from the outside and the inside, or from above and below, is sustained through the text's insistence that the ruler should see himself from 'low ground', as the dedicatory letter puts it.

The notorious chapter XVIII, on the ruler's need to have recourse to the force of a lion and the cunning of a fox, itself begins with a view from the ground:

> Everyone knows how praiseworthy it is for a ruler to keep his
> promises, and live uprightly and not by trickery. Nevertheless,
> experience shows that in our times the rulers who have done
> great things are those who have set little store by keeping their
> word, being skillful rather in cunningly confusing men; they
> have got the better of those who have relied on being trust-
> worthy.   p. 61

Whether the 'everyone' here refers mainly to previous writers
on statecraft or to some broader and vaguer common view,
Machiavelli is continually quoting some form of popular
opinion in order to raise his ruler above it. At the end of the
chapter, the achievement of this aim is registered in a series of
(again) confident reductions of the 'common people' to a homogeneous, gullible and easily mastered entity:

> With regard to all human actions, and especially those of rulers,
> who cannot be called to account, men pay attention to the
> outcome. If a ruler, then, contrives to conquer, and to preserve
> the state, the means will always be judged to be honourable and
> be praised by everyone. For the common people are impressed by
> appearances and results.   chapter XVIII, p. 63

Having begun with the common opinion that it is praiseworthy to keep promises, the chapter ends by fuelling the ruler's
sense of superiority by exposing for him the folly of common
opinion. What 'everyone believes' may change throughout the
chapter, and indeed throughout the book: 'men' are on some
occasions seen as highly moral, on others as selfish and greedy.
But by the end of the chapter these apparent contradictions
have been swept aside, so as to allow the Prince yet another
panoramic view, an insight into the 'real', as opposed to the
popularly imagined, nature of things.

It is, of course, significant that the means of elevation is
itself unusual, un-common, for it is not achieved by placing the
ruler in a position of moral superiority. The 'frisson' that *The
Prince* instead allows its select reader is based on the ruler's
freedom from customary moral constraints. The slick, worldly-
wise Prince sees through the traditional signs and symbols of
authority and exploits them to his advantage:

> [A ruler] should seem to be exceptionally merciful, trustworthy,
> upright, humane and devout. And it is most necessary of all to
> seem devout. In these matters, most men judge more by their eyes
> than by their hands. For everyone is capable of seeing you, but
> few can touch you.   chapter XVIII, pp. 62–3

Machiavelli's ruler does not have to commit himself finally to
any one of these virtuous, morally iconic 'characters'. They are
purely for the benefit of that everyman figure for whom politics and ethics are inseparable, and for whom appearances are
reliable signs of moral qualities: 'Everyone can see what you
appear to be, whereas few have direct experience of what you
really are' (chapter XVIII, p. 63). The dramatic possibilities of
The Prince mainly arise from this treatment of moral character
as a manipulable fiction, a theatrical mask to be put on and off
by the adept actor. Ethical language for the Machiavellian ruler
mainly belongs to the realm of fiction or public theatre; the
'real' Prince is invisible to the many, and visible, or rather
'touchable', as those rather odd images of eyes and hands
suggest, only to the 'few'.

It is at this point, perhaps, that Machiavelli's princely
reader might well begin to wonder what *The Prince* is doing to
and for him. For the sporadic use in Machiavelli's text of a
theatrical metaphor which insists on a resemblance between
acting and ruling itself has multiple effects. While it may
support the ruler's sense of himself as a kind of behaviourist
puppeteer, inputting stimulae in the form of stock moral 'characters' (the devout ruler, the merciful ruler, etc.) and getting
the required reactions from a gullible audience, the theatricalising of the Prince's identity has various other, more humbling
implications. Not the least of these is again the destabilising of
princely identity and authority that comes about as a result of
identifying the ruler with a form of protean role-playing. Machiavelli unmasks for the Prince what he might already sense but
be reluctant to admit to: that the moral and metaphysical foundations of authority are, at best, legitimising fictions, at worst,
a sham; that power is no more and no less than a theatrical spectacle. Stephen Greenblatt has suggested that the theatricalising
of Renaissance culture 'arose from conditions common to almost
all Renaissance courts: a group of men and women alienated

from the customary roles and revolving uneasily around a centre of power'.[18] In Machiavelli's text, the Prince is likewise alienated from a stable social and moral universe of which he is the centre. Machiavelli's ruler instead approximates the marginal, motley character of the stage fool. Obliged 'to vary his conduct as the winds of fortune and changing circumstances constrain him' (chapter XVIII, p. 62), he is permanently alienated from any one single, stable identity. And although the fool is often granted special insight, this insight is based not just on the stripping away of illusions in the name of a more solid sense of the real, but, beyond this, on undermining any fixed sense of reality.

The 'special insight' granted to the Prince fluctuates between these two options. In the passage quoted above, for example, Machiavelli seems once again keen to establish a solid sense of reality for his Prince, and introduces that odd distinction between the eyes that merely see the Prince's projected appearance and the hands that actually touch, and so grasp the reality of, the Prince. But the reality to which Machiavelli is referring here remains enigmatic. What is it that the 'few' who 'can touch you' really know about the Prince: that he has a solid knowledge of political reality (if so then might there not have been a more solid way of saying this?); or that he is a fraud, a trickster? Or, more speculatively, that his body is the only substantial thing about him? It is odd that such an image inviting speculation should be used at the moment when Machiavelli is once again winding up a chapter, offering clarificatory generalisations, and seemingly on the verge of setting the private 'reality' of the Prince's identity against the illusory world of public theatre and public appearance.

Machiavelli thus raises speculation and doubt despite himself – 'it seems to me better to concentrate on what really happens than on theories and speculations' (chapter XV, p. 54). The advice to cultivate appearances, for example, is glib. Opportunities (akin to today's photo-opportunity) to look good can, it seems, be planned – and written about – with the same efficiency as the military campaign. Yet even as Machiavelli sets about simplifying the art of image-making ('A ruler, then, should be very careful that everything he says is replete with

the five above-named qualities', chapter XVIII, p. 62), there is
a keen sense of the text leaving unresolved problems, questions
and enigmas in its wake. The text's linear movement, its neat
formulation of one rule after another, is impeded. Moral questions persist despite the text's attempt to dissipate them; so, too,
does speculation about the kind of world inhabited and
presided over by the Prince. Amongst the consequences of the
text's insistent use of the language of role-playing, for example, is the emergence of a stark emotional landscape for the
Prince, one in which he continually observes himself, sees
everything in terms of strategy and carefully measures the
effects of performances. The cost of such calculative behaviour
is not explicitly discussed by Machiavelli, for the kind of practice to which he is trying to reduce politics will not allow him
to. The austerity of the Machiavellian world is sometimes all
the more noticeable because of this.

A similarly sparse emotional world is described in chapter XVII
on 'Cruelty and mercifulness; and whether it is better to be
loved or feared' (p. 58). Again the advisory mode is glib; love
and fear are spoken of dispassionately, in the same voice as the
military man speaks of military tactics. Love and fear may be
of use to the Prince and it is the text's task to point to their
uses. At no point is the problem of such a disengaged attitude
to love and fear registered as a problem:

> A controversy has arisen about this: whether it is better to be
> loved than feared, or vice versa. My view is that it is desirable
> to be both loved and feared; but it is difficult to achieve both and
> if one of them has to be lacking, it is much safer to be feared than
> loved.   chapter XVII, p. 59

Fear is preferable to love because it is a more efficient tactic, a
surer means of maintaining support: 'fear is sustained by a
dread of punishment that is always effective' (p. 59). As
William Kerrigan and Gordon Braden have suggested, love is
'an inferior bond' in Machiavelli 'because it so difficult to exact,
and the Prince's emotional universe is kept systematically bleak
by his rigorous calculus of power: I can make you fear me much
more reliably than I can make you love me'.[19] Yet despite, or
perhaps in this case because of, Machiavelli's spare, methodical

approach to the topic, we are again drawn to speculate about the problematic psychic and moral issues which Machiavelli's streamlined version of political practice is attempting to exclude in order to constitute itself as such. To think of love and fear only in these strategic terms is perhaps to put too high a price on effective politics.

Likewise the agenda set by Machiavelli for his multiple-role-playing Prince seems impossibly exacting. Since power in Machiavelli is not a single dominative force but pluralised across numerous different stages and settings, there are too many, potentially conflicting, roles for the Prince to play, too many situations for him to control. Even that exemplary figure 'whom I never hesitate to cite' (chapter XIII, p. 49), Cesare Borgia, is finally a casualty of unforeseen, probably unforeseeable, circumstances. Having 'used every means and having done all those things that a far-seeing and able man should do' (chapter VII, p. 23) to maintain his acquired territories, Borgia's total mastery of circumstance is impeded by 'two things': 'the shortness of Alexander's [his father's] pontificate and his own illness' (chapter VII, p. 28). After all of Borgia's effort, scheming and 'necessary' cruelty, there is still a recalcitrance about circumstances which Borgia cannot subdue. If we remove those controls which encourage us to find in this story an (almost) exemplary Machiavellian career and a clear agenda for a practical politics, it is difficult not to read the account of Borgia's life as a 'sick' joke. Is power really worth all the effort required to acquire and maintain it? Is it worth all the alienation of self into tactical role-playing, and calculated performance?

It is noticeable that at the end of the story of Borgia, a personal or inter-personal note is sounded:

> Everything would have been easy for him, if he had been well when Alexander died. And he told me himself, on the day Julius II was elected, that he had thought about what might happen when his father died, and had provided against everything, except that he had never thought that, when his father was dying, he too would be at death's door. chapter VII, p. 28

With Machiavelli's more usual presentation of the self as role-player, each temporarily adopted persona becomes totally extrinsic to the self that manipulates them; there is no question of persona impinging on personality. Similarly, other people are objectified through their assignment to predictable roles. The eruption above into this emotionless, rigorously controlled regime of an unplanned, unscheduled event seems to me to expose, momentarily, a different order of subjectivity: having a conversation with another person with no regard for strategy or for the advantage to be gained is something of a novelty for the Machiavellian ruler.

The Borgia story is not, then, simply illustrative. There are more ways of reading the story, and the lesson it teaches, than Machiavelli himself appears to allow for when he innocently suggests that Borgia 'seems to me worthy to be held up as a model' (chapter VII, p. 28). In particular, the question of what kind of model Borgia provides is highlighted in the account of Borgia's use of the 'cruel and energetic' Remirro de Orco to 'introduce efficient government' (p. 26) in Romagna. The account ends with the following description of the public spectacle Borgia finally made of Remirro to absolve himself, Borgia, of all responsibility for the recent cruelties:

> availing himself of an appropriate opportunity, one morning the Duke had Remirro placed in two pieces in the square at Cesena, with a block of wood and a blood-stained sword at his side. This terrible spectacle left the people both satisfied and amazed.
>
> chapter VII, p. 26

In the dedicatory letter, Machiavelli says that speculation will form no part of the text's 'realist' project. The point I have been drawing from this is that the reader will not need to deliberate over or speculate about the use of the text. The advice it offers will be of immediate value. So how are we to read the above account of Remirro's execution? Is Machiavelli merely handing on this example of a brutal publicity stunt as yet another possible strategy? Is Borgia's act to be unproblematically imitated in a similar situation? Is it 'ready', if not for instant, then for prudent (re)use?

It seems unlikely, given Machiavelli's careful intensification of graphic detail ('the Duke had Remirro placed in two pieces …'), that this kind of writing is not intended to stir or shock, or to invite speculation as to the narrator's point of view. And it is difficult to move immediately on from this account in the way that the next sentence encourages us to, 'But let me continue from where I left off' (p. 26), without pausing to consider what precept to attach to this particular episode in Borgia's career. The attempt to effect a smooth transition in any case only draws attention to the interruption caused by the Borgia/Remirro tale. It is as if the 'Machiavelli' who likes to shock enjoys citing Borgia because he knows Borgia's transgressive career will be difficult to normalise or naturalise as part of any official agenda or ideology. What self-respecting state would care to admit as its model men like Borgia?

Although Machiavelli makes Borgia look respectable in the career synopsis he gives at the end of chapter VII, there is no simple one-to-one correspondence between the example and the lesson to be drawn from the example. Borgia's life will not deliver a monolithic message about the need for a practical politics. Cynical manipulation, wasted effort, prudent statesmanship, brutality masquerading as prudent statesmanship, heroic mastery of circumstance, and an abhorrent egoism can all be read into Borgia's career. Borgia might easily have found his way into the next chapter, 'Those who become rulers through wicked means' (chapter VIII, p. 30).

Conversely, the career of Oliverotto, which is recounted there, might with some slight changes of emphasis have replaced Borgia's.[20] Instead of functioning as solid, experiential proofs, there is an arbitrariness about Machiavelli's use of examples; and no amount of rational calculation by Machiavelli of the extent to which 'cruel deeds are committed well or badly' (chapter VIII, p. 33) can erase the sense of arbitrariness or totally 'desubjectivise' the issue of the use of necessary brutality. Neither can the reified categories and distinctions, which are used to assign characters to one or another illustrative narrative, subdue the feeling that Machiavelli's stories are interpretable in a number of different ways.

The consideration of such 'literary' devices as narrative point of view, the use of story and example and so on is also at odds with one of the stated aims of the book which is to expunge the 'literary', to remove 'politics' from the realm of speculation and interpretation. In this sense *The Prince* is a failure. There is too much going on in the text for it to be straightforwardly effective. In the case of each of the interweaving textual and ideological strands of *The Prince* discussed – the emphasis upon a definite use and reader for the text, the realist approach to statecraft, the methodical treatment of topics, the use of examples and citations – the possibility of a double perspective, or of a 'return' of the excluded, undermines the text's aspirations towards the systematic clarification of politics.

What it means to practise the art of politics therefore remains an open question. Politics is at once theatre (itself a divided image), specialised art, rationalized business, cynical game, and in the concluding 'Exhortation to liberate Italy from the barbarian yoke' (chapter XXVI) it is re-aligned with a form of idealism. Seen in 'literary' terms, Machiavelli is not so much the author of a canonical text on politics as an 'unreliable narrator', on the one hand retaining a moral perspective by exposing the seamy side of statecraft and, on the other, freeing the practically minded statesman from the need to worry about moral questions. It is equally difficult to determine the kind of application, particular or general, which Machiavelli imagines for his text, and the view of politics which arises from these different levels of application. Written out of and for a particular set of circumstances, *The Prince* constructs politics as the art of pragmatism; attempting to make the best of a (temporarily) bad situation, the politician is as virtuous as the times allow him to be. In the culminating vision of a strong, independent nation-state, he is also elevated to the position of redeemer of the times. On the other hand, in his desire to formulate general rules and principles, Machiavelli's view of politics lays claim to universality and timelessness. The world of politics is a mirror of the larger, irredeemably fallen world of 'man': 'For this may be said of men generally: they are ungrateful, fickle, feigners and dissemblers, avoiders of danger, eager for gain' (chapter XVII, p. 59). 'Men' therefore get the politicians they deserve.

Although in recent years the meaning of the word politics has extended into sexual, personal and everyday contexts, a dominant meaning still persists: politics is a distinct, specialised field, the domain not of the ordinary citizen or of everyday life but of the professional politician.[21] While it is possible to see in

Machiavelli the precursory signs of a specialisation of politics from which literary, emotive and ethical languages have been expunged, it is equally possible to see politics as a site of contestation in *The Prince*. Refusing to be of immediate use-value to the practising politician through the separation of practice from theory and speculation, *The Prince* is not, and was not, definable solely as a form of apparatus-writing, which helps to create politics as an autonomous institution, profession, science or technique. In the end it gives the lie to its own compartmentalisations and reductions, and renders problematic any single appropriation of a practical politics.

Notes

I am extremely grateful to Martin Coyle and Debbie Mousley for their encouragement, advice and comments in the drafts of this essay.

1 Margaret Scott, 'Machiavelli and the Machiavel', *Renaissance Drama*, new series, 15 (1984), pp. 147–74 (pp. 157–8).

2 Edmond Beame, 'The Use and Abuse of Machiavelli: The Sixteenth-century French Adaptation', *Journal of the History of Ideas*, 43 (1982), pp. 32–54 (pp. 33–4).

3 For further discussion of the widely held view of Machiavelli as founding figure, see Robert Hariman, 'Composing Modernity in Machiavelli's *Prince*', *Journal of the History of Ideas*, 50 (1989), pp. 3–29 (p. 3); and Maurizio Viroli, 'Machiavelli and the Republican Idea of Politics', in Gisela Bock, Quentin Skinner and Maurizio Viroli (eds), *Machiavelli and Republicanism* (Cambridge University Press, 1990), pp. 143–71 (pp. 143–5). On the diversity of sixteenth- and seventeenth-century readings of Machiavelli, see Beame, 'The Use and Abuse of Machiavelli'; and Peter Donaldson, *Machiavelli and Mystery of State* (Cambridge: Cambridge University Press, 1988).

4 J. N. Stephens, 'Ciceronian Rhetoric and the Immorality of Machiavelli's *Prince*', *Renaissance Studies*, 2 (1988), pp. 258–67 (p. 261).

5 Raymond Williams, *Marxism and Literature* (Oxford: Oxford University Press, 1985; first published 1977), p. 126.

6 Niccolò Machiavelli, *The Prince*, ed. Quentin Skinner and Russell Price (Cambridge: Cambridge University Press, 1990; first published 1988), p. 4. Further references are given within the text.

7 Desiderius Erasmus, *Apophthegmes*, translated by Nicholas Udall (Amsterdam: Theatrum Orbis Terrarum, 1969; first published London, 1542), p. 29 of Erasmus' preface 'unto a dukes soone of his countree'.

8 For further discussion of humanist concepts of method, see Victoria

Kahn, 'Humanism and the Resistance to Theory' in Patricia Parker and David Quint (eds), *Literary Theory/Renaissance Texts* (Baltimore: Johns Hopkins University Press, 1986), pp. 372–96; and Walter Ong, *Ramus, Method, and the Decay of Dialogue* (Cambridge, Mass.: Harvard University Press, 1983; first published 1958).

9 For further discussion of politics understood as 'verbum' as opposed to 'res', see Robert Hariman, 'Composing Modernity'. According to Hariman, Machiavelli 'marks the transition from politics understood as a text to the modern understanding of a political text as something awaiting realization in the material world' (p. 3).

10 It is Machiavelli's emphasis on military strength which, according to Quentin Skinner, differentiates him from earlier humanists. See Quentin Skinner, 'Political Philosophy' in Eckhard Kessler and Quentin Skinner (eds), *The Cambridge History of Renaissance Philosophy* (Cambridge: Cambridge University Press, 1988), pp. 389–452 (p. 432).

11 In post-Saussurean literary theory, the (grammatical) term 'subject' is preferred to the terms 'self' or 'individual' as a way of countering the notion that our sense of ourselves as individuals precedes or transcends language. It seems to me that the subjectivity of the Prince is at once 'centred' and 'de-centred' by Machiavelli, rendered simultaneously transcendent and non-transcendent: if the continual refashioning of identity according to changing circumstances and discourses is the key to autonomy and independence, it is also the way to protean mutability and self-division.

12 John Donne, 'Satire 1', in *The Complete English Poems*, edited by A. J. Smith (Harmondsworth: Penguin, 1984; first published 1971), p. 155.

13 Thomas Greene, 'The End of Discourse in Machiavelli's *Prince*' in Parker and Quint (eds), *Literary Theory*, pp. 63–77 (p. 64). Greene's insights into *The Prince*, particularly into its attempt to repudiate rhetoric in favour of 'the curt distinctions of a new, embracing political science' (p. 64), form the basis of my own discussion of Machiavelli's realist, programmatic approach to politics.

14 See the similar point made by Greene, 'The End of Discourse'. The reader, he suggests, is 'down on the ground of history, watching the author clear away limited areas of general truth, moving not inward from universal principles but outward from concrete events' (p. 64).

15 J. G. A. Pocock, *The Machiavellian Moment* (Princeton: Princeton University Press, 1975), p. 163. See also Pocock's discussion of innovation, pp. 159–64 and *passim*.

16 *The Machiavellian Moment*, p. 53.

17 *The Machiavellian Moment*, p. 53.

18 Stephen Greenblatt, *Renaissance Self-Fashioning* (Chicago: University of Chicago Press, 1984; first published 1980), p. 162.

19 Gordon Braden and William Kerrigan, *The Idea of the Renaissance*

(Baltimore: Johns Hopkins University Press, 1989), p. 57. Braden and Kerrigan also discuss theatricality in *The Prince*.

20 A similar point is made by Braden and Kerrigan, *The Idea of the Renaissance*, pp. 59–60.

21 For an interesting discussion of the distance of modern politics from everyday life, see Bernard Sharratt, 'In Whose Voice? The Drama of Raymond Williams', in Terry Eagleton (ed.), *Raymond Williams: Critical Perspectives* (Cambridge: Polity Press, 1989), pp. 130–49.

8

Machiavelli's political philosophy in *The Prince*

MAUREEN RAMSAY

Trying to place Machiavelli's *The Prince* in the history of political thought involves confronting a bewildering array of conflicting interpretations of his political views.[1] This can be all the more perplexing when what is initially striking about *The Prince* is its brevity, clarity and, though intense and dynamic, its *ad hoc* nature, its lack of philosophical rigour. Although there are those who imply the opposite, by claiming that Machiavelli was the founder of political science, it is now generally agreed that he was not a systematic, analytic political thinker. His methodology was consistent only in so far as it yielded a number of artistic, intuitive generalisations made by reflection on personal experience and observation, and supplemented by the inaccurate and selective use of historical evidence. As Isaiah Berlin writes:

> Machiavelli's theories are certainly not based on the scientific principles of the seventeenth century. He lived a hundred years before Galileo and Bacon, and his method is a mixture of rules of thumb, observation, historical knowledge and general sagacity, somewhat like the empirical medicine of the pre-scientific world. He abounds in precepts, in useful maxims, practical hints, scattered reflections, especially historical parallels, even though he claims to have discovered general laws, especially *regole general*.[2]

The fact that Machiavelli bases his conclusions on observation and experience is not sufficient to describe him as a political scientist. His methodology was not systematic or intellectually coherent enough to be afforded such a title, but it would not be seriously misleading to see in Machiavelli an embryonic form of more modern methods of political analysis. Machiavelli certainly saw himself as an innovator, radically breaking with medieval and ancient thought and with its theological and meta-physical underpinnings. In chapter XV he defiantly announces that in departing from 'the methods of others' he is blazing a new trail of philosophical analysis in order to reach the truth of practical politics.[3] This new approach aims to apply directly to the problems of the real world. His purpose is to 'write some-thing useful to him who comprehends it'. For this reason he writes that 'I have decided that I must concern myself with the truth of the matter as facts show it rather than with any fanci-ful notion' (chapter XV, p. 100). Machiavelli claimed the novelty of his work lay in talking about 'man' and the state as they exist in reality, as they are, not as they ought to be. And it is the content of these observations and conclusions deduced from the way in which 'men' actually behave that have led to the rival interpretations on the significance of their import.

The political reality described by Machiavelli helped foster the idea in popular imagination that he was the author of the doctrine that 'the end justifies the means'. Although Machiavelli never articulates his descriptions or prescriptions in this formulation, the means–end relationship and the rela-tionship between politics and morality are the central issues which have inspired most interest in his political philosophy.

If any means can justify any end, then it is not difficult to see why many writers from Machiavelli's own time onwards have castigated him variously as a man inspired by the devil, as an immoral writer and a teacher of evil. This was the view of most of the Elizabethan dramatists and was shared by Cardinal Pole, Bodin and Frederick the Great. In recent times it has been re-stated by Jacques Maritain[4] and Leo Strauss.[5] For other commentators, however, assessment of the Machiavellian dictum is tempered by consideration of the morality or desir-ability of the end to be justified. These have been held to be those of a passionate patriot, a democrat and a believer in liberty. According to Spinoza[6] and Rousseau[7] it is this fact that makes *The Prince* not an immoral work, but a satire on princes written to forearm and forewarn the people on what rulers actually did and could do.

For commentators following Croce[8] it is precisely the applicability of the doctrine that 'the end justifies the means' which marks Machiavelli's greatest contribution to a philosophy of politics. It was he who recognised the 'autonomy of politics'. Such a doctrine is appropriate and necessary to the realm of politics where evaluations of actions must be made without reference to extra-political or moral factors. Ends–means considerations are especially relevant to the political sphere in its proper concern with the interests of the state. Chabod holds that Machiavelli 'swept aside every criterion of action not suggested by the concept of raison d'état'.[9] Meinecke portrayed Machiavelli as the founding father of this concept in his discovery of the element of necessity in political conduct and the irrelevance of private morality in political affairs.[10]

Other writers have taken a slightly different approach and have seen Machiavelli's portrayal of means and the ends they were designed to achieve as accurate descriptions of the political practice of his own time and of ours, and as key insights into the nature and realities of political power.[11] The means–end dichotomy has also been interpreted not as justificatory or descriptive but as a hypothetical, technical imperative of the form – if you want X, do Y. It is neither moral nor amoral. The ends themselves are not justified as rational or good, the means to achieve them are neither praised nor blamed. They are advocated only as what is necessary to achieve the end in question. Thus Machiavelli is ethically neutral and politically uncommitted.[12] Since this technical imperative can apply to a variety of political actors – princes, tyrants, democrats, republicans – it follows that it can be put to the service of many ideologies in justifying or achieving a variety of ends – liberatory, revolutionary, democratic, nationalistic or despotic.

The purpose of this chapter is to attempt to clarify Machiavelli's position on the means–end relationship and the relationship between politics and morality. In particular the chapter will examine the originality and uniqueness of Machiavelli's views in relation to past and present political and ethical thought, and argue that, despite their notoriety, his ideas and their attendant problems are a common feature both of political thought and practice and also of personal and political life.

Ends and means, politics and morality

Whether or not Machiavelli conceived of the means–end relationship as justificatory, as descriptive or as a technical imperative is a matter of dispute. In a sense, his glaring illustration that there is no escape from the weight of means and ends combines all three aspects of the relationship. This is because this is the way people do behave: people constantly act as though the end justifies the means, and, without judging any particular end to be good or bad, practical necessity dictates that certain means will be required to achieve them. Whether there are some means so evil that they should never be used, or whether there are some ends so good that they justify any means, is a separate question, but not one Machiavelli avoided. In fact, it is precisely his testament to these permanent questions that generates interest in Machiavelli.

For Machiavelli, the ends of political life were the acquiring and holding down of power, the stability of the state, the maintenance of order and general prosperity. To say that Machiavelli was a scientist or a technician of political life because he was not concerned with whether such ends were rational or good is to overstate the case.[13] He never explicitly justified these ends, but simply accepted them as given, because he assumed that order and security were universal ends that all human beings aspire to, and that these were necessary for human welfare. If this is so, then it is plausible to see Machiavelli as implicitly concerned with ends, the moral purpose of which is to secure the good for human beings, given what he took to be in human interests and the context of human desires. However, if the ends of order and stability are to be achieved, what means are morally permissible as well as practically expedient?

Machiavelli was not concerned to define moral rules and explain why they should be obeyed, or to define the rights, duties and obligations of princes or citizens. Rather he was concerned in *The Prince* with those qualities (capacities and dispositions) rulers must have to establish, restore or maintain

order and stability. These qualities were psychological and
social rather than traditional moral traits. In chapter XV he lists
some of the qualities that normally bring praise or blame and
admits that it would be praiseworthy for a prince to exhibit
those qualities which are considered good. Machiavelli here is
not denying that liberality, mercy, honesty, kindness, chastity,
reliability and tolerance are virtues. He is, though, drawing
attention to the fact that no ruler can possess or fully practise
them because the realities of the human condition dictate
behaviour which by normal standards would be condemned as
immoral. The irony of the political situation is such that 'when
we carefully examine the whole matter, we find some qualities
that look like virtues, yet if the prince practises them – they
will be his destruction, and other qualities that look like vices,
yet – if he practises them – they will bring him safety and well-
being' (chapter XV, p. 101). Chapters XVI–XVIII illustrate in
detail this point, that morally good human actions can lead to
evil results, and immoral actions may have beneficial consequences. The classical virtue of liberality is considered to be a
good, yet the consistent practice of it can be damaging. A
liberal prince may use up all his resources and be forced in the
end to tax his people excessively and so make him hateful to
his subjects. His liberality injures the many and rewards the few
as well as bringing ruin to himself. Whereas if a prince is mean
initially, he will have enough income to carry out his enterprises
without harming the people or becoming extortionate. Similarly
with cruelty and mercy. In chapter XVII, Machiavelli writes:

> Cesare Borgia was thought cruel; nevertheless that well-known
> cruelty of his reorganised the Romagna, united it, brought it to
> peace and loyalty. If we look at this closely, we see that he was
> more merciful than the Florentine people, who, to escape being
> called cruel, allowed the ruin of Pistoia. A wise prince, then, is
> not troubled about a reproach for cruelty which keeps his
> subjects united and loyal because, giving a very few examples of
> cruelty, he is more merciful than those who, through too much
> mercy, let evils continue, from which result murder or plunder,
> because the latter commonly harm a whole group, but those
> executions that come from the prince harm individuals only.
>
> p. 104

Here Machiavelli is making three points. First, as in the case of liberality, he is not denying that mercy is a virtue. Just as in order to be liberal the Prince might have first to be mean, so in order to be merciful the Prince might have to be cruel. What is valued here is still the traditional virtue. Second, the selective use of cruelty can bring about the benefits of unity, peace and loyalty, whereas too much mercy can lead to ruin. This is not simply an appeal to the good consequences cruelty might promote *per se*, but a recognition that well-intentioned failure to act may have consequences far more cruel than the original inaction was designed to avoid. Where omissions have worse consequences, then cruelty is the preferable course of action. The aim is to avoid cruelty, not to promote it. This is obvious in the third point, that the lesser evil consists in harm to individuals rather than to a whole group. In political situations where choices between two evils have to be made, it is more morally responsible to act to choose the lesser evil. Machiavelli is not just simply saying that good ends outweigh immoral means; that moral squeamishness in abstaining from immoral means does not absolve responsibility for the bad consequences which result from omissions; or that in some situations the best course of action is that which avoids the worst excesses of violence and cruelty; or even that the Prince cannot conform to conventional moral standards if the interests of the state or the common good are to be preserved. He is also saying that sometimes, in employing immoral means, the Prince will be closer to displaying the virtues of conventional morality than those who, by embodying these virtues, achieve the opposite. The quality of mercy might be cruelty in disguise – we may have to be cruel in order to be kind.

Machiavelli does not disregard conventional morality as such. He exhorts his Prince to act according to the accepted virtues of truth, charity, humanity and religion when he can. That is, when the political situation is stable and secure. In these circumstances public and conventional morality are identical. However, the Prince must be adaptable and 'have a mind ready to turn in any direction as Fortune's winds and the variety of affairs require yet, … he holds to what is right when he can and knows how to do wrong when he must' (chapter XVIII,

p. 108). This is because politics poses questions for which conventional morality is inappropriate. In times of necessity the Prince must be unconstrained by normal ethical ideals and adopt methods which, though contrary to these ideas, will lead to beneficial consequences. Here there seems to be a split between private and public morality, so that, in certain circumstances, the latter has its own distinctive ethic.

However, there are passages where Machiavelli seems to indicate that the distinction he is making is not between private and public morality itself but rather between conventional morality and what people actually do in both the public and the private sphere. This is seen in his comments on human nature and human behaviour. These suggest it is partly because people do not act according to the dictates of conventional morality in the daily business of their lives that the Prince must behave in a similar fashion. In chapter XVIII, for instance, he argues for the breaking of promises on two grounds. The first is with reference to a consequentialist ethic, for experience shows that princes who do break their promises have done great things. The second is with reference to the corrupt nature and behaviour of human beings in general. A prudent prince cannot keep his word, first, when it works against him and, second, 'when the reasons that made him promise are annulled. If all men were good, this maxim would not be good, but because they are bad and do not keep their promises to you, you likewise do not have to keep yours to them' (chapter XVIII, p. 107). Here, the Prince is not to act as he ought, according to abstract, conventional virtues, but as other people act. Similarly, when discussing cruelty and mercy, and whether it is better to be loved than feared, Machiavelli advises it is safer to be feared, given the nature of human beings:

> Because we can say this about men in general: they are ungrateful, changeable, simulators and dissimulators, runaways in danger, eager for gain; they offer you their blood, their property, their lives, their children ... when need is far off; but when it comes near you, they turn about. A prince who bases himself entirely on their words, if he is lacking other preparations, fails; because friendships gained with money, not with greatness and nobility of spirit are purchased but not possessed, and at the right

times cannot be turned to account. Men have less hesitation in injuring one who makes himself loved than one who makes himself feared, for love is held by a chain of duty which, since men are bad, they break at every chance for their own profit; but fear is held by a dread of punishment that never fails you.

chapter XVII, pp.104-5

'Men' in general do not exhibit the qualities of conventional morality. The Prince can deceive because he 'always finds men who let themselves be deceived' (chapter XVIII, p. 107). The Prince need only appear to have the conventional virtues of mercy, faith, integrity and religion 'because in general men judge more with their eyes than with their heads, since everybody can see but few can perceive' (chapter XVIII, p. 109). It seems, too, that the Prince must adopt a consequentialist ethic because it is the case that 'as to the actions of all men and especially those of princes, against whom charges cannot be brought in court, everyone looks at their result' (chapter XVIII, p. 109).

In order to bring about beneficial results the Prince must cultivate not conventional virtue but Machiavellian *virtù*. There is much scholarly dispute as to whether Machiavelli attached a precise or consistent meaning to *virtù*. Russell Price has shown that Machiavelli used *virtù* as a complex cluster concept which includes traditional, Christian moral virtue, military *virtù*, political *virtù*, a combination of military and political *virtù*, an instrumental *virtù*, cultural virtue as well as ancient and modern *virtù*.[14] It is clear, though, that princely *virtù* for Machiavelli was a consistent concept in so far as it embodied those qualities, capacities and dispositions necessary for the Prince to establish, restore or maintain the stability of the state, to win honour and glory for himself and to overcome the blows of fortune.[15] The quality of *virtù* is displayed in a mode of conduct which Geerken argues underlies the plurality of meanings and has three components: '(a) suitability to prevailing circumstances, (b) adequate deliberation regarding options, priorities and consequences, and, finally, (c) timely and successful action'.[16]

Virtù, then, will consist of different qualities at different times given what is necessary to attain goals in particular circumstances. Qualities which manifest *virtù* include fortitude in adversity, foresight and insight, willingness to take risks, resourcefulness and firmness of purpose. The qualities of *virtù* can be displayed in evil actions as well as good. Hence Machiavelli's admiration for Cesare Borgia who, though cruel, was an exemplar of these qualities.

However, Machiavelli did not admire all actions simply because they were bold, resolute and effective. When discussing Agothocles, the tyrant of Sicily, in chapter VIII he makes the distinction between cruelty 'well' and 'ill' used . 'Well-used' cruelties are those that are necessary and constructive, those which a conqueror must carry out and 'then does not persist in' and which he then 'transmutes into the greatest possible benefit to his subjects' (chapter VIII, p. 82). 'Ill-used' cruelties are those which persist with time and which are unnecessary and destructive. Agothocles showed fortitude in adversity and was bold, resolute and resourceful, but his 'outrageous cruelty and inhumanity together with his countless wicked acts do not permit him to be honoured among the noblest men'. Acting in this manner may bring success and 'sovereignty but not glory' (chapter VIII, p. 81). The difference between the deeds of Agothocles and Borgia was that if Borgia had succeeded his deeds would have resulted in a strong state and so the common good (whether or not the latter was his intention). Agothocles' deeds involved uneconomic and gratuitous cruelty and led to a worse state of affairs than before. Machiavelli is reluctant to admit that Agothocles' deeds were worthy of the name *virtù*. *Virtù* is ascribed to actions consistent with the acquisition of glory, when dictated through necessity and where they serve common interests and the needs of the public realm.

When evaluating the relationship between means and ends and between politics and morality in *The Prince*, it is necessary to see the problematic against the backdrop of Machiavelli's pessimistic assumptions about the timeless and unchanging nature of human motives and aspirations. Machiavelli's view of human beings as natural egotists with a lust for domination and power led him to see history as an arena of conflict involving deceit, treachery and violence. The roots of this conflict were psychological, but the solution was social and political. The ends of political life were to achieve the order and stability necessary to secure the fundamental human desires of self-preservation and security. Therefore political morality must be one designed to achieve these ends. Conventional morality in many circumstances is inappropriate and seems to defeat these purposes. This is because the consistent practice of traditional virtues may lead to outcomes which are not virtuous, even according to that tradition's own standard, and because observing these virtues may not lead to good consequences. Conventionally immoral actions may bring beneficial results, whereas an action done for a good motive or a well-intentioned inaction may have bad or worse consequences than the supposed immoral action. Failing to act for reasons of moral purity does not lessen the responsibility for bad consequences which result from the omission. At certain political conjunctions, it is morally necessary to employ evil means to achieve the desired result. This is not because conventional virtues are not good in themselves or desirable for both public and private practices but because people are not by nature good and do not live according to these abstract virtues in either the public or the private sphere. In order for people to live according to the virtues, certain conditions of political security and stability must pertain. When this is the case moral questions can be raised and moral virtues can be pursued within the accepted values of the established and stable community. When this is not the case, conventionally immoral actions are necessary to establish the conditions for morality and what is politically and ultimately personally valuable depends on prudential calculation. Here conventional values are questioned against the criteria of human interests and desires and the result is a consequentialist ethic. An effective political morality must be one designed for human beings as they are, in the circumstances they find themselves in, in order to create a situation where human beings will be fit for morality.

Originality and uniqueness of Machiavelli's views

Precursors

The question arises as to how far Machiavelli's views on the relationship between ends and means, morality and politics is all that unique to either past or present political thought. Since ancient times political writers had been concerned with princes and princedoms. In the princely literature from the Middle Ages to the Renaissance, political theorists compiled a list of cardinal and princely virtues which it was the duty of a good ruler to acquire. The prince, like his subjects, was advised to be liberal, generous, merciful, truthful, kind, chaste, reliable, tolerant and devout. It was assumed that it was rational to act morally; that public virtue was identical to private virtue; that ethics and politics were interrelated and inseparable. Since these abstract virtues were delineated and endorsed without reference to the social or political context in which they were to be cultivated, Machiavelli complained that such advice applied to perfect princes living in perfect states, neither of which exists in reality. Machiavelli's unique contribution to princely literature was his discussion of actual political situations with the aim of formulating rules for political conduct useful for those who govern the state. As we have seen, in chapters XV to XIX he forcefully overturns the idealised conception of the virtues found in traditional humanist catalogues. He begins by tacitly agreeing that it would be admirable for the Prince to have such virtues, and that in times of stability their practice was possible. However, he shows that necessity forces rulers to commit deeds which are not by conventional standards moral. In this he rejects the humanist conception that moral means achieve desirable ends. In order to attain the ends of political life, it cannot be rational to adopt moral means when this will defeat ultimate purposes. Practical rationality demands that the Prince must act according to necessity, regardless of abstract moral imperatives. In real life, force of circumstances are such that political morality must be divorced from conventional morality and from what would be desirable in private moral behaviour.

Although earlier writers did not directly anticipate Machiavelli's views, all but the most naive and utopian could not help but be aware of the moral problems and the element of expediency involved in successful political action. Sidney Anglo has argued:

That Machiavelli has come to be particularly identified with the divorce of politics from private morality, with the doctrine of expediency in political actions, and with the mode of justifying all political means on grounds of reasons of state, is less due to his uniqueness than to the dynamic way in which he expressed these ideas.[17]

Other writers have shown that the kind of issues Machiavelli's political theory raises had been aired at least since the time of Aristotle and were raised more explicitly in the princely literature of the fifteenth-century Italian humanists.[18] In chapter III of *The Politics*, Aristotle describes how the problem of immoral means necessary for political survival concerns all forms of government, whether or not they adopt such policies to further their own interests or for the common good.[19] Here there is a clear awareness of the realities of political action and a suggestion that there may be different moral criteria for judging public and private affairs. In the same chapter Aristotle writes that 'the virtues of the good citizen and the virtue of the good man cannot be always the same, although in some cases (i.e. in the perfect state) they may'.[20] Aquinas in his *Commentary on Politics* took this directly to mean that 'it follows, therefore, that the virtue of the good citizen and the good man are not the same'.[21] Aristotle and his followers, in their accounts of the means used by tyrants to maintain their position, outlined the methods Machiavelli took to be essential, not just for the tyrant but also for the Prince. So, for example, in the fifth book of *The Politics*, the tyrant, like Machiavelli's prince, is advised to cultivate a reputation for the virtues, to appear to be religious, and to produce the impression that he acts in the character of a statesman if he wishes to maintain his power to rule.[22]

The political realism reflected in the internal and external affairs of the medieval state highlighted the problem of justification. This had not escaped the notice of medieval theologians and legal theorists who had frequently used the notion 'necessity has no laws' to justify extraordinary means in exceptional circumstances. The problem was accentuated by the changing politics of Europe and demonstrated in the practices of emerging states, if only because they were more powerful. It was acknowledged by the fifteenth-century Italian humanists, whom

Gilbert views as forerunners to the more explicit formulations of the problem by Machiavelli. These writers, though they endorsed the traditional princely virtues, recognised that beneficial political consequences may necessitate or excuse immoral means. Gilbert quotes Pontano:

> It is the act of a wise man, when two ills are put before him, always to choose the smaller one. Hence it is permissible, for the sake of the State and of a king who is father of his people sometimes to tell falsehoods; though when time and circumstance require silence about the truth, especially when the safety of the king, the kingdom, and the fatherland is in question, he who prudently keeps still certainly does not seem to be a liar. Or if he uses deception he does not seem straight away to be a liar, since he acts like a prudent man who balances utilities and necessity with the true and the false.[23]

Other writers, too, had indicated that the standard of public utility was at stake when the breaking of promises was permissible. Platina allows for breaches of faith in abandoning foreign treaties when the interests of the native subjects are threatened by common enemies or the threat of war. He suggests that in these circumstances even the private citizens commit no fraud if they breach agreements.[24] Patricius implies the public interest when he commends those times when a ruler must simulate and dissimulate. The Prince must not appear gloomy and morose because this makes his subjects anxious. Since it would be disastrous to let the subjects know of some impending disaster, for the ruler 'it is proper that by simulation and dissimulation he should often show the contrary to the truth'.[25] The importance of the ruler appearing to preserve religious and other virtues had been recognised by Aristotle. Egidio, Beroaldus and Campanus, too, demonstrated the necessity of simulating the appearance of being good to win the respect and admiration of the people.[26] When a ruler could not be loved because of the unpopular measures he imposed, Carafa advises that, to avoid being hated, the ruler should make it clear to his subjects that 'necessity and not desire, induces you to do it'.[27]

Therefore, within the political and theoretical context in which Machiavelli wrote, there already existed an awareness of expediency when faced with political realities. But for earlier writers these questions usually had been touched upon with reference to extraordinary situations and they had never fully articulated a specific doctrine, justificatory, explanatory or descriptive of political necessity and morality. For Machiavelli, expediency was not just a feature of abnormal situations but was generally the norm of political activity, given the nature of human beings and the uncertainty which prevailed in human affairs. In order to ensure the good life for human beings a stable, political order was required. To the realisation of this end, and with it the very possibility of the merging of morality and politics, the practice of traditional moral virtues was obsolete.

Machiavelli is unique, then, in that he took the suggestions, hesitations and implications in other political thinkers' advice to princes to their logical and most extreme conclusion. He shamelessly and powerfully 'blurted out' what they had whispered and what any reflecting person must have known, but did not dare or care to admit.

Other traditions in political and ethical thought

If Machiavelli was the first political theorist explicitly to endorse a prudential and consequentialist ethic based on beliefs about human nature and society, he certainly was not the last. Two dominant traditions in the history of both political and ethical thought take on board, albeit in more sophisticated form, certain features of Machiavelli's assumptions and conclusions.

Aspects of Machiavelli's ideas pave the way for the rise of liberal thought which opens up with the development of capitalism and which begins in a systematic, theoretical form with Hobbes. In this tradition, the abstract pre-social individual is the most fundamental and important social unit, while power and stability are the ultimate goals of social and political life. For Machiavelli, and the liberal tradition, the individual stands apart from society. Society is the backdrop against which individuals separated from their social relationships and roles act to achieve their own ends. Human beings, their motives and aspirations are defined independently of the specific social context in which these are formulated and experienced. They are essentially the same at all times and places because they are motivated by the same insatiable passions. Human beings are

self-assertive, self-preserving, infinitely desirous and endlessly
ambitious in a world of scarcity and limited satisfactions. The
realisation of the most fundamental human desires for self-
preservation and security can be achieved by creating a strong
and stable state. Human psychology thus becomes the cause of
external conflict and the remedy for social cohesion. Self-preservation is the overriding motivational factor in creating or maintaining political arrangements which promote human desires. It
follows, then, that if human beings are solely motivated by such
desires, morality can be imposed by force, derived from fear
of sanctions or observed only because doing so leads to their
satisfaction. Moral injunctions now take the form of technical
imperatives and become factual statements about the means
necessary to achieve the given and required end. Reasoning in
moral matters is concerned not with questioning or revising
these ends but with prudential calculation, assisting human
beings to attain their ends – the most basic of which is security.
In brief, notwithstanding the differences in and the developments
of political and moral thought, the liberal tradition continues to
have at its core the key dichotomies and assumptions found in
Machiavelli: the separation of the individual and society and
also of the private and public sphere; the sovereignty of the
individual; the pre-social, pre-political notion of an unchanging human nature; the instrumental nature of rationality and
morality.

Continuities with the issues Machiavelli raises, however,
are nowhere more apparent than in traditions of ethical justification and their ongoing problems. It would be absurd to
attribute to Machiavelli a systematic ethical theory, but in so
far as the doctrine of political expediency embodies his views
on politics and morality, this has parallels with all forms of
normative and political theories which rely on a utilitarian or
consequentialist ethic. For Croce and his followers to argue that
Machiavelli divorced morality from politics is to make a false
antithesis. Isaiah Berlin suggests that what Machiavelli distinguishes is not moral from political values but two incompatible
ways of life and therefore two moralities. For Berlin, these are
the morality of the pagan and heroic world versus Platonic–
Hebraic–Christian morality, each with its own values and claims

to ultimacy. Machiavelli was not rejecting Christian values but showing the need 'to choose either a good, virtuous private life or a good, successful social existence, but not both'.[28] Dante Germino[29] has proposed that Machiavelli's position can be seen as similar to the contrast made by Weber (in *Politik als Beruf*) between 'ethics of responsibility' and 'ethics of intention', in which it is irresponsible in politics to act out of pure motives of individual conscience, without weighing the consequences which actually result. But, broadly speaking, the legacy of Machiavelli is the contrast not between the political and the moral but between consequentialist ethics and all other forms. Consequentialist ethics contrast with Christian, traditional and Kantian ethics; any kind of moral purism or idealism; any ethic that has as its source and criterion of value the word of God, eternal reason or the dictates of conscience; ethics which focus on the salvation of the individual soul or the individual as an end in themselves; ethics which stress intentions, or which embody abstract conceptions of justice, fairness and rights. In short, consequentialist ethics conflict with any ethic that, in formulating rules governing how people should be treated, places restrictions on the means no amount of good consequences would sanction or permit. Machiavelli demonstrates and highlights the incompatibility of consequentialist ethics from other systems of value, and it is this collision which persists between rival ethical positions.

Though Machiavelli justified public morality on grounds of reasons of state, and though varieties of utilitarianism may differ on what ends are justified, all moral theories which justify actions according to outcomes suffer from the problems of condoning means that on other standards are bad or undesirable. The problem of means and ends is not unique to Machiavelli but is relevant to all justifications which rely on a consequentialist ethic. These range across and pervade diverse ideological frameworks and apply to all areas of public and private life. This is seen in theological and Christian formulations of just war theory; defences of *raison d'état*, imperialist and populist, Catholic and Protestant; Marxist justifications for revolution, defences of the market economy and in arguments for and against a variety of issues such as legal punishment, discrimination, abortion, infanticide and euthanasia. Consequentialist calculation is also an intimate feature of our daily lives, since in all the small lies we tell and the promises we break we constantly act as if the end justified the means. Moreover, in practical politics there has always been the problem of adopting anything other than a version of utilitarianism, when ends that are judged good (on whatever grounds) cannot be achieved without recourse to means, which judged according to the principles of alternative moral traditions would be impermissible but which, if adhered to, would make the end unrealisable. Even regimes which stress the importance of individual rights and liberties have been more than ready to sacrifice these to achieve a desired outcome. Such acts as the bombing of Hamburg and Dresden, Hiroshima and Nagasaki and American involvement in Vietnam could be justified only by appeal to their consequences, despite the fact that the perpetrators of such deeds did not subscribe to a consequentialist ethic.

The pervasiveness of means–end reasoning in moral and political, private and public life illustrates the diverse situations in which moral demands or principles conflict and the frequency with which choice has to be made between one or the other. Action directed to outcomes can involve sacrificing moral principles, but the case against moral purity does not deny that this is a sacrifice. Machiavelli acknowledges that it cannot be called good to lie, cheat, be cruel and faithless. He, like many Marxist and revolutionary thinkers following him, thought such actions were necessary to achieve a better, more humane future, but he did not deny the contradiction of achieving moral ends through immoral means. In his poem 'To Those Born Later', Brecht says that living in dark times he cannot live 'wisely', according to the morality of the 'old books', 'shun the strife of the world', 'get along without violence' or 'return good for evil'; but he laments this and makes a plea to future generations who have escaped this contradiction:

> And yet we know:
> Hatred, even of meanness
> Contorts the features.
> Anger, even against injustice
> Makes the voice hoarse. Oh, we

Who wanted to prepare the ground for friendliness
Could not ourselves be friendly.

But you, when the time comes at last
And man is a helper to man
Think of us
With forbearance.[30]

Actions which involve the sacrifice of moral values may be necessary in an imperfect world, but the efficacy of such action does not obscure their anti-moral and inhuman nature. James Connolly reiterates this point: 'No, there is no such thing as humane or civilised war! War may be forced upon a subject race or subject class to put an end to subjection of race, of class, or sex. When so waged it must be waged thoroughly and relentlessly, but with no delusions as to its elevating nature, or civilising methods'.[31]

Trotsky confirms this view of both the necessity and the immorality of the means to liberatory ends:

> Nevertheless do lying and violence in themselves warrant condemnation? Of course as does the class society which generates them. A society without contradictions will naturally be a society without lies and violence. However, there is no bridge to that society save by revolutionary, that is violent means. The revolution is itself a product of class society and of necessity bears its traits. From the point of view of 'eternal truths' revolution is of course anti-moral. But this means that idealist morality is counter revolutionary, that is in the service of the exploiters.[32]

It is not, though, just the acknowledgement of the necessity of immoral means which forms the case against idealist morality in Machiavelli or in other consequentialist justifications. The case against moral purism argued for in contemporary literature[33] and found in embryonic form in Machiavelli depends on a rejection of the acts and omissions doctrine to show that there is no escape from the dilemma of dirty hands. The acts and omissions doctrine states that failure to perform an act with certain foreseen consequences is morally less bad than to perform an act with the same foreseen consequences. Machiavelli shows, like others who reject this doctrine, that certain omissions are as blameworthy as certain acts and sometimes more so, because those who fail to act, whatever their

good intentions, are causally responsible for harm they could
have prevented. If an action which employs violent, cruel or
otherwise immoral means is the only way to change the world's
destiny for the better, then those who fail to act will be responsible for maintaining the evil of the status quo and for allowing worse consequences to result. As Machiavelli noted, it is
not the most moderate and morally pure who have provided
the fewest victims in history.[34] At certain political conjunctions
there can be no ethical neutrality in decision-making – 'all roads
lead to the mire'.[35] In these circumstances, abstaining from
immoral means is at best self-deception, at worst immoral.

It is not a particularly Machiavellian idea, nor exclusively
a Marxist one that the end justifies the means or that it is impossible to apply in politics the same moral standards that are
appropriate to the private sphere. Whatever ideology they are
informed by, all practical politics at some time or other involves
actions which would be condemned if performed by private
citizens or if judged with regard to other moral considerations.
Though the Anarchist tradition has argued against this and for
the inseparability of means and ends, requiring that political
action should be judged by personal standards, in contemporary times the emergence of radical feminism marks the sharpest
break with Western political thought in this respect by questioning the legitimacy of the distinction between the private
and public spheres of action. The radical feminist claim that
the 'personal is political' exposes the idea that male power is
not confined to the public world of politics but also extends to
areas of personal life, such as the family and sexuality, which
are normally seen as private and non-political. But for many
radical feminists, personal politics also means that women's
experience of intimate relations provides a fund of values which
should inform, inspire and regulate political life.

It is easy to see, though, why an 'ethic of care'[36] arising from
women's experience of connection and responsiveness, and
informed by love, empathy, compassion and responsibility,
would be as inappropriate to politics as Machiavelli thought
traditional and princely virtues were. This is because, in the
world as it is, with 'men' as they are, politics is about power,
albeit in both political and private life. Change depends not on

the personal reflected in the political but on the transformation of social structures which no amount of princely, personal or female virtue alone can transform or maintain.

We may agree that feminism provides insights into what is morally good. We may also agree that the mode of morality which dominates the public sphere embodies typical male views of human nature as abstract, universal and self-interested which are false to the experience of women. Though the feminist alternative virtues may be desirable in themselves, it is surely Machiavelli's point that we are involved in a world where any such morality is impossible and undesirable. Without the deceit, violence, fraud and ruthlessness that would be psychopathic in personal relations, ends cannot be achieved which make the practice of virtue possible.

We need not be committed either to a view of human nature as universal and unchanging and of conflict as endemic, nor to a view that endorses male values and conceptions to see that, in the world as it is, a consequentialist ethic and the dilemmas this brings are unavoidable if political goals are to be achieved.

And when the time comes at last and 'man is a helper to man'[37] it will still be the case that, despite the flourishing of personal virtues and their reflection in public life, there will still be occasions when these have to be sacrificed for the sake of the common good or for their very preservation itself. There will always be decisions to be made in both personal and public affairs which require prudential calculation and which will justify means which contradict those most cherished values. Traditional male conceptions of what constitute the political sphere is not the only arena in which it would be fair to say that we will still be faced with the problem of Machiavelli who has left us with 'an enigma that perhaps will never be resolved'.[38]

Notes

1 For a review article on conflicting theories about *The Prince*, see E. W. Cochrane, 'Machiavelli: 1940-1960', *The Journal of Modern History*, 23 (June 1961), pp. 113-36.

2 Isaiah Berlin, 'The Originality of Machiavelli', in Myron P. Gilmore (ed.), *Studies on Machiavelli* (Florence: Sansoni, 1972), pp. 147-206.

3 I have used the translation by Allan H. Gilbert, *Machiavelli: The Chief Works and Others* (Durham, NC: Duke University Press, 1965), reprinted in John Plamenatz, *Machiavelli* (London: Fontana 1972). Page numbers refer to this reprint.

4 Jacques Maritain, 'The End of Machiavellianism', *Review of Politics*, 4 (1942), pp. 1-33.

5 Leo Strauss, *Thoughts on Machiavelli* (Glencoe, Ill.: The Free Press, 1958).

6 Spinoza, *Tractatus politicus*, 5, section 7, in *The Political Works*, ed. and trans. A. G. Wernham (Oxford: Clarendon Press, 1958).

7 Rousseau, *Du contrat social*, 3, 4 note, ed. Ronald Grimsley (Oxford: Clarendon Press, 1972).

8 Benedetto Croce, *Elementi di politica* (Bari: Laterza, 1925), pp. 60-5.

9 Federico Chabod, *Machiavelli and the Renaissance* (Cambridge, Mass: Harvard University Press), 1958.

10 Friedrich Meinecke, *Machiavellianism*, trans. Douglas Scott (London: Routledge, 1957).

11 That Machiavelli described political practice was the view of Herder, Ranke, Macauley and Burd and is held in recent times by Gennaro Sasso, *Niccolò Machiavelli* (Napoli: Istituto italiano per gli studi storici, vol. 10, 1958). Kamenev argues that Machiavelli revealed key insights into the nature of political power. See Chimen Abramsky, 'Kamenev's Last Essay', *New Left Review* (May/June 1962), pp. 34-42.

12 See Ernst Cassirer, *The Myth of the State* (New Haven, Conn.: Yale University Press, 1946), ch.12; Augustin Renaudet, *Machiavel: Étude d'histoire des doctrines politiques* (Paris: Gallimard, 1942); Leonardo Olschki, *Machiavelli the Scientist* (Berkeley: University of California Press, 1945); Keith Hancock, 'Machiavelli in Modern Dress', *History* 20 (September 1935), pp. 197-210.

13 See Cassirer, *The Myth of the State*, ch. 12.

14 Russell Price, 'The Sense of Virtù in Machiavelli', *European Studies Review*, 31 (1973), pp. 315-46.

15 Quentin Skinner, 'Machiavelli', *Great Political Thinkers* (Oxford: Oxford University Press, 1992), pp. 1-106, (p. 44).

16 John H. Geerken, 'Machiavelli Studies since 1969', *Journal of the History of Ideas*, 37 (1976), pp. 351-68.

17 Sydney Anglo, *Machiavelli: A Dissection* (London: Victor Gollancz Ltd, 1969), p. 173.

18 Allan H. Gilbert, *Machiavelli's 'Prince' and its Forerunners* (Durham, NC: Duke University Press, 1938); Felix Gilbert, 'The Humanist Conception of the Prince and *The Prince* of Machiavelli', *Journal of Modern History*, 11 (1939), pp. 449-83.

19 Aristotle, *Politics*, III 13 1284b, 20, 5-9, trans. B. Jowett, *The Politics of Aristotle*, vol. 1 (Clarendon Press: Oxford, 1885).

20 Aristotle, *Politics*, III 4 1227a, 9, 30-4.

21 Cited in Gilbert, *Forerunners*, p. 83.

22 Aristotle, *Politics*, V 11 1314a, 19, 45-50.

23 Gilbert, *Forerunners*, p. 127.

24 Cited in *Forerunners*, p. 127.

25 Cited in *Forerunners*, p. 126.

26 *Forerunners*, pp. 127-9.

27 *Forerunners*, p. 113.

28 Berlin, 'The Originality of Machiavelli', pp. 197-8.

29 Dante Germino, 'Second Thoughts on Leo Strauss's Machiavelli', *Journal of Politics*, 28 (November 1966), pp. 794-817.

30 Bertolt Brecht, *Poems, 1913-56*, ed. John Willet and Ralph Manheim (London: Eyre Methuen, 1976), pp. 318-20.

31 James Connolly, 'The Worker' (30 January 1915) in *Selected Writings*, ed. P. Beresford Ellis (Harmondsworth: Penguin, 1973), p. 213.

32 Leon Trotsky, *Their Morals and Ours* (New York: Pathfinder Press, 1973), p. 46.

33 See, for example, Jonathan Glover, *Causing Death and Saving Lives* (Harmondsworth: Penguin, 1977); John Harris, *Violence and Responsibility* (London: Routledge, 1980); Ted Honderich, *Violence for Equality* (Harmondsworth: Penguin, 1980).

34 See *The Prince*, chapter XVI and XVII.

35 Brecht, *Poems*, p. 319.

36 See, for example, Christine Gilligan, *In a Different Voice: Psychological Theory and Women's Development* (Cambridge: Harvard University Press, 1982).

37 Brecht, *Poems*, p. 320.

38 Benedetto Croce, 'Una questione che forse non si chiuderà mai: la questione de Machiavelli', *I Quaderni della 'Critica'*, 19 (July, 1949), pp. 1-9.

Appendix

Niccolò Machiavelli's letter to Francesco Vettori,
10 December 1513

To the magnificent Florentine ambassador Francesco Vettori, his
patron and benefactor, at the court of the Pope, in Rome.[1]

Magnificent ambassador,
'Divine favours were never late.'[2] I say this, because I seemed
to have lost, no, rather mislaid your favour, since you have
gone a very long time without writing to me, and I was unsure
what the cause might be. And, of all those which came to mind,
I took little account except of one, that I feared you had stopped
writing to me because someone had written to you that I didn't
take good care of your letters; and I knew that, except for
Filippo and Paolo,[3] nobody else had seen them on my account.
I have regained your favour through your latest letter of the
twenty-third of last month, in which I am very pleased to see
in what an orderly and peaceful way you are carrying out this
public office; and I urge you to continue in this manner,
because I know that anyone who gives up his interests for those
of others loses his own and gets no gratitude for doing so. And
since Fortune wants to do everything, she wants us to let her
have her way, to be calm and not to give her any bother, and
to wait for a time when she lets men do something; and then it
will be right for you to put in more effort, to keep a closer eye
on things, and for me to leave my country house and say: here
I am. So, wishing to return equal favours to you, all I can tell
you in this letter of mine is what my life is like; and if you
think it's to be traded with yours, I'll be happy to exchange it.

   I stay in my house in the country[4] and, since that recent
business of mine,[5] I have not been twenty days in Florence, all
told. Up to now I have been catching thrushes with my own

hands. I would get up before dawn, smear on the bird-lime, set out with a bundle of cages on my back, so that I looked like Geta when he came back from the port with Amphitryon's books;[6] I would catch at least two, at most six thrushes. And so I spent all September; then this pastime, spiteful and strange though it is, came to an end to my regret; and I'll tell you what my life is like. I rise in the morning with the sun and go off to a wood of mine which I'm having cut, where I stay two hours reviewing the previous day's work and spending time with those woodcutters, who always have some misfortune on their hands, either among themselves or with their neighbours. And, about this wood, I could tell you a thousand fine things that have happened to me, both with Frosino da Panzano and with others who wanted some of this firewood. And Frosino in particular sent for some stacks of wood without telling me anything, and when it came to payment he wanted to deduct ten lire which he says I owed him from four years ago when he beat me at cards at Antonio Guicciardini's. I started to kick up a fuss; I was going to accuse the carter who had gone for the wood of being a thief; at last Giovanni Macchiavelli inter-vened and settled things between us. Batista Guicciardini, Filippo Ginori, Tommaso del Bene and certain other citizens all took a stack of wood off me when that north wind was blow-ing. I made promises to everyone; and I sent a stack to Tommaso which in Florence became half its original size, because there was him, his wife, the maids, his children, all piling it up and looking like Gabburra when he beats an ox on Thursdays with his boys. So that, seeing who was benefiting, I have told the others I have no more wood; and they have all been angry about it, and especially Batista, who counts this among the other misfortunes of Prato.[7]

After leaving the wood, I go off to a spring, and from here to an aviary of mine. I have a book with me, either Dante or Petrarch or one of the minor poets, such as Tibullus, Ovid and the like: I read about their amorous passions and their loves, I remember my own, I revel for a while in these thoughts. Then I move over to the road, into the inn, I talk to the passers-by, I ask for news of their villages, I learn various things, and I take note of the various tastes and ideas of men. Meanwhile

lunchtime comes along, when with my family I eat what food
this poor country house and my paltry patrimony allow. Once
I have eaten, I go back to the inn: here I find the innkeeper,
usually a butcher, a miller, two furnacemen. With these I turn
good-for-nothing all day long playing cards and backgammon,
and that gives rise to a thousand arguments and countless
grudges with insulting words; most of the time we're fighting
over a penny and still we can be heard shouting from San
Casciano.[8] So, wrapped up in these lice, I stop my brain from
going mouldy, and I give vent to the malice of this fate of mine,
content that she should trample on me along this path, to see
if she might be ashamed of it.

When evening has come, I return home, and enter my
study; and at the door I take off my everyday clothing, full of
mud and mire, and I put on royal and courtly clothes; and,
appropriately attired, I enter the ancient courts of ancient men,
where, welcomed lovingly by them, I partake of that food
which is mine alone, and for which I was born. Here I am not
ashamed to speak with them, and to ask them about the reasons
for their actions; and they, in their kindness, answer me; and
for four hours I feel no affliction, I forget every trouble, I do
not fear poverty, death does not make me afraid; I become
completely absorbed in them. And because Dante says that
there can be no knowledge without retaining what one has
learned,[9] I have noted what I have gained from my acquain-
tance with them, and have composed a little work *De principatibus*, in which I go as deeply as I can into thoughts on this
subject, discussing what is a principality, of what kinds they
are, how they are acquired, how they are held, why they are
lost. And if ever you liked any of my whims, this one should
not displease you; and to a prince, and especially to a new
prince, it should be welcome; therefore I am addressing it to his
Magnificence Giuliano.[10] Filippo Casavecchia has seen it; he will
be able to tell you something both about the work itself and
about the discussions I have had with him, although I am still
filling it out and polishing it.

You would like me, magnificent ambassador, to leave this
life and come to enjoy yours with you. I shall do so in any case,
but what tempts me now is certain affairs of mine which will

take me about six weeks to settle. What makes me hesitate is that those Soderini are there;[11] I would be obliged, if I came, to visit them and speak to them. I would be afraid that on my return I would expect to dismount at home but would in fact dismount in the Bargello,[12] because, although this regime has very strong foundations and is very secure, still it is new, and for this reason full of suspicion; nor is there a shortage of smart alecs who, to make an impression like Pagolo Bertini, would invite others to table and would leave me to foot the bill. Please allay this fear for me, and then I will in any case come to see you within the time stated.

I talked to Filippo about this little work of mine, whether it would be a good idea to present it or not to present it; and, if so, whether it would be a good idea for me to bring it or to send it. In favour of not presenting it, there was the fear that it would not even be read by Giuliano, and that this Ardinghelli[13] would take the credit for this latest effort of mine. In favour of presenting it, there was the need which is driving me, because I am wearing myself out, and I cannot go on for long like this without poverty making me despicable; there was also my desire that these Medici lords should begin to make use of me, even if they were to start by getting me to roll a stone;[14] for, if I were not then to win them over, I would regret it deeply; and through this work, if it were read, it would be evident that the fifteen years I have been studying statecraft have not been spent by me in sleeping or playing; and anyone should be glad to make use of someone who at the expense of others was full of experience. And about my good faith nobody should be in doubt, because, having always kept faith, I am not going to learn to break it now; and someone who has been faithful and good for forty-three years, as I have, cannot change his nature; and my faith and goodness are testified by my poverty.

I should therefore like you too to write to me with your opinion on this matter, and I commend myself to you. 'Be favourable.'[15]

10 December 1513
Niccolò Machiavelli in Florence

Notes

1 Vettori (1474-1539) had been appointed Florentine ambassador to the papal court in December 1512.

2 Petrarch, *Triumph of Eternity*, 13.

3 Filippo Casavecchia, a former colleague of Machiavelli and a mutual friend of himself and Vettori; Paolo Vettori, younger brother of Francesco.

4 At Sant'Andrea in Percussina, a village some seven miles south of Florence.

5 Like the 'north wind' later in this paragraph, probably a reference to Machiavelli's imprisonment and torture in February–March 1513, following his suspected involvement in an anti-Medicean conspiracy.

6 An allusion to the encounter between Geta, servant of Anfitrione, and Birria, servant of Anfitrione's wife Almena, in *Geta e Birria*, a Tuscan verse narrative derived indirectly from the *Amphitruo* of Plautus.

7 Batista Guicciardini (1468–after 1534) was *podestà* of Prato, near Florence, when it was sacked by Spanish troops on 29 August 1512. He was captured and held to ransom.

8 A small town about two miles south of Sant'Andrea.

9 Dante, *Paradiso*, V, 41-2.

10 Giuliano de' Medici (1479-1516), son of Lorenzo the Magnificent and younger brother of Pope Leo X.

11 Piero Soderini (gonfalonier of Florence from 1502 until forced into exile on the return of the Medici in 1512) and his brother Cardinal Francesco.

12 The *palazzo* of the Bargello (head of police), in which Machiavelli had already been imprisoned earlier in the year.

13 Pietro Ardinghelli (1470-1526), personal secretary of Pope Leo X.

14 A reference to the eternal labour of Sisyphus in the underworld.

15 The Latin phrase used by Machiavelli, 'Sis felix', seems to be cited, as a counterpart to the opening quotation on divine favours, from another poetic text which both he and Vettori knew well, Virgil's *Aeneid*, I, 330: here Aeneas, driven ashore in an unknown country, has met his mother, Venus, disguised as a huntress, in a wood, and pleads for her help.

Notes on contributors

JANET COLEMAN is Professor of Ancient and Medieval Political Thought in the Government Department at the London School of Economics. Her many publications include *Ancient and Medieval Memories: Studies in the Reconstruction of the Past* (1992).

MARTIN COYLE lectures in English at the University of Wales, Cardiff. He is joint general editor of the Macmillan *New Casebooks* series, in which he edited the *Hamlet* volume (1992), and co-editor of the Routledge *Encyclopedia of Literature and Criticism* (1990).

MAGGIE GÜNSBERG is a Lecturer in Italian at the University of Sussex. She has written articles on Pirandello, Tasso, Ariosto and Aleramo, and is the author of *Patriarchal Representations: Gender and Discourse in Pirandello's Theatre* (1994). She is currently working on a book entitled *Gender on the Italian Stage: From the Renaissance to Rame*.

ANDREW MOUSLEY is Lecturer in Literature at Bolton Institute of Higher Education. He has published essays and articles on Renaissance constructions of the self, and is the co-editor of *Literature and Nationalism from the Reformation to the Restoration* (forthcoming).

JOHN M. NAJEMY is Professor of History at Cornell University. His work on Florentine history includes studies on the guilds and a book on elections and office-holding, *Corporatism and Consensus in Florentine Electoral Politics, 1280-1400* (1982). He is also the author of *Between Friends: Discourses of Power and Desire in the Machiavelli–Vettori Letters of 1513-1515* (1993).

JOHN PARKIN is Senior Lecturer in the French Department at the University of Bristol. He has published work on a variety of sixteenth-century authors, including Rabelais, Montaigne, Pasquier and Bodin.

MAUREEN RAMSAY lectures in political theory at the University of Leeds. Her particular area of interest is normative political philosophy applied to contemporary social issues. Recent publications include *Human Needs and the Market* (1992).

BRIAN RICHARDSON is Senior Lecturer in Italian at the University of Leeds. He is the editor of Machiavelli's *Il Principe* (1979), and author of *Print Culture in Renaissance Italy* (1994).

Select bibliography

Editions of Machiavelli's works

Tutte le opere, ed. Mario Martelli (Florence: Sansoni, 1971)
Tutte le opere storiche e letterarie di Niccolò Machiavelli, ed. G. Mazzoni and M. Casella (Florence: G. Barbera, 1929)
Editions of *Il Principe*
Il Principe, ed. Arthur Burd (Oxford: Clarendon Press, 1891)
Il Principe, ed. Mario Casella (Milan: Libreria d'Italia, 1929)
Il Principe, ed. Federico Chabod and Luigi Firpo (Turin: Einaudi, 1966)
Il Principe (De principatibus), ed. Brian Richardson (Manchester: Manchester University Press, 1979)
Il Principe e Discorsi, ed. Sergio Bertelli (Milan: Feltrinelli, 1960)
Translations
Machiavelli: The Chief Works and Others, tr. Allan Gilbert (Durham, N.C: Duke University Press, 1965)
Niccolò Machiavelli: 'The Discourses', ed. Bernard Crick, tr. Leslie J. Walker, S.J. (Harmondsworth: Penguin, 1970)
'The Prince': Niccolò Machiavelli, tr. Harvey C. Mansfield (Chicago: University of Chicago Press, 1985)
Machiavelli: 'The Prince', ed. Quentin Skinner and Russell Price (Cambridge: Cambridge University Press, 1988) (has detailed notes on vocabulary and on proper names cited in the text)
Niccolò Machiavelli: 'The Prince', tr. George Bull (Harmondsworth: Penguin, 1961)
Niccolò Machiavelli: 'The Prince', tr. Bruce Penman (London: Dent, 1981)
Niccolò Machiavelli: 'The Prince', tr. Robert M. Adams (New York: Norton, 1992) (Norton Critical Edition: contains extracts from Machiavelli's other works and from twentieth-century critical writings)

Biographical studies

Grazia, Sebastian de, *Machiavelli in Hell* (Princeton, N.J.: Princeton University Press, 1989)
Hale, J. R., *Machiavelli and Renaissance Italy* (New York: Collier Books, 1960)
Ridolfi, R., *The Life of Niccolò Machiavelli* (1954), tr. Cecil Grayson (Chicago: University of Chicago Press, 1963)

General studies

Anglo, Sydney, *Machiavelli: A Dissection* (London: Victor Gollancz Ltd, 1969)

Berlin, Sir Isaiah, *Against the Current* (London: Hogarth Press, 1979) (extract in the Norton edition above)

Bock, Gisela, Skinner, Quentin, and Viroli, Maurizio, (eds), *Machiavelli and Republicanism* (Cambridge: Cambridge University Press, 1990)

Chabod, Federico, *Machiavelli and the Renaissance* (Cambridge, Mass.: Harvard University Press, 1958) (extract in the Norton edition above)

Colish, M., 'The Idea of Liberty in Machiavelli', *Journal of the History of Ideas*, 32 (1971), pp. 323-50

Fleischer, Martin (ed.), *Machiavelli and the Nature of Political Thought* (New York: Atheneum, 1972)

Gilbert, Allan H., *Machiavelli's 'Prince' and its Forerunners: The Prince as a Typical Book de Regimine Principum* (Durham, N.C.: Duke University Press, 1938)

Gilbert, Felix, *Machiavelli and Guicciardini: Politics and History in Sixteenth-Century Florence* (Princeton, N.J.: Princeton University Press, 1965) (extract in the Norton edition above)

Gilmore, Myron, (ed.), *Studies on Machiavelli* (Florence: Sansoni, 1972)

Hale, J. R., *Machiavelli and Renaissance Italy* (London: English University Presses Ltd, 1961) (extract in the Norton edition above)
Florence and the Medici (London: Thames & Hudson, 1977)

McCanless, M., *The Discourse of Il Principe* (Malibu: Udena, 1983)

Meinecke, Friedrich, *Machiavellianism: The Doctrine of Raison D'Etat and its Place in Modern History* (London: Routledge, 1957)

Parel, Anthony (ed.), *The Political Calculus: Essays on Machiavelli's Philosophy* (Toronto: University of Toronto Press, 1972)

Pitkin, Hanna, *Fortune Is a Woman: Gender and Politics in the Thought of Niccolò Machiavelli* (Berkeley: University of California Press, 1984)

Pocock, J. G. A., *The Machiavellian Moment: Florentine Political Thought and the Atlantic Republican Tradition* (Princton, N.J.: Princton University Press, 1975)

Praz, Mario, *The Flaming Heart* (New York: Doubleday, 1958)

Price, Russell, 'Ambizione in Machiavelli's Thought', *History of Political Thought*, 3 (1982), pp. 382-445
'The Senses of *Virtù* in Machiavelli', *European Studies Review*, 3 (1973), pp. 315-45
'The Theme of *Gloria* in Machiavelli', *Renaissance Quarterly*, 30 (1977), pp. 588-631

Raab, Felix, *The English Face of Machiavelli: A Changing Interpretation 1500-1700* (London: Routledge & Kegan Paul, 1964)

Skinner, Quentin, *Foundations of Modern Political Thought* (Cambridge: Cambridge University Press, 1978)
Machiavelli (Oxford: Oxford University Press, 1981)

Whitfield, J. H., *Machiavelli* (Oxford: Oxford University Press, 1947) (extract in the Norton edition above)
Discourses on Machiavelli (Cambridge: Heffer, 1969)

Wood, N., 'Machiavelli's Concept of *Virtù* Reconsidered', *Political Studies*,
    15 (1967), pp. 159-72

Bibliographical studies

Fiore, Silvia Ruffo, *Niccolò Machiavelli: An Annotated Bibliography of
    Modern Criticism and Scholarship* (New York: Greenwood, 1990)

Index